Best wishes —

[signature]

Six-gun and Silver Star

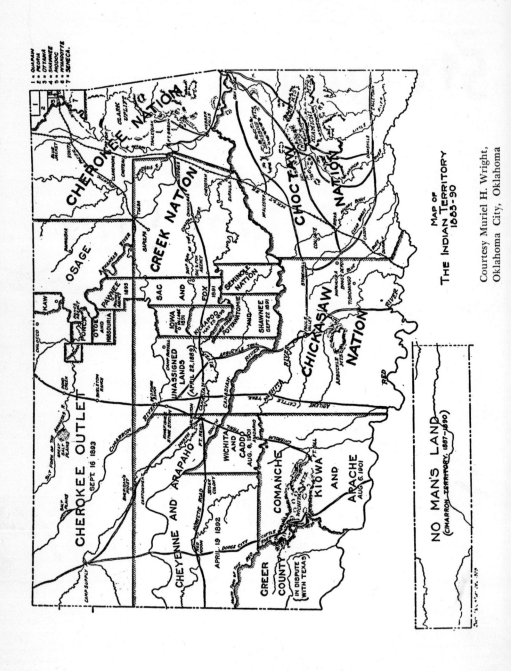

MAP OF
THE INDIAN TERRITORY
1865-90

Courtesy Muriel H. Wright,
Oklahoma City, Oklahoma

Six-gun

and

Silver Star

Glenn Shirley

UNIVERSITY OF NEW MEXICO PRESS
ALBUQUERQUE   1955

Also by Glenn Shirley
TOUGHEST OF THEM ALL

 COPYRIGHT, 1955 ● UNIVERSITY OF
NEW MEXICO PRESS ● ALBUQUERQUE
Library of Congress Catalog Card Number 55-10029

Preface

Examining court cases throughout Oklahoma, cases that were shifted from the territorial to the state courts, and before that, old federal district and supreme court dockets, one finds on almost every page remembrances of the pioneer and frontier days—names that recall in themselves all the early history of Oklahoma.

From extensive reading of these court records, supplemented by voluminous research through Indian Territory and Oklahoma Territory journals and newspapers, I have compiled the outlaw history of a great commonwealth from the first opening of the Indian country to white settlement, in 1889 to 1907, when the vast acreages of the Five Civilized Tribes were joined to the regions of the white man, and Oklahoma, the forty-sixth state, was born.

In other volumes of Oklahoma history and lore, the emphasis has been placed on the boomer, the homesteader, the politician, often giving unreality by making it too much of a story of sweetness and light. Of course, the first mad race for homes, followed by other similar races in rapid succession, building commonwealth after commonwealth into the unity of the nation's wonder territory, was so big no one could see it whole. To preserve the balance, I have set forth in these pages the criminal chapter of this most important and notable epoch —the big-scale war on outlaws from the first opening and including statehood. Nowhere in our Wild West did the outlaw problem become so great a menace.

When Oklahoma was still the "Indian Nations," the people saw the rise and fall of the most desperate gangs in the western hemisphere, and after the western part of the state had been settled, they lived under the furious reign of new, and even more vicious, gangs than they had ever known. Trains, stores, banks, and post offices were robbed; peaceful citizens were shot down in cold blood. Supplementing these terrors, the land was overrun with horse and cattle thieves, counterfeiters and whiskey peddlers. The question was whether the outlaws or the honest settlers owned it. Time came when the merchants and farmers either had to quit or bow to the will and power of the brigands. The progress of railroads into the Cherokee Outlet aroused dissension between rival townsites and added unrest and turmoil.

Grover Cleveland was returned to the White House to serve a second term as President, and with characteristic honesty and courage, he met the appeal of the people for help. He appointed Evett Dumas Nix, a Guthrie business man, United States Marshal. Nix selected one hundred and fifty field deputies on the basis of character and record alone, and told them to put an end to this reign of terror. There had been a lot of deputy marshals even worse than the outlaws. The Nix bunch, hand-picked, was of another sort. Within a few years the country was practically cleared of its thieves and robber gangs.

Fabulous names appeared in this saga, names of both good and bad men. Among those on the side of the law were John Hixon, Frank Canton, Charles Colcord, Frank Cochrane, Steve Burke, Jim Masterson, and experienced gunmen of the border like Bill Tilghman, Heck Thomas, and Chris Madsen, who became known as the "Three Guardsmen." Opposing the forward march of public and individual safety were the Dalton gang, the Doolin gang, the Caseys, Christians, Jennings, and the Wyatt and Black outlaws, with such picturesque names as

Black-Faced Charley, Arkansas Tom, Rose of Cimarron, Red Buck, Dynamite Dick, Tulsa Jack, Bitter Creek, Little Bill, Little Dick, Cattle Annie, and Little Breeches.

The battle against lawlessness in this raw country was really not a battle at all, but a long-drawn-out war, with criminals violently dropping out of the picture, and new outlaws continually taking their places, until the balance of power swung finally in favor of the lawmen.

Detailing these criminal activities is not an attempt to eulogize the outlaw or glorify the gory work of exterminating more than three score of notorious renegades and placing thousands of lesser lights behind prison bars. It is a grim story, as it must be if the truth is told, and only by recounting facts can one bring into proper distinction the splendid moral and personal courage of the marshals and other officers who tamed these early menaces and laid the foundation for peace and greatness.

GLENN SHIRLEY

Stillwater, Oklahoma

Contents

Prologue

Oklahoma is unique among all the forty-eight states. The others grew slowly, painfully, by gradual infiltration into the wilderness of settlers who built them into statehood.

But Oklahoma sprang into being in one day. The government waved a magic wand and, between the rising and setting of the sun, what had been an unpopulated prairie became a humming land of farms and cities.

Oklahoma's first settlers were not seeking political freedom. They had much more of that in the states they left than in a territory where governors and judges were appointed by the several presidents and Congress had veto power over any legislation.

It was the consuming land hunger of the American people that led to the opening.

All the best land in the older states was occupied. Thousands of homesteaders had built their sod houses and dugouts across the plains of western Kansas. In Texas, ranchmen and farmers had spread across the Staked Plains. This left Old Oklahoma and other unoccupied lands of the Indian country as a broad peninsula between them—millions of acres carpeted with buffalo grass and blue-stem grass that could easily be broken to the plow, supporting only sparse herds of cattle and nomadic Indian tribes. The press painted glowing pictures of the vast area: "In addition to furnishing the farmer a magnifi-

1

cent soil, unsurpassed even by the Illinois bottoms in produc-
tiveness, and so favorably situated that it is then and there
ready for the plow, being free of rock, swamp, and forest, this
superb addition to the public lands of Uncle Sam is blessed
with a climate so exquisitely balanced between the long win-
ters of the North and the long summers of the South, that
almost all the products of both North and South can be successfully cultivated." It was the topic of conversation around
campfires and in the villages and towns of the two states.

Nothing was said of the rights of the Indian or of the
treaties the white man had made with him. The talk was about
the waste of resources under tribal governments.

As an example, the land-hungry whites pointed to the fact
that, in 1883, the Cherokee Nation leased the Cherokee Outlet
to a group of feudal cattle barons for five years, for $100,000
per year—only a few cents an acre. Each Cherokee would
realize perhaps $3.00 per year, while 100,000 white settlers
were deprived of rich farms. In 1883, the Cheyennes and
Arapahos rented 3,117,880 acres at two cents an acre to seven
cattlemen.

"Spell that out," cried the *Oklahoma War Chief,* the
Boomer newspaper published at Caldwell, on the Kansas border. "Three million, one hundred and seventeen thousand,
eight hundred and eighty acres! Divide it up into 160-acre
farms; just 19,486 farms with 120 acres left over for a soldiers
home; on each farm a husband, wife, and three children would
be, in round numbers, a thriving, industrious population of
100,000 producers! And their vast domain leased to seven cattle kings!"

Almost directly in the heart of the reserved Indian lands
was an unassigned region of 1,888,900 acres. This region constituted an uneven quadrangular block bounded on the north
by the parallel of thirty-six degrees north latitude, the southern boundary of the Cherokee Outlet; on the east by the
reservations of the Pawnee, Sac and Fox, Iowa, Kickapoo, Pottawatomie, and Shawnee plains tribes; on the south by the

Canadian River, the northern boundary of the Chickasaw Nation; and on the west by the Cheyenne and Arapaho reservations, immediately west of the ninety-eighth meridian. Here the cattlemen had built headquarters ranches, constructed corrals for branding their animals, and established line camps for use of their men.

"These are not the only public lands thus filched from the people by the cattle kings," the *War Chief* continued. "There are other leases in Oklahoma . . . empires of public lands fenced by these monopolists from Washington territory to the Texas border, hundreds of millions of acres fattening countless herds of stock—at two cents per acre!"

It is small wonder then, in the lean days following the panic of 1873, when the Civil War inflation bubble burst, that Captain David L. Payne was able to gain increasing support for his demand that Oklahoma be opened to white settlement. From 1870 to 1879, thirty-three bills asking the formation of an Oklahoma Territory out of the Indian lands were introduced in Congress. Payne's first Boomers entered the territory in 1880, and were thrown out by federal troops again and again until his death in 1884.

In the early eighties, another lesser depression strengthened the demand for opening Oklahoma. William L. Couch, Payne's most active lieutenant, succeeded him as leader of the movement. With the same earnestness for their cause and the energy that characterized Payne, he advertized their plans widely, and the railroads with lines in the country, realizing how it would enhance their value if the homeseekers won, added their powerful propaganda and influence. Literally thousands flocked to the Kansas and Texas borders to share this enthusiasm, until military authorities found it necessary to call for reinforcements to eject them. The pressure on Congress grew steadily stronger.

The cattlemen were scared. They organized at Caldwell, in 1881, a Cattlemen's Association that wielded tremendous power for good and evil. Besides looking after the cattle business, it took a hand in politics, controlled newspapers, kept sympathetic representatives in Congress, and had much to say even in big money centers in New York.

The Five Civilized Tribes opposed the selling of their lands and the opening of the land not assigned. They were represented in Washington by delegations which included their ablest men and leaders.

Commissioner Price, of the Department of Indian Affairs, attempted to discredit the Boomers as a class of people "well armed, mostly with Winchester rifles and carbines, and among them are reported men with full wagon loads of whiskey and cigars intending to open saloons on arriving at their destination. They seem to be, with two or three exceptions, persons without visible means of support, whom the citizens, though deprecating the movement, were glad to get rid of at any price . . ."

But the plea of the Indian and the influence of their allies, the cattlemen, to keep out the white settler was doomed. Too many believed what General Nelson A. Miles wrote in his report on the Indian country to the War Department in 1885:

"The object in reserving the Indian Territory as a place where scattered tribes from Texas, Missouri, Kansas and other states and territories could be congregated and removed from before the advancing settlements was humane and judicious and it has accomplished its mission. The Indian Territory is now a block in the pathway of civilization. It is preserved to perpetuate a mongrel race far removed from the influence of civilized people—a refuge of the outlaws and indolent of whites, blacks and Mexicans. The vices introduced by these classes are rapidly destroying the Indians by disease. Without courts of justice or public institutions, without roads, bridges or railways, it is simply a dark blot in the center of the map of the United States. It costs the government hundreds of thousands to peaceably maintain 60,000 to 80,000 Indians there, when the territory is capable of supporting many millions of enlightened people."

The federal government so far realized the ultimate capitulation to settlement that Congress authorized negotiations with the Creeks, Seminoles, and Cherokees to relinquish their claims to all unoccupied lands and appropriated $5,000 for expense of such negotiations. The Dawes Act, of 1887, cleared the way for the western half of the Indian country—all land except that occupied by the Five Civilized Tribes—to be settled by the white man. In the same year, the Santa Fe was permitted to build a line across the territory from Arkansas City south to Fort Worth; and on March 2, 1889, the news spread over the land that Congress had passed the Indian appropriation bill for the forthcoming fiscal year with a "rider" opening the unassigned area to white settlement under the homestead laws.

President Cleveland was forced to choose between two evils. Veto of the bill would wreck Indian administration finances. His signature on the bill meant the end of all hope for a future Indian commonwealth. Repudiated by the voters the preceding November, worn out by the stress of a turbulent administration, he "chose to relieve immediate necessity" and signed the bill on his last day in office. Three weeks later, on March 23, his successor, President Harrison, issued a proclamation announcing April 22 as the opening day and twelve o'clock noon the earliest hour at which one could legally enter the land. Any settlers entering Oklahoma before that time would be considered "sooners" and forfeit all right to homestead any of the land, and the military was ordered to keep them out. The people were to gather at the border around the unassigned area. The first man on the land was the one to homestead it.

CHAPTER
1

Hell's Fringe

"It was a great day to commence the building of an empire. The sky was as blue as in June. A tonic air, as exhilarating as wine, was fanning down from the north with just force enough to make exertion of man and beast effective and pleasant. Mighty possibilities, sightly lands, fertility equalling the fabled Nile, the garden of the gods, were fenced in by an anxious human wall on that immortal 22nd of April, 1889. No region had been so thoroughly advertised, so favorably advertised. The frequent heroic efforts of the Boomers by the military, at the behest of greed, wakened the world to the belief that a wondrous land was here. The very name Oklahoma was a poem, an inspiration, an invitation irresistible, impossible to ignore or refuse—Oklahoma! A slogan for conquering and conquest! Oh, yes, Oklahoma was advertised. The denizens of all civilization came; came from the hills, from the valleys, from the prairie and forest; came from the caves of the earth, from the isles of the sea and, seemingly, from the clouds of the air. They were here in all tongues, in all colors, in all garbs, with all kinds of profanity and every imaginable odor; were here at high noon."[1]

They were lined up by the thousands, mile upon mile, north to south, east to west. The rich and the poor, the refined

[1] Dr. Delos Walker, *Daily Oklahoman*, April 22, 1909.

6

and the ignorant—all touched elbows in this horde who waited for the sound of the starting guns.[2]

Most of them were making the run on horseback. There was everything from mules to race horses, some saddled, many bareback. Top or open buggies, fringed carriages, prairie schooners, light farm wagons, carts, racing sulkies, and even a few five-foot bicycles stood wheel to wheel in that curious line. Hundreds had come on foot, trusting sturdy legs and good lungs to win a piece of land.

The Santa Fe had assembled all spare equipment it could find. On the northern border, roughly one mile north of Orlando, trains from Arkansas City, eleven in all, were backed as far as the eye could see. Every coach bulged with passengers who sat in the seats, windows, and aisles. Others rode the platforms and clung desperately to the sides and tops of the cars. The Gulf Line sent up six trains from Texas to Purcell, on the South Canadian River, "just as jammed."[3] One woman, who had made up with the engineer of the lead train, rode the cowcatcher.[4]

2 "All the poor people west of a line drawn through Fort Worth, Wichita and Lincoln, Nebraska, went to Kingfisher (on the west border of the Unassigned Lands) to make the Run. . . . Ten thousand people had gathered a mile and a quarter west on Kingfisher Creek. . . . There was not an average of $10 for each man, woman and child. . . . While we were loafing, we had nothing to do except get information and visit. We took an invoice of Democrats and Republicans from the states, and No Man's Land showed up with no party but what they called Presbyterians and sons-of-bitches. We rode up and down the line, asking all Republicans to get on a certain line or street. Pat Nagle [later to become United States Marshal] unhitched one of his mules and got on bareback and rode up and down the line, asking all Democrats to line up. The Republicans lined up and outnumbered the others about three to one. Then Fatty Smith went up and down the line asking all of the sons-of-bitches to line up, and Dr. Overstreet, riding a fine bay horse, asked the Presbyterians from No Man's Land to line up on his side. There were about three sons-of-bitches and one Presbyterian."—C. M. "Cash" Cade (Ltr. to the *Kingfisher Free Press*, April 17, 1939) .

3 James Marshall, *Santa Fe, The Railroad That Built An Empire*, p. 233.

4 Nannetta Daisey, a newspaper woman of note and correspondent for the Dallas and Galveston *News*. She rode the train past Oklahoma City, and when opposite a fine piece of land near Edmond, jumped off the cowcatcher, struck an attitude of defiance, flung her shawl to the wind saying: "This claim is mine against all the world, take it who dare."

Out in front, the soldiers rode back and forth. Two-hundred cavalrymen policed the west line, near Hennessey, holding back nearly 2,300 vehicles and 7,000 people. Occasionally an impatient rider would cross the line, but scamper back with amusing alacrity when challenged by the troops. Every few minutes scouts could be seen bringing out sooners who had slipped into the country the night before. On the north and east lines, the same procedure was repeated. On the south jump-off line, at Purcell, infantry troops stalked strategic points along the river. A few minutes before twelve everybody crowded the front lines until it was almost impossible to hold them back. "In all that legion of '89'ers, there was not one Joshua who could have forced the sun to stand still, but every devil of them could force their watches ahead and they did. Then, a moment of bated breath, a hush till hearts could be heard to beat. . . ."[5]

A call from the bugle, the crack of revolvers and carbines of the cavalrymen, and a "human flood deluged the wonder land."[6] The great lines surged forward with a mighty rush.

[5] Walker, *op. cit.*

[6] The best pen picture of the race is given in the following eye-witness accounts written in 1890:

"It was a typical Bull Run. . . . Thousands uncorked their exuberance in shouts and cheers that fairly shook the ground. . . . It was a race free for all. None was barred. Neither sex nor circumstances were imposed as conditions. . . . Cheers and shouts from ten thousand souls, a refrain to the bugle notes, sent echoes o'er hill and plain. Fleet racer and plow horse were given free rein and plied with whip and spur.

"The long railway trains, too, with ear-piercing shrieks from the engine whistles joined in. . . . From the windows of every coach came shouts of cheer and the waving of rags and handkerchiefs to those who were racing to the south on either side of the fast-flying trains. The ranks of the racers are diminishing on every side; they are seen to leap from their horses; a happy shout, a waving of the hat, the setting of a flag or stake. They have taken a homestead. Oklahoma was the home of the white man!"

* * *

"In the race for homes from the south at least a score of fords had been selected by which to reach the Oklahoma side of the Canadian, and as the hour of twelve drew near, hundreds mounted on fleet horses formed in line at those different fords. . . . Like well-trained jockeys, these long lines of riders were seeking for an advantage in the start. All, or many at least, knew the treacherous

Pandemonium. A din of confusion. Vehicles overturned and broke down. Horses, freed from their encumbrances, galloped madly with flying harness. As the trains rolled over the prairie, hundreds leaped from the platforms and windows and dashed off in search of claims. Victorious shouts as they drove identification stakes into the ground, rising above the thunder of hoofs, the roar of locomotives, the clatter of vehicles careening from side to side in wild, uncertain courses, the scream of a man thrown from his mount and trampled to death.[7]

By nightfall, the wild flowers in the new spring grass nodding in the morning breeze had been crushed under the feet of hurrying, excited people, the land scarred deeper with horses' hoofs and iron wheels and furrows plowed around new homes and cities that sprang from the prairie with hundreds and thousands of inhabitants.

A great state had been born. The twenty-second of April, 1889, was a happy day for those lucky enough to secure a claim. "The possibility of failure or disappointment did not enter into the consideration of a single individual . . . but, for

---

quicksands of the Canadian, yet all were eager to be first in plunging into its waters. They saw the signal officer, watch in hand, away on the opposite shore, and just as the second-hand told the hour of twelve he gave the signal, and ere the stirring notes from the bugle reached the ears of those in the furtherest end of the column, the foremost horsemen, with yells that would have done credit to a band of Pawnee warriors, dashed into the fords, followed by hundreds of other equally excited riders. It was a furious dash, the horses and riders were drenched with water and covered with sand. Wagons and carriages, as thick as they could be crowded together, followed pell mell the column of horsemen through the fords. The opposite bank gained, the immense throng spread out like a great army, covering the entire country for miles, the advance only falling out of the race as they reached claims that suited them. And so the race went on until all had driven a homestead stake into Oklahoma soil."—Marion Tuttle Rock, *History of Oklahoma*, pp. 20-28; Charles Evans, *Lights on Oklahoma History*, pp. 179-183.

7 "Many never reached their claims at all. . . . Those on horses paid little attention to those on foot . . . ran over them and in a number of instances killed them. . . . It is hard to understand the condition of the minds of the people in a time like this. It seemed they had lost all reason and judgment except to achieve and to attain the purpose for which they had long waited and suffered many privations. . . ."—J. A. Newsom, *Life and Practice of the Wild and Modern Indian* (Chapter VI, "The Opening of Oklahoma"), pp. 106-107.

many, the anticipations were 'April hopes, the fools of chance.' "[8] Many went away with an empty purse and a broken heart because they had spent so much time and money trying to get a piece of property and failed. Many picked claims that were not what they expected and left them. Others, who got good claims, found that they could not make a crop and disposed of them for little or nothing. Some filed on claims and left them, never returning. Others tried to hold all the lots they could stake, "settling in the names of their sisters, their cousins, and their aunts, or in sheerly fictional names, hoping to hold them for the arrival of relatives or friends, or to sell their 'possessory rights' after a few days' accretion of value."[9] Most of the misery resulted from finding choice claims already occupied by sooners.[10]

The soldiers had made a diligent effort to keep them out. A negro named Jackson was so persistent in getting into the country ahead of schedule that he was arrested several times, but would be back on the property again when the soldiers returned. Finally, they placed a rope around his neck and another around his body beneath the arms, then hoisted him into a tree, tightening the rope around his neck just enough to make him think he was being hanged. They took a picture of him hanging in the tree before they let him down, and that photograph became his undoing when he appeared at the land office to prove he had not been in the country prior to the opening.[11]

Several attempts to beat the proclamation were made by organized gangs. One outfit, under the leadership of a smart Bohemian, divided itself into two parties. Half of them crossed the river near Purcell and managed to get to Mustang Creek, along which lay some of the most fertile country. Each

8 Hamilton S. Wicks, "The Opening of Oklahoma," *Oklahoma Daily Capital,* April 27, 1890; *Chronicles of Oklahoma,* IV, June, 1926.

9 Angelo C. Scott, *The Story of Oklahoma City,* p. 11.

10 Victor E. Harlow, *Oklahoma,* p. 256.

11 Chris Madsen (army scout and later famous as a United States marshal), Guthrie *Leader,* April 16, 1939.

staked two claims—one for themselves, the other for one of the party which had remained at the line to prove the ones in the country were with them at Purcell until the opening. The plan worked until special agents from the Interior Department secured evidence which caused the violators to be indicted in the federal court at Wichita. Capiases were ordered for their arrest and the marshals served warrants on twenty-eight of the offenders and took them to Topeka. All except the leader pleaded guilty and were given jail sentences, and he was tried at Wichita and sentenced to two years in the penitentiary.[12]

In spite of the vigilance of the troops, however, great numbers had sneaked into the country and hid in ravines and timber until the opening hour when they popped from their hiding places and occupied the land they had already marked with stakes.[13]

The prairie grass was alive with them, crawling out of ditches, dropping from trees, squirming from beneath freight cars full of raw lumber, hardware, furniture and farm implements that had been allowed entry previous to the opening and stood in long rows on hastily built sidetracks, fifteen or thirty miles inside the border. Before 12:15 a dozen men from the Seminole Land and Town Company, having made fifteen miles from the border in fifteen minutes—in theory—were staking out a townsite [Oklahoma City]

12 *Ibid.;* Dan W. Peery, "The First Two Years," *Chronicles of Oklahoma,* VII, September, 1929, pp. 285-286.

13 "There were many who were not disposed to play the game fair . . . and slipped into the forbidden land the night before 'by the light of the moon.' . . . Those people were called 'Moonshiners' and the word 'sooner' was not applied for five or six months afterwards. You may imagine the disappointment of a man who had run his horse ten or twelve miles and into some beautiful valley and there finding a man on every quarter and sometimes two or three to the quarter. We knew that they were 'Moonshiners' but they would all claim that they started from the line at high noon and had just beat us to it. . . . They had come to the country together and had organized a conspiracy to each swear for the other. . . ."—Peery, *op. cit.,* pp. 284-285.

"The manner of opening Oklahoma has been subject of numerous criticisms, yet, if the people had obeyed the law, a more fair or equitable system could not have been devised. The fault was not in the manner of the opening, but in the shameful manner in which the law was violated. And it was in this, as in all other violations of law, honest men suffered through the dishonest acts of their fellow men."—Rock, *op. cit.*

around the Santa Fe depot . . . and unloading freight cars into wagons. At 12:40 more than forty tents were up, and one settler was busy driving a stake in the center of the Santa Fe tracks and defying the agent and soldier-guards.[14]

" 'At dawn a trackless virgin prairie with no human habitation; at sunset a city of tents, homes for a multitude'; 'At sunrise a trackless wilderness, at eventide a settled community'; 'Rome was not built in a day, Guthrie was'—these and many kindred catch lines had headed our advance stories of the founding of Guthrie," wrote Fred Wenner, correspondent for the Kansas City *Star* and one of the first newspaper men to arrive on the scene the day of the Run. "Theoretically and rhetorically they were fine, but historically they failed of realization for, when our train arrived carrying the first legal settlers, the townsite was swarming with sooners who came in on Sunday, the 21st, or early the morning of the 22nd, staked off most of the choice lots, put up their tents, and at one minute after 12, just about the time the law-abiding settlers were starting at the north line, offered two townsite plats for record at the land office!"

The homeseekers who made the run from the borders did not give up without a fight. Many rows with sooners were settled with fists, others with six-shooters and the rest in the land offices.

On the other hand, arriving on a piece of land first did not always hold it.

We had to let many others who claimed they had done the same thing know we were the first ones on the claims. Hundreds of people were passing, and we were kept busy riding like the devil seeing to it that others did not stop. . . . A creek ran through the claim I took. . . . A man riding a gray mule came through the brush about five minutes after, and I saw him driving a stake. I rode up and asked him what he was doing. He said, "Staking this

14 Marshall, *op. cit.*, pp. 232-233; L. L. Waters, *Steel Trails to Santa Fe*, pp. 161-162.

claim." I jumped off my horse, pulled up the stake and told him to look some other place and he left. Just then another man came up to me and said he had seen me when I got off my horse and that he was on the claim as soon as I was. He said we would have to divide it up, he to take eighty acres and I to take eighty. I told him it was 160 or six feet, I didn't give a damn which . . . that I had a Winchester pump shotgun and it was loaded with buckshot. . . . The man soon left. Then I saw two men near the creek and rode down to them. One man with a Winchester rifle across his arm said, "I'll stay with you till hell freezes over." I told him he would have plenty company, there or any other place, and he and his partner left.[15]

A number of these land hunters were not so easily dissuaded as evidenced by reports received during the first days.

On April 23, a settler named Goodwin appeared at Fort Reno and made a sworn statement to the post commander that his party of four had been fired upon by twelve Texans, who claimed their location by priority of selection, having come there several years before with Captain Payne. Goodwin escaped only by hiding in the thick brush along the river, making his way in the darkness to the fort. The rest of his party were slain. A detachment of Company C, 13th Infantry, under Lieutenant Buck, was quickly dispatched to the scene to recover the bodies and arrest suspicious persons in the vicinity.[16]

Deputy Marshal J. G. Varnum rode into Oklahoma City with a report that Martin Colbert, a wealthy half-breed cattleman of the Chickasaw Nation, had been killed in a quarrel over a claim by a man named Nolan. About fourteen miles west of Oklahoma City, he had found another man dead on a claim and a settler named Martin taking the matter "coolly and quietly." Three miles west of Guthrie, a man who arrived on the first train had staked a quarter section. When a second claimant refused to leave, he levelled a Winchester and fired

[15] Evan G. Barnard, *A Rider of the Cherokee Strip*, pp. 142-143.
[16] Dispatch from Fort Reno, April 24, to *Oklahoma City Times*, April 29, 1889.

three shots into his body. Two boomers, engaged in a dispute over a lot, attracted the attention of the soldiers. Charles Qinly, one of the contestants, warned them to keep out of the trouble. When one of the troopers interfered, he deliberately drew his revolver and killed him.[17]

Another cold-blooded murder occurred near Guthrie when three "desperate characters" seeking a claim shot down J. C. Chyland, of Franklin County, Missouri. A posse of thirty settlers cornered one of the slayers in some brush near the river. He refused to surrender and was promptly riddled with lead. "The posse made no effort to conceal the killing of the assassin and rely upon the community to sustain them in their efforts to overawe the turbulent and lawless element of the camp."[18]

There were other difficulties with "professional crooks who stood in with some lawyer as crooked as they were," who would file a contest with or without reason. This forced the poor landholder into a lawsuit to defend his claim before the land office, where the person contesting the homesteader generally would relinquish his suit for a consideration. The amount depended on the homesteader's purse. A "friendly" attorney, selected by the contestant, would be recommended to the homesteader by some other member of the gang and, apparently, would represent the homesteader when, in fact, he was "one of the gang out to skin him."[19]

There were others, vicious outlaws, who had come for no home, nothing but to prey off the fat of the land. . . .

[17] *Oklahoma City Times*, April 29, 1889.
[18] *Ibid.*
[19] "When one considers that just three and a half years after the opening a claim of 160 acres within the limits of Guthrie, which must have cost the original owner a total sum (including all fees) of $258 . . . is now worth from one hundred thousand to a quarter million dollars, it is easy to understand with what furious greed the sixty thousand would-be settlers must have been urged almost to any deed of violence. To take and keep possession of desirable city lots or particularly well situated farm land; to have one's entries made upon the official records—those two ambitions which might, if successfully attained, make a Croesus out of a pauper, aroused within this motley and decidedly wild assemblage the worst passions dormant within every human being. . . ."—*The Dalton Gang* (Anonymous), pp. 38-40.

"Law? For thirteen months there was no law but what we made ourselves."[20] The "rider" measure of the act approved March 2 contained no provision for territorial government. "Congress must have registered amazement on April 23, when they read the headlines of the morning press which proclaimed that sixty thousand settlers had occupied every available foot of this million and a half acres . . . with no government to restrain their actions and no authority to establish one."[21]

The only law was a few scattered deputy marshals and the squads of blue-shirted troops assigned to keep order. Even what little protection they afforded was looked upon with contempt by these people who considered them hated tools of an arbitrary government that had so long deprived them of their right to occupy public domain.

On the score or more townsites where hundreds and thousands had crowded together on lots twenty-five and fifty feet wide, quick, serious action was necessary to prevent wholesale bloodshed. In Guthrie alone were settled more than eight thousand people, and every man was armed with a revolver, often plus a bowie knife and a Winchester.

"Perhaps it was the psychology created by this preparedness that prevented many more brawls than occurred," wrote Frank H. Greer, a young editor from Kansas who established one of Oklahoma's first newspapers, the *State Capital*. "The second hectic day of Guthrie's existence a general assembly was held on the government square.[22] The people gathered around a big farm wagon. Colonel Constantine who had been speaker of the house of the Wisconsin legislature presided. He had a voice that reached to the utmost confines of the vast crowd and his kindly genius kept everybody in good humor. A provisional committee of fifty was elected to select a mayor and other officers to be approved by an assembly meeting a

[20] Dennis T. Flynn, lawyer and journalist, who lived through Guthrie's first three turbulent years as its postmaster and for eight years served as delegate from the territory to Congress.
[21] John Alley, *City Beginnings in Oklahoma Territory*, pp. 9-10.
[22] An acre of land set aside for use of the government on each townsite.

week from that date. Colonel D. B. Dyer, a prominent business man of Kansas City and a gentleman of the highest standing, was selected as mayor, with a de facto council and other officers, all being approved by the second assembly meeting. Soon ordinances were passed, a city marshal and policemen appointed, and an occupation tax levied for the expenses of the government. The gamblers were fined, and that was the way we got enough money to run the town."

This amounted to a fair sum considering that "between the land office and the railroad, flanking each side of what is now Oklahoma Avenue, also on Second and Harrison streets, covering every available foot of ground, were tents and booths . . . where every game of chance from the simple throwing of dice to faro was openly plied night and day." [23] "In one big tent, ninety feet wide and 125 feet long, every kind of gambling from chuck-a-luck to faro and poker was going every hour of the day and night," [24] and scores of games like blackjack and the shell game operated on tables outdoors. [25] Other places of sort made contributions:

The house of ill fame next to the Elephant Dance Hall in East Guthrie was being prospered without contributing to the city revenue. (City) Marshal Gebke told the inmates that he wished to see the landlady, the purpose being to arrest and fine her; but the various inmates declined to disclose who the landlady was and, moreover, Frank Scott told the marshal that he would blow a hole through anybody that arrested a person in the house. Being asked his authority, Scott said *he* was the owner of the place and told the marshal to go. Marshal Gebke is a man that means business and accordingly did not do as Scott told him. Instead, he gets four men to help him and provides them with Winchesters. Going back to the house the party boldly broke down the door which had been locked and arrested seven of the inmates. Scott was put under guard. A large crowd assembled and excitement ran high. How-

23 Rock, *op. cit.*
24 Statement of Frank H. Greer, Editor, *Daily Oklahoma State Capital.*
25 Evett Dumas Nix, *Oklahombres,* p. 21.

ever, Marshal Gebke safely housed his prisoners in jail, and all the girls paid $7.50 fines without further demurrer. Scott, who refused to recognize the court or enter a plea of any kind, was locked up.[26]

The absence of a constituted government to preserve order was not the only oversight of a dilatory congress. This august body had also failed to visualize the sudden building of cities and had enacted no provisions to meet the situation. The statutes in existence, framed to fit normal conditions of development, provided that a townsite plot on public domain must be filed with the registrar of the land office by the corporate authorities of the town if incorporated; if no incorporated town existed, then the plot must be filed with the judge of the county court in which the townsite was situated.[27]

There being no corporate authorities, no counties and no county judges, there was no legal authority to lay out streets and alleys, blocks and lots. In Guthrie, everyone had staked lots without regard to streets, locating wherever they could find a vacant spot. The tents were so thick their ropes crossed and the passages were mere wagon tracks or foot paths winding between them.

The provisional government was forced to take drastic steps to open them for traffic. Mayor Dyer had streets laid out by competent surveyors, then issued a proclamation declaring Oklahoma Avenue would be cleaned on a certain date and other streets as designated cleaned daily afterwards until all were opened.

At 10 a. m., on the day set, two great logs which had been brought from the woods were fastened together with chains and on each end were put four mules. In front of four of these mules was Bat Masterson, one of the most famous gunmen of the old Dodge City days, and on the other end before the mules rode Bill Tilghman, who had been city marshal of Dodge City and was famous

26 *Guthrie Daily News,* August 1, 1889.
27 Roy Gittinger, *The Formation of the State of Oklahoma,* p. 189.

then as afterwards as a deputy United States marshal. Each was mounted with a rifle on his saddle and two sixes showing on each side of his belt. Each made speeches to the people saying that the streets had been fairly surveyed, that no town could be without streets, that they were going right down Oklahoma avenue and were sending men down the street ahead to tell the people to get their tents and luggage out of the way before the mules were ridden over it or it was thrown out.

There were great mutterings. Men stood with their Winchesters and revolvers in hand, saying that they had the same right to their lots in the street as others who were lucky enough not to locate in the street and that no one could drive them out without suffering the consequences.

At the appointed time, Tilghman, Masterson, the mules and logs started. In an hour, there was not a tent or piece of luggage in Oklahoma avenue, and for the first time since the occupation of Guthrie you could stand on the hill and look straight down the avenue to the Santa Fe station.[28]

The history recorded here of Guthrie was being re-enacted in provisionally organizing the other towns, as citizens held mass meetings in streets, tents, or saloons and elected officials to steer them through their first raw, wild days and nights. Kingfisher boasted:

Chicago avenue is half a mile long. . . . The town is spreading over the whole section. Unless Guthrie or some other of the eastern Oklahoma towns beats this town, this is the liveliest place in America today. . . . Almost every man wears a six-shooter and wears it where he can get it very easily . . . but matters will probably be settled by law.[29]

The first civil government of the booming community that was to become the largest city in the state to be Oklahoma saw the greatest excitement. In Oklahoma City it was necessary for the military to remain on duty to help enforce the laws even

28 Greer, *op. cit.*
29 *Oklahoma City Times,* April 29, 1889.

after provisional government was established. It seemed that most of the inevitable horde of riffraff that came to prey upon this great flood of citizenship had settled here, and robberies, gambling, and the sale of liquor were rampant.[30]

Some of the lawless events were amusing, others tragic. For instance, a gambler named Cole, from Chicago, took possession of the only town pump, demanding five cents a drink tribute and enforcing his demands with a pistol. As "dry tongues began sagging," an appeal went to the troops to run

[30] In his book, *Thirty Years of Hell*, the first chapter of which is devoted to the beginnings of Oklahoma City, D. F. MacMartin gives the following account of his personal contact with the camp followers and hangers-on who settled as dregs in the lower levels of this fast-moving community:

"History has never recorded an opening of government land whereon there was assembled such a rash and motley colony of gamblers, cutthroats, refugees, demi mondaines, bootleggers and high-hat and low-pressure crooks. . . . The spectacular array embraced the Kansas Jayhawker, the Arkansas swamp angel, the Texas ranger, the Illinois sucker and a heterogeneous smear from every state in the Union. To be specific . . . there would be discovered units of humanity who were nesters, horse thieves, train robbers, hijackers, bank raiders, yeggmen, vagabonds, brand blotters, broncho busters, sheep herders, cow-punchers, spoofers, bull-whackers, range riders, four-flushers, chevaliers, d'industrie, montebanks, 'con' men, butterfly chasers, bubble-blowers, blue sky promoters, sour doughs, bumpkins and goofs. Also soldiers of misfortune just liberated from the stir, who had ugly corners in their life to live down and marksmen who were quick on the draw, who could throw a half dollar in the air and clip it with a bullet four times out of five . . .

"I do no violence to the truth when I say that the throng included ancient maidens, withered amazons, foolish virgins, scoundrels and camouflage slickers—scum of the earth and spawn of the devil who would not scruple to take unfair advantage of their bosom friends; slippery bunco-steerers, gunmen with stipulated fees for the midnight performance of pillage; and post-graduate, glass-blown, plush-lined, all silk, bottled-in-bond, fire-baptized, bullet-proof, ball-bearing, extra lubricated perjurers. . . . Some of these settlers had left families, creditors and in a paucity of instances even officers of justice, perplexed and lamenting. Some had deserted their wives for the wives of others, for this sanctuary. It is no grotesque assertion to say that some of the best men had the worst antecedents, some of the worst rejoiced in spotless, puritan pedigrees.

"Immediately upon human freight's deposit, gambling dens were opened, first in tents, and these rapidly metamorphosed to gaming parlors, approached by no passage or guarded entrance, where the rattle of coin and the sweeping of boards brought the senses under the dazzling spell of an agony of greed . . . and adventurous spirits risked their all with the ace in the hole and the high card to win as against velvet money represented by a flash roll big enough to stuff a feather pillow . . .

"Honky-tonks and hurdy-gurdies of salacious flavor opened their flaunting portecocheres, wherein racy floozies dwaddled about and separated the novice

the racketeer out of town. If they didn't, leaders of the angered citizens warned, Cole would be hanged. The soldiers "chased Cole off his perch."

Two hundred and fifty armed men attempted to jump a claim adjoining the city on the north. Ten armed men on the claim opposed them. Troops arrived just in time to prevent a pitched battle. Another group of five hundred armed men raided a claim on the west side of the city, staked it in town lots and named the site "West Oklahoma." They were run out by a detachment of cavalry. On June 14, the newly appointed city marshal of South Oklahoma was shot and killed by the man he succeeded in office.[31]

A group called the "Kickapoos" sought to dethrone the city administration, set up an entirely new government and rewrite the charter. They called an election for July 16, which was in violation of city ordinances, but the "Kickapoos" boasted of open defiance to the government and "pooh-poohed" the threat of possible arrest if they carried out their plan. Four companies of infantry on duty in the city were reinforced by two troops of cavalry. On the day of the proposed election more infantry arrived, and all troops, with guns loaded, stood ready for a free-for-all fight. The "Kickapoos," sizing up their number, called off the election. However, they started several riots, which were "nipped at the roots." Several were wounded and a dozen more arrested.[32]

As soon as the community showed itself able to cope with

---

from his diamonds and velvet. No exception was made here as between the case hardened cowman, plainsman, drunken soldiers, sheep herder, mule-skinner and the general indiscriminate driftwood of western civilization. The wide open element was in the saddle and was prepared to furnish dynamic throbs and thrills or any brand of frontier excitement the exacting visitor might demand. . . . It was the effervescent moment when everything floated on top that was foul. It was the home of mad excess with the lack of restraint that characterizes all new utopias."

31 Gittinger, *op. cit.*, p. 191.

32 *Oklahoma City Times*, September 19-27, 1889; Scott, *op. cit.*, pp. 43-45, 65-67; Peery, *op. cit.*, pp. 297-315.

its own rapid development the troops were withdrawn. But lawlessness continued, and other incidents of the day lent their color to the creed of the era: Let the best man live—to hell with weaklings![33]

The first brick building, situated in the heart of the city, boasted a liquor store on the first floor, police headquarters and police court on the second, and a jail in the basement. At the front door of this building Sheriff John Fightmaster killed Scarface Joe, an Indian who tried to flee from his cell. Doctor Falsom, a half-breed Cherokee, tried to knife Phil Rogers to death. Ike Steel, deputy United States marshal, bounced the butt of his gun off Falsom's head in time to save Rogers' life. George Shields, known in Texas as "Satan" Shields, learned that several members of the Wolf gang of killers were in town "to get his friend." The killers were in a saloon. Shields went to a store and bought a hickory axe handle, then proceeded to "mop up" on the gang in the saloon. When the battle ended, the six outlaws lay unconscious on the floor. They were tried before Police Judge Bent Miller and fined $100 each on a charge of "attempting suicide." Kid Bannister, a bad man of repute, finally was too slow on the draw and his notorious career ended from a gun in the hand of a citizen who seldom used a pistol. The crowd that witnessed the "execution" cheered when they found Bannister dead. When two Texas bad boys, Bud and Ping Fagg, went on trial for a misdeed, Police Chief Oscar Lee had to clear the courtroom because it wouldn't hold all the spectators. One man who objected, Bill McMichael, told Lee to "Go to hell!" McMichael landed at the bottom of the courthouse steps. Lee gave him back his gun, fully loaded, and told him not to come back or "I'll have to use force."[34]

Such lawlessness was destined to be wiped out as the cities

[33] "Oklahoma City Was Born in One Day," *Daily Oklahoman*, January 3, 1943.
[34] *Ibid.*

welded themselves into peace-loving, God-fearing people. But
outside the cities, where there was not even provisional government, and no laws except such as were generally applicable
to federal territory, gangs of outlaws were organizing swiftly.

Outlaw bands from the Indian Territory to the east and
south rode into Oklahoma, raided trains and the towns, and
fled back to their haven across the border. All along the line
of the Indian Territory, in which intoxicating liquor had long
been prohibited, saloons sprang into being. Red whiskey
flowed freely to those willing to cross into the Oklahoma country and get it, and "Poor Lo, the Indian whose untutored mind
sees God in cloud and hears him in the wind, was soused with
this brand of tailor made hell broth to the brink of going on
the warpath."[35]

When Congress met in December, 1889, the settlers demanded immediate organization of Oklahoma Territory. A
memorial drafted at Guthrie by a territorial convention of one
hundred delegates proclaimed in part:

> The laws at present in force in the territory relate only to
> crimes against the United States and the primitive forms of
> violence, such as murder and stock stealing. . . . There is no
> provision of law as to child stealing, attempted rape, poisoning,
> abortion, libel or blackmail, reckless burning of woods or prairies,
> burglarious entry of houses, trespass, embezzlement, rioting, car-
> rying deadly weapons, disturbing public meetings, seduction, pub-
> lic indecency, profanity, gambling, lotteries, drunkenness, bribery,
> destroying legal process, official negligence or malfeasance, creating
> or maintaining a public nuisance, selling unwholesome, diseased,
> or adulterated provisions or drink, introducing diseased or in-
> fected stock into the territory, swindling, false weights or measures,
> obtaining money or property under false pretense, making or using
> counterfeit labels; nor for many other offenses. . . .

By the exceptional and intelligent employment of United States
troops and United States marshals, and by the force of an excep-
tionally cool and intelligent and honest public opinion, there has

[35] MacMartin, *op. cit.*

been a degree of public order so far preserved . . . but it cannot be hoped that such conditions shall permanently continue.[36]

On May 2, 1890, President Harrison affixed his signature to a bill[37] creating six counties and six county seats,[38] extending the territory to include all that part of the former Indian Territory except the tribal reservations proper of the Five Civilized Tribes, the seven small reservations of the Quapaw Agency northeast of them[39] and the unoccupied part of the Cherokee Outlet;[40] but including the Public Land Strip (No Man's Land),[41] and Greer County (which was in dispute between the United States and Texas) in case the title thereto should be adjudged vested in the United States.

The government prescribed was republican in form, consisting of an executive, legislative, and judicial branch. The chief executive was to be a governor, appointed for a term of four years by the President. The legislative assembly was to consist of two houses, a council of thirteen members and the house of representatives with twenty-six members. The act placed the judicial power in a supreme court, district courts, probate courts and justices of the peace, the supreme court to consist of a chief justice and two associate justices, each of the three justices to be assigned to duty as a district judge as well as serving as a member of the appellate court. A large portion

---

[36] "Agitation for Territorial Government" (Joseph B. Thoburn and Muriel H. Wright, *Oklahoma, A History of the State and Its People*) Appendix LVI-2.

[37] Organic Act (U. S. Statutes at Large, XXVI, pp. 81-100; Oklahoma Statutes 1951, I, pp. 18-44).

[38] The counties were Logan, Oklahoma, Cleveland, Canadian, Kingfisher, and Payne; the seat towns, Guthrie, Oklahoma City, Norman, El Reno, Kingfisher, and Stillwater, respectively.

[39] Quapaw, Peoria, Ottawa, Shawnee, Modoc, Wyandotte, and Seneca.

[40] The portion of the Outlet occupied by the Ponca, Tonkawa, Otoe and Missouri, and Pawnee tribes was included.

[41] Cattlemen had occupied No Man's Land shortly after the Civil War. In 1887 they had sought to create the Territory of Cimarron, but had gained no encouragement from Congress. To meet their needs, Congress now added the strip to the Territory of Oklahoma as Beaver County with the county seat at Beaver.—Carl Coke Rister, *No Man's Land*, pp. 102-159; Leroy R. Hafen and Carl Coke Rister, *Western America*, p. 596; Harlow, *op. cit.*, pp. 250-251.

of the general statutes of Nebraska was adopted for temporary use, and Guthrie was designated the seat of the territorial government until such time as the Legislative Assembly and governor of the territory might see fit to establish it elsewhere.

Under the provisions of the act a full complement of officers was provided by President Harrison, who appointed George W. Steele, of Indiana, as governor. Judge Robert Martin, of El Reno, was appointed secretary of the territory; Horace Speed, of Guthrie, became United States district attorney; and Warren S. Lurty, of Virginia, was named United States marshal. Within a few weeks, Lurty resigned his office and was succeeded by William Grimes, of Kingfisher. Appointed as justices were Edward B. Green, of Illinois; John G. Clark, of Indiana; and A. J. Seay, of Missouri. Judge Green was named chief justice and, on May 29, the court was formally organized. The first district, assigned to Judge Green, held court at Guthrie and Stillwater. The second district, Judge Seay, met at Beaver (No Man's Land), El Reno, and Kingfisher. The third district, Judge Clark, sat at Norman and Oklahoma City. Guthrie remained the headquarters for the court's appellate function.

Governor Steele assumed office at Guthrie May 23. The boundaries of the counties were defined, their population enumerated, and representatives to the first legislature elected July 8. The first legislative assembly met August 27. Guthrie was declared the territorial capital; a code of laws taken from the statutes of different states was passed; and provisions were made for farming out the territory's convicts to the Kansas state penitentiary, at Lansing, and its insane to Illinois.[42]

The area along the boundary between the two territories, meanwhile, had become infested with every class of criminal from the most deadly and ruthless man killer to the petty, cowardly thief. It became known as "Hell's Fringe."

Its most desperate band of outlaws was the Dalton Gang.

---

[42] Oklahoma prisoners worked in the Kansas coal mines to pay the cost of their maintenance. This arrangement continued until statehood.

The Daltons Go Wild

☆ Too long have the outlaws on the Oklahoma frontier been defended as products of conditions; that as former cowboys with little or no education, forced out of work and driven from the freedom of the range by the division of the land into farms, they could not adjust themselves easily to agricultural conditions. "They had acquired more of the dare-devil spirit than they had been endowed with by nature; when the call came for them to join with other outlaws, they went wild," write the legend builders, and this explanation has been accepted. It catches the fancy of the reader and delights the collector of Western lore. But look at the facts.

When the farmer took over this region in the late eighties and early nineties, the cattle business still held its own in Texas and areas to the west and north. Moving was not hard for the average cowboy. Those with no stomach for such humble work as tilling the soil went with the migrating herds. Many who stayed took claims and became rich in land and fruits of their labor. Some went into the towns and cities and became merchants and bankers and, later, leading men of the state. They accepted the changed conditions and made the best of them. The few who took the outlaw trail could have found a niche to fit into had such been their choice.

Which brings us to the second legendary fallacy that nearly every bandit in the territory had been a cowboy before becoming a lawbreaker. Again the facts are: For two decades fugitives from all over the country had found refuge in the Nations so long as they violated no tribal statutes. The cattle and horse thieves and daring gunmen of the territory before the opening remained in the same class in which they had operated after the settlement of Oklahoma. They were joined by a few disgruntled cowboys who had listened to the lurid tales of easy money, but most of them came from the rabble who flocked to this last frontier. Legend has it that Bob, Grat, and Emmett Dalton, the three brothers who organized the Dalton gang, were of the few who could not bring their nature to the subjection of such a change from the wild, free life. They were of the venturesome spirit of the old Southwest and could not be tamed, it is argued. A sober investigation into their background reveals that they, like many outlaws to gain wide notoriety in their footsteps, "had a taint of outlaw in them all along, but it did not come to the surface until the occasion called it forth."[1]

Lewis Dalton, their father, was a gloomy-looking, dull, and morose individual, with a gruff disposition, but whose laziness and love of ease smothered a viciousness which lacked determination to become assertive. He was a Kentucky man who fought in the Mexican War. At the close of hostilities he returned to his native state, and in 1850 moved west, settling at Independence, Missouri, near the home of the notorious James and Younger boys. In 1851, he married Adeline Younger, aunt of the Younger boys, they moving, in 1860, to Lawrence, Kansas, and later to Montgomery County, near Coffeyville. Fifteen children were born them, nine sons and five daughters. Two, a boy and girl, died in infancy. The remaining thirteen grew up on the border of the Indian Territory. The three older brothers, Charles, Henry, and Littleton, migrated to Texas and Montana. Another son, William Marion (Bill), went to California, where he married and settled down in apparent respectability. In 1862, Lewis Dalton

1 Newsom, *op. cit.* (Chapter X, "Outlaws of Oklahoma and Indian Territory"), p. 103.

moved the rest of his family to the Cherokee Nation, leasing some land near Vinita until 1889, but was unsuccessful in obtaining a farm in the Oklahoma rush. His temper soured, he returned to Coffeyville, working at odd jobs about the country until his death in 1890. Mrs. Dalton came to live with her sons, Charles, Henry, and Littleton, who had returned to Oklahoma and obtained good claims near Kingfisher. Three of her daughters, Eva, Leona, and Nannie, married and located on good farms in the western part of the territory. Another son, Frank Dalton, had served as deputy marshal under the famous "Hanging Judge" Isaac C. Parker at Fort Smith, Arkansas, as early as 1884, and was known as a brave and trustworthy officer. In 1887, he was slain in a gun battle with bootleggers in the river bottoms west of Fort Smith.[2]

Gratton (Grat) Dalton took Frank's place as deputy marshal. He immediately appointed Robert (Bob) as a posseman. Emmett, still a boy, was working on the Bar X Bar ranch, near the Pawnee Agency.[3] He never held a federal commission, but when Bob and Grat organized the Indian Police for the Osage Nation, in 1888, he became a posseman. During 1889 and 1890, the Daltons made Pawhuska their headquarters. They nabbed no famous bad men, but brought in much criminal small fry, and were respected citizens until a controversy arose over their wages and Bob resigned as chief of police and Grat and Emmett refused amounts offered them as policemen.

The three brothers could have turned to farming then had they desired, for there already was land in the family and more to be had in subsequent openings. Bob and Grat could have continued to earn fees as federal marshals, and Emmett, without doubt, soon would have been added to the staff. But in either occupation the work was hard, the hours long, and really big and easy money was seldom to be had. They made their last trip as officers for the Fort Smith court June 20, 1890.

[2] Emmett Dalton, *When the Daltons Rode*, pp. 24-25; S. W. Harman, *Hell on the Border*, pp. 633-635; Emerson Hough, *The Story of the Outlaw*, pp. 375-376; Newsom, *op. cit.*, (Chapter X, "Going Out of the Outlaws") pp. 157-158.
[3] Dalton, *op. cit.*, p. 35.

They left here (Fort Smith) and went to Claremore, where they remained until after the 4th of July, when they visited the Osage country and stole seventeen head of ponies and a pair of fine mules. This stock they brought to Wagoner, and one or both of the boys (Bob and Emmett) came down here and tried to sell the stock to local buyers in this city, proposing to deliver it at Wagoner or opposite this city in the Cherokee Nation. They failed to make any trade, and started to Kansas, trading the mules to Emmett Vann, in the Cherokee Nation, and disposing of the ponies in Kansas.

They next showed up in the neighborhood of Claremore and boldly rounded up and drove away some twenty-five or thirty head of horses belonging to Frank Musgrove, Bob Rogers, and other citizens. This stock they sold at Columbus, Kansas, to a horse trader named Scott, referring him to some of the best men in the Territory as to their standing. He gave them a check for seven hundred dollars, which they cashed, endorsing it with their proper names. Scott took the stock to a pasture near Baxter Springs, where the owners afterward found it. In the meantime the boys had gathered up another bunch of horses, and on the very day Rogers and others were at Baxter Springs for the purpose of recovering the stolen property, the Dalton brothers arrived with them. A posse was hurriedly gotten together for the purpose of capturing them, when they hurriedly saddled fresh horses out of the stolen bunch and lit out with a crowd in hot pursuit. Emmett's horse gave out, and meeting a man driving a team, they took one of his horses, leaving him the jaded steed and Emmett's saddle, bridle and coat, which was tied to the saddle. They were being so closely pressed that they had no time to transfer the saddle from one horse to the other. They made good their escape, however, and their brother Grat was arrested while taking them fresh horses. Grat was lodged in the U. S. jail here, where he remained for several weeks, and Emmett and Bob escaped to California where a brother is residing. There being no evidence implicating Grat in the horse stealing business with his brothers, he was released and also went to California.[4]

The activities of the trio after joining brother Bill on the West Coast is described in the following circular from San Francisco, dated March 26, 1891:

4 *Fort Smith Elevator,* May 8, 1891.

$3600 REWARD

Supplementing circular letter of W. E. Hickey, Special Officer Southern Pacific Company, dated San Francisco, February 26th, 1891, wherein is offered a reward of $5000 for the arrest and conviction of all parties concerned in the attempted robbery of train No. 17 on the night of February 6th, 1891.

The Grand Jury of Tulare county have indicted Bob and Emmett Dalton as principles in said crime, and William Marion Dalton and Gratton Dalton as accessories; the two latter named being now in jail at Tulare county awaiting trial.

The Southern Pacific Company hereby withdraws said general reward in regard to Bob and Emmett Dalton, and in lieu thereof offer to pay $1,500 each for the arrest of Bob and Emmett Dalton, *upon their delivery to any duly authorized agent or representative of the State of California, or at any jail in any of the States or Territories of the United States.*

In addition to the foregoing the State and Wells, Fargo & Co., have each a standing reward of $300 for the arrest and conviction of each such offender.

The robbery had occurred at eight o'clock in the evening, near Alila. The express messenger had resisted, and in the exchange of shots, Fireman G. W. Radcliff was wounded in the abdomen and died the following day.[5] On March 2, railroad detectives learned that Bob and Emmett Dalton had left San Luis Obispo on horseback, and on March 8 disposed of their horses at Ludlow, a station on the A & P Railway about one hundred miles east of Mojave, where they purchased tickets on the east-bound train.

The pair made their way to their mother's home in Oklahoma, where they spent one night, secured horses and headed north into the Cherokee Outlet. In the latter part of April, it was reported they were in hiding near Tulsa.

The country up there is full of detectives and officers who are endeavoring to secure the big reward. Parties from there state that the Daltons range up in the Turkey Track ranch neighborhood,

5 C. B. Glasscock, *Bandits and the Southern Pacific,* pp. 38-40.

which is in the Sac and Fox reservation. No one lives in that section, it being 35 to 50 miles from one habitation to another. Deputy Marshal Heck Thomas is out there, and all manner of rumors reach Tulsa and Red Fork as to the movements of the fugitives and those in pursuit of them. The Daltons are desperate, are thoroughly acquainted with the country, and have friends who will keep them posted. Bob Dalton is recognized as one of the best shots with a Winchester rifle in the Indian country. That they will never surrender without a fight is a foregone conclusion . . .[6]

While Bob and Emmett Dalton were worrying the officers in the Oklahoma and Indian territories, their brothers in California were making it lively for Tulare County officials. Grat's horse had fallen with him in his ride from the Alila holdup, and he had been badly bruised in the accident. Since he was comparatively unknown this side of the Rockies, he boldly rode to his brother's place in the same county of Tulare. A chain of circumstances enabled detectives to trace him from Alila Canyon to Bill Dalton's home, and the messenger and engineer both declared under oath it was his voice they heard that eventful night of February 6, and that his size and general outlines corresponded exactly with those of the robber left in charge at the engine. This fact saved Grat Dalton from the gallows, for the shots that killed Radcliff had been fired by the two bandits who stood at the express car. On the other hand, Bill Dalton furnished an alibi which made Grat an "apparently total stranger" at the holdup. The fact that Bill had sheltered his wounded brother "could hardly be counted against him." The Tulare County jury acquitted Bill Dalton, but found Grat guilty of complicity in the robbery and the judge sentenced him to twenty years in the state penitentiary. That same day, in Visalia, Bill Dalton boasted that it would take the entire state militia to get his brother to San Quentin. Perhaps if the officials had heeded his warning, they might have avoided another "extraordinary occurrence" which "changed

[6] *Elevator,* May 8, 1891.

the course of events and set Grat one step nearer the terrible death he was to meet twenty months later at the hands of infuriated citizens."[7]

Two deputy sheriffs had been entrusted with the task of bringing Grat Dalton from the Tulare county jail to the state penitentiary. Knowing the man to be an athlete and a fearless desperado, they had decided to have his feet tied together with a leather thong, allowing their prisoner to take short steps only, while by turns each of the deputy sheriffs would link one of his wrists to one of the man's wrists by means of a double manacle. Thus it seemed that no possible escape could be effected. By using a day train, full of people, there was no danger of an attempt at rescue by Grat's confederates.

So the trio started on its trip on a fine morning in early April, 1891. The temperature was very hot . . . and the window next to which sat the prisoner had been thrown open. While the train was running at full speed between Fresno and Berenda, the deputy sheriff who was tied to the prisoner felt so drowsy that he let his head droop upon his breast in a delightful doze. His companion was having a chat and a smoke with a friend at the far end of the car.

Suddenly Grat Dalton rose from his seat with a jerk that awoke his bewildered neighbor. By a magic that has never been explained to this day, the bracelet around the prisoner's wrist fell upon the seat, while the man pitched headforemost and with lightning rapidity through the open window. A great noise of water was heard outside, and the excited passengers, now all shouting and crowding to that side of the train, could just see the form of the escaped prisoner swallowed up in the blue waters of a running stream.

The whole thing had not lasted five seconds, and the officers were gazing at each other with comic desolation, without even thinking of having the train stopped, when it slacked speed upon the conductor's spontaneously pulling the bell-rope.

The deputy sheriffs started out in hot pursuit, but their search was fruitless.

All they found on the river bank, close to the point where this

[7] *The Dalton Gang*, pp. 60-61.

incredible plunge had taken place, was the leathern thong and fresh hoofprints of a couple of horses that had evidently been kept waiting for the pre-arranged escape of Grat Dalton.[8]

In Oklahoma, Grat Dalton re-joined Emmett and Bob. Bob, a beardless youth hardly of age, impulsive but shrewd and inventive, became their leader. "The die was indeed cast; the bridges cut behind the trio; they were to bloom now into full-fledged desperadoes, and, all other means of living being thus rendered unavailable by their own fault, they would have to find their subsistence as open and daring violators of the law."[9] They added four members to the gang: Bill Doolin, who was later to become leader of a worse and more dangerous band than the Daltons; "Black-Faced" Charley Bryant (named for a scar on his cheek, the result of a duel with a cowboy);[10] Bill Powers; and Dick Broadwell.

Charley Bryant came from Wise County, Texas. He was small and slender, insignificant in appearance, but he had spent his last eight years in the Indian country in association with the most desperate characters and he had no superior among men beyond the law.[11]

Little is known of Powers except that he was a typical territory renegade, always ready to follow the Daltons in any crime, and sometimes went under the alias "Tom Evans."

Dick Broadwell's career in crime is blamed on a woman. In 1889, he homesteaded a choice 160 acres on the Cimarron. A good looking young woman took the quarter section next to him and they soon became friends. In a short time Dick found himself very much in love with the girl and asked her to marry him. She said she would, but did not want to live on a farm, as

8 *Ibid.*, pp. 62-63.

9 *Ibid.*, p. 50.

10 His face had been dangerously close to the cowboy's exploding gun. A bullet had creased his cheek, causing the scar, and the burned black powder had buried itself beneath the skin, making a splotch of dark dots.—Sam P. Ridings, *The Chisholm Trail*, p. 464; A. B. MacDonald, *Hands Up!*, p. 273; Nix, *op. cit.*, p. 37.

11 Ridings, *op. cit.*, p. 468.

she had taken the claim only as an investment. Finally, she persuaded him to sell both claims and go to Fort Worth with her to be married. Dick consented, placing the money in her care. Shortly after their arrival in Fort Worth, the girl and money disappeared and, in spite of his frantic efforts, he never found a trace of her. From then on, the tale continues, "Dick began to change." He returned to the territory, stole horses and committed one crime after another until he joined the Dalton gang.

How much of this story is true one can only surmise. It is sure-fire entertainment if one desired to build up this outlaw as a frontier hero. Obviously it is another attempt of the sentimentalists to excuse an outlaw's misdeeds by claiming he was sinned against. No mention is made of the fact that he enjoyed greater profits from operating with the Daltons than operating alone.

On May 9, 1891, the gang committed the first act to bring them into prominence after becoming organized. They held up the Santa Fe passenger train at Wharton, in the Cherokee Outlet, sixty miles south of the Kansas line, and looted the express car.[12] While passing the station window, they observed

12 A special from Guthrie gives the following account of the robbery:

"When the robbers boarded the train, the messenger was looking out the door of his car, and seeing what was going on, immediately . . . closed and locked the door and commenced to hide the money and valuables in his keeping. While the bandits were detaching the engine and express car from the rest of the train and were running it to the place where the robbery occurred, two miles distant, the messenger disposed of most of the valuables in places of safety. Then he locked the safe.

"When the robbers appeared at the door . . . he made a show of resistance, but finally admitted them. They made for the safe and demanded that it be opened. . . . With feigned reluctance the messenger opened it and handed over the contents, among which was a package of worthless papers which he told the robbers was a valuable package of money. Most of the money had been hidden in the stove, which was not being used for its legitimate purpose. In the search of the car, the robbers overlooked that hiding place, but stumbled upon a package of $500. . . ."

A dispatch from Topeka says: "An official report of the robbery has been made to the headquarters of the Santa Fe railway. The details made public are very meager, but coincide with the report from Guthrie. The amount secured by the robbers is given out by the Santa Fe as $1500. . . ."—Elevator, May 15, 1891.

the young station agent sending a message for help, and
Charley Bryant shot him through the head.[13]

A search for the gang spread at once; but the country was
ideal for their escape. Only a few railroads traversed it. The
Indian reservations surrounding it were wild and practically
uninhabited.[14] After leaving the railroads and settlements
"the bandits were as well hidden as were the robbers of old in
the fastness of a wilderness."[15] In the months that followed,
the Dalton name became a terror to all whose business and
daily vocations compelled them to travel across the territories.

Following the Wharton robbery, the Daltons were never
seen by those who knew them, at least by those who would
have informed the officers of their whereabouts. They made
long, hard rides. They would pull a job in one place and scatter. By the time the officers arrived to pick up their trail, they
were miles away, each in a different locality.

These rides required fresh horses frequently, and many
farmers in Oklahoma Territory lost their best saddle stock.
In one raid the gang stole ten horses from a colony of Missouri-
ans who had settled on Beaver Creek, near Orlando. The farmers quickly organized and trailed the thieves to a canyon camp
near Twin Mounds in eastern Payne County on the border of
Hell's Fringe. As the posse approached through the dense
timber along the bank of a creek, the outlaws opened fire
from ambush. The farmers quickly took cover and poured a
deadly fire in the direction from which the shots had come,
but the outlaws were well concealed. They killed the leader

13 MacDonald, *op. cit.*, p. 274; Hough, *op. cit.*, p. 379; Nix, *op. cit.*, p. 40,
admits this slaying but claims it happened during the Red Rock robbery, which
occurred nearly a year after Bryant had been captured and slain.

14 Except for cattlemen who had leased the land for grazing purposes,
there were only 70 Indians in the Cherokee Outlet. Some of them had farms or
ranches, others were with the Indian police. John W. Jordan, a Cherokee, was
one of the famous policemen appointed by the government to keep boomers
and outlaws out of this strip. He had built a fort out of heavy timber and logs
on his ranch for the protection of his family against the white man and the
other Indians. Bob and Grat Dalton were members of his force before they
became deputy marshals.

15 Zoe A. Tilghman, *Outlaw Days*, pp. 32-33.

of the posse, W. T. Starmer, and badly wounded another farmer, named William Thompson. The rest were quickly routed without further fight, and the gang escaped with the best horses from the stolen herd, scattering again to parts unknown.[16]

The search for the Daltons continued under the personal leadership of Marshal Grimes. Charley Bryant was staying at a cow camp near Buffalo Springs, just over the Oklahoma Territory border, in the Outlet, seven miles north of Hennessey. He would leave camp occasionally, saying nothing to anyone. At the time of the Wharton robbery he had been gone several days. The men in camp figured him for a slow, easy-going fellow with the wandering habit. No one thought of him in connection with the Dalton gang.[17]

Ed Short, a blond man of large, robust physique and commanding appearance, was deputy marshal, with headquarters at Hennessey. He had come west from Indiana and sought employment where his services in the interest of law enforcement were desired. He had been city marshal at Woodsdale, Kansas, during the memorable Stevens County War, of 1886 and 1887, when several persons were killed and the state militia called to quiet the contention and violence. He had been at Caldwell prior to the opening of Oklahoma, and was considered a fearless officer.[18]

In the latter part of July, Bryant returned from one of his trips dangerously ill with fever. The men at the camp persuaded him to let them take him to Hennessey for medical treatment. The doctor, upon making an examination, ordered him to bed. He was placed in a room on the second floor of the Rock Island Hotel.

Ed Short saw Bryant when the cowboys brought him in. Looking over a list of pictures and warrants for men he was

16 Nix, *op. cit.*, pp. 37-38.
17 Barnard, *op. cit.*, p. 193.
18 Ridings, *op. cit.*, p. 464; Rister, *op. cit.*, p. 130; Hough, *op. cit.*, pp. 235-237; George Rainey, *No Man's Land*, pp. 203-204.

hunting, the deputy read a description of Black-Faced Charley on a notice offering $1,000 reward for his capture as one of the most dangerous members of the Dalton gang.

Short watched the hotel. He talked with the nurse who carried Bryant his meals and medicine and learned when he had recovered. On August 2, he went to the room, opened the door, and leveling his six-shooter at Bryant's head, commanded him to throw up his hands. Bryant started to reach for a revolver under his pillow, but saw that Short had the drop on him and surrendered.

The capture had been made. The question was what to do with the prisoner. There were few jails in the territory, none at Hennessey. Short could take his prisoner across country to the federal jail at Guthrie, but this meant almost certain delivery by other members of the gang. He decided to take him to Wichita.

At five o'clock the evening of August 3, Short boarded the northbound passenger train with his prisoner. At first, he had handcuffed the outlaw's hands behind him, but Bryant complained so much about this position hurting him because of his recent illness that the marshal changed them, placing his hands in front.

This gesture of comfort to a renegade killer was to cost Ed Short his life.

For this trip, the deputy armed himself with a Winchester rifle besides the six-shooter he carried. The Dalton gang was as desperate a bunch as he had known and might go to any extent to rescue a member of their band. It had been rumored in Hennessey, before his departure, that they might even rob the train during the operation.

As an added precaution, Short, instead of taking his prisoner into the coaches, placed him in the baggage car. This car, used also as a mail car, was equipped with pigeonholes for sorting letters. In one of these the baggage agent kept a .45 Colt revolver.

The first stop before reaching the Kansas border was at Waukomis, in the Outlet, thirteen miles north of Hennessey. If an attempt were made to rescue his prisoner, it would be at Waukomis, Short reasoned. As the train approached the station, he directed the agent to keep an eye on Bryant, while he went out on the platform with his rifle to search for signs of an attack.

He scarcely had gone from the car when Bryant, unnoticed by the agent, reached into the pigeonhole and seized the revolver in his shackled hands. Ordering the agent to say nothing, the outlaw stepped to the doorway.

Short had just finished his inspection when he glimpsed his prisoner standing with a gun pointed at him. Jerking his rifle to his hip, he started firing as fast as he could lever and pull the trigger. Bryant's revolver roared at the same instant, and the outlaw kept firing until all six shots were gone before he died on the platform.

Short lived long enough to help carry the outlaw back inside the car and lie down on a cot. When the train stopped at the station a few minutes later, he was dead.[19]

Word of the killings was wired ahead and arrangements made to remove the bodies at Caldwell. An examination revealed one fatal wound in each man. A bullet fired by Bryant had entered the marshal's shoulder and ranged down into the vital organs. A ball from Short's Winchester had struck Bryant in the center of the breast even with the heart, severing the spinal column.

The bodies were prepared for burial by the Schaeffer Undertaking Parlors. Relatives claimed Bryant's. The body of Ed Short was shipped east to his mother, with the reward for the capture of Black-Faced Charley.[20]

[19] *Indian Chieftain*, August 27, 1891; *Daily Oklahoma State Capital*, January 24, 1894; "Ed Short, Fearless Gunman," *Daily Oklahoman*, February 29, 1920; *The Dalton Gang* pp. 95-96; Ridings *op. cit.*, pp. 466-468; Barnard, *op. cit.*, pp. 194-195.
[20] Ridings, *op. cit.*, p. 468.

The killing of Bryant sent the Daltons into hiding. The legend builders have credited them with having a cave somewhere deep in the mountain fastness which commanded a view of the only approach and from which the occupants could "stand off a regiment."

It is readily apparent to the discerning person that while one man could withstand assault for a time in a cave with a single approach, the same factors that kept anyone from coming in also kept the occupants from getting out. A siege could last only as long as food and water. Finally the outlaws would be forced to surrender or come out shooting and be cut down by the besiegers.

The Daltons had no such cave or stronghold. They did have a hideout; two, in fact. Bob, the leader, worked on the theory that if one hideout was discovered and they were forced to vacate, they should have another into which to move. Both places were so constructed that the gang could leave whenever they were ready, unless they happened to be surrounded by several score of pursuers, which was not likely in those days. A posse of six was considered large, and twice that number was a rare exception.

Both hideouts were in small clumps of trees surrounded by open country so they could view the surroundings for a distance on all sides. The outlaws excavated about four feet below the surface and built up walls three feet with logs and cut saplings, camouflaged with tree branches and underbrush for roofing, so that at a distance of a hundred yards it would have escaped notice unless someone had been deliberately led to the spot or stumbled upon it by chance.

These dugouts were about eighteen feet square and consisted of a single room. Around the walls were six bunks. After the death of Charley Bryant, there were never more than six in the Dalton gang, and seldom more than four stayed in either hideout at any one time. Loopholes were provided on all sides of the room, so that they could repel attack from any angle. These loopholes were at a height convenient for the best shooting with rifles, and the gang always kept a good supply of ammunition.

One of these dugouts was located southwest of Kingfisher, on a high bluff in the cedar brakes above the Canadian River. The other lay in the edge of the Creek Nation, just over the eastern border of Payne County, in the highland above the Cimarron, on Hell's Fringe.

For months the territory was left surprisingly undisturbed. The southbound passenger train on the Missouri, Kansas, and Texas railroad was flagged at Lillietta, a cattle station north of Wagoner, the night of September 15, 1891, and the express robbed of $3,000. Reports were conflicting. It was the general opinion that the Daltons were "in it."[21] In his book, *When the Daltons Rode,* Emmett Dalton credits the gang with committing this holdup.[22] But the identity of the robbers was never established. On the night of June 1, 1892, the gang came out of hiding to hold up the Santa Fe train at Red Rock, a depot in the Otoe reservation forty miles south of Arkansas City.

This robbery, which occurred at 9:30 P. M., met with strong resistance from E. S. Whittlesey, the messenger, and John A. Riehl, an express company guard. More than sixty shots were fired by the bandits through the windows and wooden sides of the express car before the two defenders gave up the unequal contest. Three of the gang then entered and ordered the messenger to open the safe. Whittlesey assured them he did not know the combination. The robbers secured a sledge hammer and caved in the door and took out the contents. They next went through the merchandise and took what they wanted. They even appropriated the lunch baskets and took the firearms of the two men who had successfully held them at bay for more than a quarter of an hour, then mounted their horses and rode off into the night.[23]

As soon as the gang had disappeared, the train proceeded

21 *Elevator,* September 18, 1891.
22 pp. 131-134.
23 *Elevator,* June 10, 1892.

on its run. At the first telegraph station, Conductor Harry
Wilcox wired the news of the holdup to the dispatcher's office
at Arkansas City. Deputy Marshal Heck Thomas and a posse
hurried to the scene and trailed the gang west into the Outlet.
A wide search was made by other posses.[24] But all efforts to capture the outlaws again failed.[25]

The Daltons had doubled back and retired to their dugout
on Hell's Fringe. Riding out from there on the night of July
15, less than two months after the Red Rock job, they appeared over in the Cherokee Nation at Adair, near the Arkansas line, and held up the "Katy" northbound passenger and
express.

This act was the most audacious and daring of any in their
career up to that time. A large force of armed railroad detectives and Indian police were on the train and "poured a
withering fire upon them," but the robbers succeeded in carrying away all valuable contents of the express car and escaped

[24] "On June 4, Sheriff John W. Hixon of Logan county returned from the
trail of the Red Rock train robbers. When he left the pursuers of the gang, they
were sixty miles west of Red Rock. There were twenty-five deputies in the party
and he said they would press on until the trail ended or the robbers were over-
taken. United States Deputy Marshals Ransom Payne and Chris Madsen were
in the Panhandle country at that date with a posse watching to prevent their
escape. The two posses are now pursuing a northerly course through the strip.
A party has started from Caldwell, Kansas, going south in sufficient numbers
and fully armed to do good battle in case they intercept the fleeing road agents.
The latest reports state that the robbers were on the trail leading to Fort
Supply and their pursuers were following them very close. A posse had started
from Fort Supply to intercept them. . . ."—*Stillwater Gazette,* June 10, 1892.

[25] "Deputy Marshals Kress and Severns returned yesterday from the pursuit of the train robbers. On the same train with them were the posse of marshals from Purcell en route home. All of the pursuing party have now returned
and the chase of the bandits has been entirely abandoned. Marshals Kress and
Severns, with eleven others, chased the robbers over two hundred miles before
they gave up and then their horses gave out so they saw it would be no use to
go further. They first chased the robbers into the Cimarron hills in the strip,
then south into the Cheyenne and Arapaho country and finally back into the
Cimarron hills. The bandits had obtained a relay of fresh horses and it was then
very easy for them to ride away from their pursuers whose animals were completely tired out. Four horses which the robbers had abandoned were picked up
and brought back by the marshals. They believe the train robbers are the same
men who stole the horses at Orlando several months ago and afterwards murdered W. T. Starmer. They had every arrangement completed to make sure
their escape. . . ."—*Stillwater Gazette,* June 17, 1892.

unharmed. Several police and passengers were wounded and a physician, who resided in Adair, slain.[26]

News of this holdup—the incredible details and the startlingly easy success of the Daltons' bold raid in the face of armed forces which they must have known to be on the train—caused great concern throughout the territories and the border states: Was there no security left for railway passengers? Was money in transit to be henceforth at the mercy of this dangerous band of robbers?

[26] "The coolest and most desperate train robbery ever perpetrated on the Missouri, Kansas and Texas railroad took place at Adair station on the Cherokee Division of the road about 9:30 o'clock last night, resulting in the killing of one man, the wounding of several others and the loss to the express company of a large sum.

"The notorious Dalton gang, who had been camped in the Indian Territory between Adair and Pryor Creek for several days, made their way to Adair about 9 o'clock last night and at the muzzles of Winchesters, pointed in the face of the station agent, ransacked the office of the station of all money and valuables. Having accomplished this, the robbers sat down at the station and coolly waited the arrival of passenger train No. 2, due there at 9:42 o'clock.

"When the train was slowing up at the station, the robbers covered Engineer Glen Ewing and his fireman with Winchesters and no sooner had Conductor George W. Scales and his porter stepped off the train than both of them were also forced to face Winchesters.

"Three of the robbers then compelled the fireman to leave the engine and with his coal pick aid them in securing admission to the express car. Up to this time Messenger George P. Williams had persisted in his refusal to open the door. One of the bandits then shouted that he had placed dynamite under the car and would blow it to atoms if the door was not opened. He fired, by way of emphasis, several shots into the car, which passed uncomfortably near the head of the messenger and he gave in and opened the door.

"The three men sprang into the car and while one covered the terrified messenger with his gun, the other two turned their attention to the safe. The messenger was threatened with death if he did not open it. He finally succeeded and the robbers made short work of its contents, taking everything they could find, even things that were of no value to them. After relieving the messenger of his watch, the robbers bound him and dumped him in a corner of the car. While the three robbers were in the express car, another was seen to back a spring wagon up to the door of the car and the contents of the safe were thrown into the wagon.

"When the train stopped at Adair, Captain J. J. Kinney, chief of the detective force of the Missouri, Kansas and Texas, Captain LaFlore, chief of the Indian police, and seven other guards were in the smoking car of the train, expressly to protect the train from any attack from robbers. The robbers, the moment the train stopped, began firing their Winchesters and kept the firing up until they had accomplished their aims. Kinney and his men opened fire on the robbers and for a few minutes bullets were flying thick and fast. In the

The time had come for "a gigantic effort to wipe out this triumphant band." In addition to rewards already offered for the Daltons, the Missouri, Kansas, and Texas railroad announced that $5,000 would be paid for the capture and conviction of each member of the gang, an aggregate now of $33,600—the largest sum ever offered for a single outlaw band in America.

There were "great stirs" in top political circles. From Washington came orders for the territorial governor to use every means at his disposal to apprehend these bandits who had become "a menace to Oklahoma's march of progress."

The wildest rumors concerning the lightning rapidity and secrecy with which Bob Dalton conducted his operations spread until every act of particularly bold outlawry was placed to his credit. It has been the general, though perhaps erroneous, opinion that the Daltons were the gang which attacked the bank at El Reno shortly after the Adair robbery. One morning while the streets were crowded with people, six bandits entered the leading bank of the city. The only person inside was the wife of the president, who fainted at the sight of their weapons. The bandits took all the money in sight and escaped. The raid netted them $10,000, which was such a loss to the bank that it was forced into liquidation.[27]

"Of the many crimes laid at the doors of the Daltons," said Superintendent C. H. Epplesheimer, of the Pinkerton Detective Agency, in an interview with a Kansas City reporter, "I doubt they were guilty of this one. I am not defending them in the least, but in this respect they resembled the James boys.

---

melee Kinney received a flesh wound on the right shoulder, LaFlore had one arm burned and a guard by the name of Ward suffered a slight flesh wound. None of the robbers were injured as far as known. Stray bullets entered a drug store up town and struck Drs. Youngblood and W. L. Goff, who were sitting in the building. Goff has since died of his wounds and Youngblood is in a dangerous condition.

"After the robbers had loaded their plunder into the spring wagon, they headed for the woods, and after firing a parting shot at the train, were soon lost to view."—*Stillwater Gazette,* July 16, 1892; also Harman, *op. cit.,* p. 637; Nix, *op. cit.,* p. 43; Newsom, *op. cit.,* p. 163.

27 Hough, *op. cit.,* p. 380.

In their time every robbery and crime committed in this section was laid to them, while it is an unquestioned fact that they knew nothing of many of the occurrences. So it was with the Daltons."

Superintendent Epplesheimer likely was correct, for by this time, within six weeks after the holdup at Adair, the ground had become too hot for the gang to circulate—the indignation of territorial officials, a seething citizenship, rewards so great to cause even their trusted friends to turn against them. Bob Dalton realized that, sooner or later, they would be captured, and laid plans for a last big raid from which they could gain a fortune and retire.

Encouraged by their successful robberies and escapades, young Bob's mad ambition was fired with a desire to commit a robbery so daring and so sensational that the entire country would be shocked, and that would establish the Dalton gang as more to be feared than the James boys or the Youngers had ever been. Having been reared near Coffeyville, Kansas, the Dalton boys knew the little town, its inhabitants and their habits intimately. Young Bob decided that Coffeyville should be the scene of his *coup de theatre*. They would rob two banks in the same town simultaneously. That would eclipse anything the James or Youngers had ever done. He visualized himself as a romantic hero and he developed a super-ego and an unreasonable confidence that was to lead him to his destruction.[28]

What happened the few days preceding the Coffeyville raid is related in Emmett Dalton's confession, which he gave Deputy Marshal Ransom Payne at the Farmer's Home, a little hostelry where the bandit lay badly wounded the day following the famous battle:

On the first of October, 1892, I met the boys south of Tulsa, and they asked me how much money I had. I told them about twenty dollars. I asked them how much they had, and they said

<hr>

[28] Nix, *op. cit.*, p. 44; also Tilghman, *op. cit.*, pp. 39-40.

about nine hundred dollars. I asked them what they were going to do, and they said this town, Coffeyville, had been talking about them and some of the people had been trying to get them captured. I told them I knew it was a lie, that they used to have lots of friends here.

Bob said he could discount the James boys' work and go up and rob both banks of Coffeyville in one day. I told him I did not want any of it at all. He said I had better go along and help get some money and leave the country; that if I stayed around here I was sure to get caught or killed.

On the morning of the 3rd of October we saddled up north of Tulsa in the Osage Nation and rode about twenty miles toward Coffeyville, and we talked it over that day. I tried to prevail on the boys not to come up, for the people here had done us no harm. They said all right, if I didn't want to come that the rest would come and give the town a round-up. I told them if that was the case I might as well come with them. . . . I knew I would be chased just as hard if I didn't come as I would if I did, and I had no money to get out of the country on.

We camped in the timbered hills on the head of Hickory Creek about twelve miles from Coffeyville the night of the 4th, and in the night we saddled up and rode to the Davis farm in the Onion Creek bottoms, and that morning (the 5th) as we fed our horses I asked them if they were still coming up here. They said they were. . . .

I asked them how they were going to do it. Bob said we would ride in about half-past nine o'clock, that there would not be so many people in town and we wouldn't have to hurt anyone.

He told me he would like to have me go with him because I was quick on foot and that he and I would go to the First National Bank and let the others go to C. M. Condon's. He said he would ride in and hitch at the old C. M. Condon building. We all would hitch so the people would not see us until we got into the banks. . . .

The six members of the gang rode out from Onion Creek bottoms, but only five rode into Coffeyville. Bill Doolin's horse went suddenly lame and the outlaw, bitterly disap-

pointed, left his companions to go to the ranch of a friend
several miles off the trail to obtain another mount. It had been
planned to have three men enter each bank, and Doolin promised Bob Dalton he would rejoin them just below the Kansas
line.

How the battle might have ended had Doolin been with
the band is a matter of conjecture. Perhaps it would have
ended in the Dalton's favor; on the other hand, he would
probably have shared their defeat and death. As it was, Doolin
arrived at the meeting place too late. It already was past
9 o'clock, and the gang had not waited for him.

So many versions of what happened during the next few
minutes of that eventful day have been told and written that
it has been difficult to separate facts from fiction.[29] The most
reliable account covering all activity and parties involved is
given by David Stewart Elliott in *The Last Raid of the
Daltons:*[30]

They rode into Coffeyville over a piece of road that was rarely
traveled . . . talking in ordinary tones to each other and gaily
laughing. . . . A marked change had come over the personal appearance of each of the men. The smooth-faced leader had somehow or other acquired a heavy black moustache and goatee. The
youngest of the number had been transformed into a heavily
bearded man. One had grown a moustache and whiskers that gave
him the look of an ancient pirate. The remaining two were

29 Newsom, *op. cit.*, pp. 164-167; Nix, *op. cit.*, pp. 45-51; Dalton, *op. cit.*,
pp. 237-261; Harman, *op. cit.*, pp. 637-642; Glasscock, *op. cit.*, pp. 60-64; The
Dalton Gang, *op. cit.*, pp. 127-169; Tilghman, *op. cit.*, pp. 40-46; Richard S.
Graves, *Oklahoma Outlaws*, pp. 44-53; William Ward, *The Dalton Gang*, pp.
135-163; Harry Hawkeye, *The Dalton Brothers and Their Gang*, pp. 174-182;
Pete Fanning, *Great Crimes of the West*, pp. 186-189; Arthur H. Lamb, *Tragedies of the Osage Hills*, pp. 34-38; Hough, *op. cit.*, pp. 382-391.
30 David Stewart Elliott was editor of *The Coffeyville Journal* in October,
1892, and was in the Plaza area when the gun battle with the Dalton gang
started. He was an eyewitness to the whole fight and the first man to reach
Emmett Dalton, the lone survivor of the gang, after the latter had been shot
from his horse in the alley. Elliott published this book on the Dalton raid
October 22, 1892, in a limited edition which has become exceedingly rare and
a collector's item.

unchanged and were seemingly regardless of the change in the others. . . . [They might have been taken] for a deputy United States marshal and posse, who frequently came up from the Indian country in such numbers and similarly equipped. No arms were visible on any of them. Their coats were closely buttoned and their broad-rimmed black slouch hats set forward on their foreheads.

Reaching the junction of two section lines, near the cheese factory and dairy farm, they changed their course for the first time since leaving the Verdigris below Nowata. The horses' heads were turned east, and the animals urged into a brisk, swinging trot. They were now on one of the principal thoroughfares leading into Coffeyville . . . riding in files of three in front and two in the rear. They were soon within one block of the business portion of the city. A number of residents on both sides of the street observed them as they passed, but no one was particularly attracted to them at the time. The deputy U. S. marshal and posse idea seemed to have taken possession of the minds of the people who saw them. The party never paused, but wheeled into Maple Street in a semi-military manner and rode south. Passing the Long-Bell Lumber Company office, they suddenly diverged into the alley that runs east and west through the block, from Walnut street to Maple, and halted in the rear of the lot of Police Judge Munn, and within thirty feet of his residence, dismounted and hitched their horses to the fence at the north end of his lot, within fifty feet of Maple street and three hundred and fifty feet from Walnut, the main business street of the city, and the same distance from the Plaza, or public square. Quietly forming in lines as they had been riding, three in front and two following, the men walked at an ordinary pace down the alley, in an easterly direction towards the Plaza. A stone-cutter, a comparative stranger in the city who was examining some rock for curbing purposes that was piled in the alley near the jail, walked closely after them. He saw that they were armed with guns, which they were carrying on the inside, so as not to be visible. He thought nothing of it, and as the men passed across the street, in the direction of the bank of C. M. Condon & Co., he turned toward his work at the north end of the block. . . .

A member of a well-known firm of general merchants was standing on the pavement in front of a dry-goods store when the men, followed by the stone-cutter, came out of the alley between the building and the drug store of Slosson & Co. The party passed within five feet of where he was standing. An oil wagon or tank of the Consolidated company, drawn by two horses, pulled into the alley about the same time and stopped about one hundred feet from the front street. The gentleman was close enough to detect the disguises on the men, and he recognized one of them by his well-known walk and the peculiar shape of the back of his head.

After crossing the pavement, the men quickened their pace, and the three in the front file went into C. M. Condon & Co.'s bank at the southwest door, while the two in the rear ran directly across the street to the First National Bank and entered the front door of that institution. The gentleman was almost trans-fixed with horror. He had an uninterrupted view of the inside of Condon & Co.'s bank, and the first thing that greeted his vision was a Winchester in the hands of one of the men, pointed towards the cashier's counter. He quickly recovered his lost wits, and called out to the men in the store that "The bank is being robbed." Persons at different points on the Plaza heard the cry and it was taken up and quickly passed around the square. At the same time several gentlemen who saw the two men enter the First National Bank, suspecting their motive, followed close at their heels and witnessed them "holding up" the men in this institution. They gave the alarm on the east side of the Plaza. A "call to arms" came simultaneously with the alarm, and in less time than it takes to relate the fact a dozen men with Winchesters and revolvers in their hands were ready to resist the escape of the unwelcome visitors. . . .

Entering the Condon & Co. bank by the southwest door, the robbers found Mr. C. T. Carpenter, one of the proprietors, at the west front counter, engaged in making remittances. Mr. Tom C. Babb, the bookkeeper, was at his desk, at the east front near the doors of the vault. Mr. Charles M. Ball, the cashier, was in his private office, which occupied the northwest portion of the room, and had a door leading out to Walnut street. The three men quickly closed the front door after them as they entered, and quickly disposed themselves in different portions of the room. Mr. Carpenter, from his position, could not see the men as they came through the door. Attracted by their footsteps, he turned towards them, and was horrified to find the muzzles of three Winchesters pointed directly at his person. The man who acted as the leader, and who it was afterwards ascertained was Grat Dalton, called out in quick tones: "We have got you, God damn you! Hold up your hands!" The other two men, who proved to be Bill Powers and Dick Broadwell, stopped in the front part of the bank, Broadwell being closer to the southeast entrance, and Powers stationed himself near the southwest door. Mr. Babb, the bookkeeper, discovered the character of the men before they discovered him, and he quickly and quietly stepped into the vault. Mr. Ball, the cashier, hearing the noise in the front part of the bank, came into the room, and was at once put under the surveillance of the Winchesters in the hands of the daring men. Grat Dalton then ran to the private office door, passed through the office and into the front part of the bank, behind the counter. He had in his hands a two-bushel seamless grain sack, which he gave Mr. Ball, with directions to hold it open and at the same time he ordered Mr. Carpenter to put all the money on the counter and in the drawer into the sack. The latter reluctantly complied. After this was done, the robber asked: "Where is your gold?" Not receiving a satisfactory reply, he ordered Mr. Carpenter and Mr. Ball to go into the vault and as they turned to comply he for the first time discovered the presence of Mr. Babb. He gave the young man a terrible cursing and made him hold up his hands and come out from behind the book-rack, where he was secreted. The burglar-proof chest was closed and locked with a combination lock. The two front doors and the two sets of outside doors of the hall burglar-proof safe were standing open. There were three canvas bags filled with silver, containing one thousand dollars each, in the safe. These fell under the eye of the robber, and he directed Mr. Carpenter to empty them into the sack which Mr. Ball was holding. While this was going on he asked: "What is that you are putting in there?" Mr. Ball replied, "Silver dollars." Looking around quickly and nervously at Mr. Ball with an oath he said: "Open up that door," pointing to the burglar-proof chest. Mr. Ball replied: "It is not time for that to open."

Grat Dalton—"What time does it open?"

Mr. Ball—"Half past 9 o'clock," guessing at the time.

Grat Dalton—"What time is it now?"

Mr. Ball (looking at his watch)—"Twenty minutes after 9 o'clock."

Grat Dalton—"We can wait ten minutes."

It was actually twenty minutes of ten, and Mr. Ball had missed his guess just twenty minutes. In the meantime Mr. Carpenter had turned the handle of the door of the chest in order to show that it was locked. Waiting a moment or two with evident impatience, Grat Dalton exclaimed:

"God damn you! I believe you are lying to me, I've a mind to put a bullet through you. Open it up or I will shoot you; you have been blowing too much about what you can do. Where is your gold?"

Mr. Ball—"We haven't any."

Grat Dalton—"How much in this sack?"

Mr. Ball—"Four thousand dollars."

Grat Dalton—"How much cash did your books show last night?"

Mr. Ball—"Four thousand dollars; one thousand dollars in currency and three thousand dollars in silver, all of which you have in your sack. There is nothing in the burglar-proof chest except some nickles and pennies; we ordered some currency, but it has not been delivered yet; it is over in the express office."

In the meantime, Mr. J. D. Levan and Mr. D. E. James, two customers of the bank, had entered at the southwest door, and had been captured by one of the fellows on the outside of the counter. Just at this critical juncture the citizens opened fire from the outside and the shots from their Winchesters and shot-guns pierced the plate-glass windows and rattled through the bank. Bill Powers and Dick Broadwell replied from the inside, and each fired from four to six shots at citizens on the outside. The battle then began in earnest. . . . Grat Dalton asked whether there was a back door through which they could go to get to the street. He was told that there was none. He then ordered Mr. Ball and Mr. Carpenter to carry the sack of money to the front door. Reaching the hall on the outside of the counter, the firing of the citizens through the windows became so terrific and the bullets whistled so close around their heads that the robbers and both bankers retreated to the back room again. Just then the one at the southwest door was heard to exclaim: "I am shot; I can't use my arm; it is no use, I can't shoot any more." Grat Dalton then ordered Mr. Ball to go and bring the sack into the back room, which he did. He next ordered him to cut the string with which it had been tied shut, and take out the currency. Mr. Ball poured the contents

on the floor and assorted the currency from the silver and handed
the former to Grat Dalton, who immediately went out at the southwest door, by which he had entered, his companions following
immediately after him.

. . . At the First National Bank a similar scene was enacted.
The two masked men came in at the front door, which was protected by a screen. They closed the heavy doors after them. Messrs.
J. H. Brewster, A. W. Knotts and C. L. Hollingsworth, customers
of the bank, were in the front part of the room at the time. Mr.
J. E. S. Boothby stepped into the door a moment or two after the
robbers, and was about to back out when one of them motioned
to him with his Winchester to step inside, which he did. The taller
of the two men with his Winchester covered Mr. Thomas G. Ayres,
the cashier, who was at his window, and with a horrid oath called
upon everyone present to hold up their hands. He ordered the
customers present to stand still right where they were. The smaller
one covered with his Winchester the teller, Mr. W. H. Shepard,
who was at a desk near the vault, and also assisted in keeping
those present in a state of nervous excitement by his dreadful profanity and the reckless manner in which he flourished his gun.
These two men proved to be Bob Dalton, the leader of the gang,
and his brother, Emmett Dalton, the youngest member of the
band. . . . Leaving Emmett to take care of the men in front, Bob
passed through the hallway into the private office in the rear of
the bank room (which had) a door that opened into a lot leading
to the alley (and was) protected by a heavy iron grating with a
spring lock on the inside. He found Mr. B. S. Ayres, the bookkeeper, at his desk in the office, and peremptorily ordered him to
go to the front, behind the counter, and hand out the bank's
money. The younger man obeyed, but not with sufficient alacrity
to suit the Daltons, so they undertook to hurry him by swearing
at him and threatening to shoot him. After young Ayres had
handed over all the money on the counter and in the drawer,
Bob ordered him to bring out the money in the safe. He told him
that he did not know the combination. Turning to the cashier,
Ayres, he said:

"Damn you, go and get it."

Mr. Ayres went and got some currency and put it in a sack
which the men had brought with them. Bob asked them if that was

all. Mr. Ayres replied that there was some gold in the vault, and asked if he wanted that. Bob replied:

"Yes; every damn cent of it."

Mr. Ayres then got the gold and gave it to him. He inquired a second time if that was all. Mr. Ayres pushed the safe door shut and replied that it was. Determined to see for himself, Bob went into the vault, opened the safe doors, and taking out two packages of currency containing five thousand dollars each, he inquired: "What's this?"

He threw them into the sack, and turning again to the vault emptied the silver on the floor, but did not take any. He picked up a box containing gold watches that belonged to a customer but the bankers told him there was nothing but papers in it, and he placed it back again. He then ordered the three bankers to walk out from behind the counter in front of him and they put the whole party out at the front door. Before they reached the door Emmett called to Bob to "look out there at the left." Just as the bankers and their customers had reached the pavement, and as Bob and Emmett appeared at the door, two shots were fired at them from the doorway of the drug store of Rammel Bros., which adjoins the banks on the north, by George Cubine, from a Winchester and C. S. Cox from a revolver. Neither one of them was hit. They were driven back into the bank and Messrs. B. S. Ayres and W. H. Shepard sprang in after them. Bob stepped to the door a second time, and raising his Winchester to his shoulder, took deliberate aim and fired in a southerly direction. Emmett held his Winchester under his arm while he tied a string securely around the mouth of the sack containing the money. They then ordered the young men to open the back door and let them out. Mr. Shepard complied and went with them to the rear of the building, when they passed out into the alley. It was then that the bloody work of the dread desperadoes began.

The hardware stores, where guns and ammunition are kept for sale, quite naturally became the rallying points for the alarmed citizens. The store of Isham Brothers & Mansur, hardware merchants, was a large one story brick building, with basement and heavy plate-glass windows and doors. The front was protected by an awning supported by iron columns. It was situated on the east side of Union street, immediately opposite the bank of C. M.

Condon & Co., and adjoined the First National Bank on the north. It had two entrances from Union street, and when the fight began the heavy front doors were all wide open. The men who visited the First National were compelled to pass immediately in front of this store on their way to the bank. The store of A. P. Boswell & Co., hardware merchants, was a large two-story brick with basement. The lower front was of plate-glass, and was protected by an awning similar to that of Isham Brothers & Mansur. The proprietors of these stores most willingly passed out their guns and ammunition to the eager citizens. John J. Kloehr, of the firm of Lewark & Kloehr, liverymen, was among the first to obtain a Winchester at the store of Boswell & Co. Some one handed him the gun and he went behind the counter and selected his own cartridges and loaded the piece. In company with several others, he took a position on the pavement in front of the store, where a good view of the Condon bank could be had, and from this point a number of shots were fired at the robbers in that building and as they passed out. Parker L. Williams secured a Colt's forty-four calibre revolver and got out upon the awning in front of Boswell's, from which point he opened on the robbers in Condon's bank. The one who stood at the southeast entrance, and who afterwards turned out to be Richard L. Broadwell, alias "Texas Jack," placed the muzzle of his Winchester against the heavy glass in the door and fired at Mr. Williams, but missed. . . . Mr. Williams abandoned his conspicuous position, but not until his enemy on the inside of the bank was seen to drop his gun and grasp his right arm. . . .

Charles T. Gump, who was driving his team on the street at the time, sprang from his wagon when the alarm was given, ran into Isham's store, grabbed a shotgun and returned to the outside edge of the pavement and took a position behind the iron awning post, facing the First National Bank. He held his gun in a position of "ready" and awaited the exit of the robbers. A shot from Bob Dalton's rifle, and the first one fired by that individual, struck Mr. Gump on the hand with which he had the gun clasped, cutting away the wood surrounding the pinion on which the gun was operated in loading, and made a dent in the barrel. The gun fell in several pieces at his feet, and Mr. Gump was seized by friends and drawn into the store. His hands were torn by the bullet, and he was found to have sustained a severe wound. He retired as the first victim of the dreadful fight that followed.

About the time that Mr. Gump was wounded, Lucius M. Baldwin, a clerk in the store of Read Brothers, general merchants, a noble, generous-hearted, brave and loyal young man, came from his employer's store on the west side of the Plaza, and entering Isham's store, seized a small revolver that came within his reach, and passed out at the back door of the store, into the alley. As he reached the alley, Bob and Emmett Dalton came to the rear door of the First National Bank, having Mr. Shepard, the teller, in charge. The latter opened the door for them and they passed out. Mr. Baldwin, holding the pistol down at his side, started forward with the evident purpose of joining the men when both leveled their Winchesters at him and commanded him to stop. He either did not hear the command or else failed to understand it, and continued to move toward them. . . . "I'll have to get that man," exclaimed Bob Dalton, and his deadly rifle rang out a second time upon the morning air. Young Baldwin fell . . . within fifty feet of his assassin . . . a bullet through his heart. . . . The Daltons turned and ran northward on the alley and disappeared on Eighth street . . . turning west toward Union. Arriving at the corner of the street, they fired two shots up the pavement without results. Moving on westward to the middle of the street their eyes fell upon the brave and intrepid George B. Cubine, who was standing in the doorway of the drug store of Rammel Bros. with a Winchester in his hand and his gaze fixed on the doors of the First National Bank. Four shots rang out, and Cubine fell dead. . . . Charles Brown, an aged gentleman whose place of business was immediately north of the drug store was the first person to approach the prostrate form. Discovering that his fellow mechanic was dead, he seized his gun and turned upon his slayers. Four more shots came from the middle of the street below, and the brave old veteran fell bleeding and dying within two feet of the prostrate form of his friend. . . .

All this bloody work was accomplished in an incredibly short space of time. The shots were fired by the Daltons at a distance of from forty to fifty yards from the objects of their aim. When Thomas G. Ayres, the cashier of the First National Bank, was turned out of the bank by the Daltons, he immediately ran into Isham's store, and seizing a Winchester, took a position in the north doorway of that establishment where he could command a view of the front of the bank. He expected the Daltons to force their way out by the front entrance, and he watched the building where he had left them a few moments before. In the meantime they had passed around the north end of the block and accomplished the death of three men in their hasty movements. They had reached the west side of Union street and were ascending the steps of an elevated pavement that surrounded the brick building in the center of the Plaza, where Bob's eye caught sight of Mr. Ayres in the door. Taking deliberate aim, at a distance of over seventy-five yards, he sent a ball crashing through the face of the cashier . . . who fell bleeding and unconscious to the floor. At the same moment Grat Dalton and his companions reached the alley in their efforts to escape, and before the prostrate form of Mr. Ayres could be removed the fleeing robbers fired nine shots into the front of the building where he lay. . . . Bob and Emmett Dalton had disappeared behind the buildings and were not seen again until they reappeared at the junction of the two alleys. . . .

When the alarm was first given that the banks were being robbed, Henry H. Isham, senior member of the firm Isham Brothers & Mansur, and his two clerks, Lewis A. Dietz and T. Arthur Reynolds, grapsed Winchesters and stationed themselves in the front part of the store where they could see all that was going on in front of Condon's bank, and at the same time command an excellent range of the alley on the opposite side of the Plaza. N. M. Anderson, a carpenter who was at work two blocks away, had arrived at the store and took up a Winchester. Charles K. Smith, a young Kansan and the son of the proprietor of a barber shop near Isham's store, procured a Winchester and joined the forces. . . . The moment that Grat Dalton and his companions, Dick Broadwell and Bill Powers, left the bank, they came under the guns of the men in Isham's store. Grat Dalton and Bill Powers each received mortal wounds before they had retreated twenty steps. The dust was seen to fly from their clothes, and Powers in his desperation attempted to take refuge in the rear doorway of an adjoining store, but the door was locked. He kept his feet and clung to his Winchester until he reached his horse, when another ball struck him in the back and he fell dead at the feet of the animal. Grat Dalton, getting under cover of the oil tank, managed to reach the side of a barn that stood on the south side of the alley. Here he stood for a few moments, firing several more shots, either waiting for Bob and Emmett to join him, or else because he was unable to go any further. . . .

After the robbers entered the alley at Slosson's, they were lost to the sight of the men at Boswell's store. John J. Kloehr, the liveryman, with Carey Seaman and Marshal Connelly, who were on the south side of the Plaza, near Read's store, started up Ninth street for the purpose of intercepting them before they could reach their horses. Marshal Connelly was in the hall on the third floor of an adjoining building when the firing commenced. He had left his revolver at his residence that morning; hence was unarmed. As they were passing up the street, the marshal ran into the machine shop of Swisher Brothers and procured a small Winchester, then ran across a vacant lot to an opening in the fence at the alley, at the corner of the barn where Grat Dalton was still standing. The marshal sprang into the alley with his face toward where the horses were hitched. His back was to Dalton, who raised his Winchester to his side and without taking aim fired a shot into the back of the officer. Marshal Connelly fell forward on his face and died. Dick Broadwell in the meantime had reached cover in the Long-Bell Lumber Company's yards, where he laid down for a few moments. He was wounded in the back. A lull occurred in the firing after Grat Dalton and Bill Powers had fallen. Broadwell took advantage of this and crawled out of his hiding place and mounted his horse and rode away. A ball from Kloehr's rifle and a load of shot from a gun in the hands of Carey Seaman overtook him before he had ridden twenty feet. Bleeding and dying he clung to his horse and passed out of the city over the route by which the party had entered not more than twenty minutes before. His dead body was found alongside the road a half-mile west of town, and his horse and trappings captured near where he fell.

Almost at the same moment that Marshal Connelly went down before the deadly rifle of Grat Dalton, Bob and Emmett emerged from the alley by which they had left Eighth street in their effort to join the rest of the party at their horses. The men at Isham's took deliberate aim at them and fired. The notorious leader of the gang evidently received a severe if not fatal wound at this moment. He staggered across the alley and sat down in a pile of dressed curbstones near the city jail. True to his desperate nature, he kept his rifle in action and fired several shots from where he was seated. His aim was unsteady and the bullets went wild. While sitting on the rocks he espied John Kloehr on the inside of the fence near Slosson's store. He tried to raise his Winchester to his shoulder but could not, and his shot, intended for Kloehr, struck the side of a small building. Bob Dalton then made his supreme effort. He arose to his feet and sought refuge alongside an old barn west of the city jail, and leaning against the southwest corner, brought his rifle into action again and fired two shots in the direction of his pursuers. A ball from Mr. Kloehr's rifle struck the bandit full in the breast and he fell upon his back among the stones. . . .

After shooting Marshal Connelly, Grat Dalton made another attempt to reach his horse. He passed by his fallen victim and had advanced probably twenty feet . . . when he turned to face his pursuers and again attempted to use his Winchester. John Kloehr's rifle spoke in unmistakable tones another time, and the oldest member of the band dropped with a bullet in his throat and a broken neck. . . .

Emmett Dalton had managed to escape unhurt up to this time. He kept under shelter after he reached the alley until he attempted to mount his horse. A half-dozen rifles sent their contents his direction as he undertook to get into the saddle. The two intervening horses belonging to Bob Dalton and Bill Powers were killed by some of the shots. The two horses attached to the oil tank, being directly in range, were also shot. Emmett succeeded in getting into the saddle, but not until he had received a bullet through the right arm and one through the left hip and groin. All this time he had clung to the sack containing the money they had taken from the First National Bank. Instead of riding off as he might have done, Emmett boldly rode back to where Bob Dalton was lying, and reaching down his hand, attempted to lift his dying brother on the horse with him. "It's no use," faintly whispered the fallen bandit, and just then Carey Seaman fired both barrels of his shotgun into Emmett's back as he was leaning over the prostrate form of his leader and tutor in crime. He dropped from his horse, carrying the sack containing over twenty thousand dol-

lars with him, and both fell near the feet of Bob, who died a
moment after. Citizens who had followed close after the robbers,
and some who were nearby when they fell, surrounded their
bodies, Emmett Dalton readily responding to the command to
hold up his hands by putting up his uninjured hand and making a pathetic appeal for mercy. Lynching was suggested for the
wounded one, but wiser counsel prevailed and he was taken to a
surgeon's office and his wounds dressed.[31]

Before he was sent to the penitentiary, Emmett Dalton confessed all the different crimes the gang had committed. Marshal Charles Connelly and the little group of citizen heroes
won for themselves the everlasting gratitude of law-abiding
people, not only of Coffeyville and the Oklahoma and Indian
territories, but everywhere. John Kloehr, the liveryman whose
ready aim sent three of the bandits to their deaths, received
special recognition. The bankers and citizens presented him
with a magnificent gold badge set with a large diamond and
engraved: The Emergency Arose, The Man Appeared. On
the back were the words: "Presented by friends who admire
nerve and courage when displayed in defense of social order."

So ended in blood the career of as desperate a band as yet
had existed in the robber history of this land or time. Oklahoma Territory was soon to see leagues of renegades worse
than the Daltons, gangs with hands more red in blood. In one
short month a new reign of terror spread through the Southwest, and this new frontier government grew trembling and
uncertain before the onslaughts of a vicious and unholy gang
led by Bill Doolin.

31 Pp. 16-42.

CHAPTER
3

Doolin Takes Over

Bill Doolin's story of how a lame horse kept him out of the Coffeyville fight is questionable. At the same time he told several friends that he and Bob Dalton had a "disagreement" over the latter's plan to rob two banks simultaneously. That some friction developed is evidenced by Emmett Dalton's confession to Deputy Marshal Payne, in which he expressed his own concern about the matter. There is no doubt that Doolin admired the daring of young Bob, but Doolin, being an older head, obviously felt the plan too foolish to participate. Perhaps his mount did go lame and he seized upon this coincidence as an excuse that would have kept him in good standing with Bob Dalton had the raid been successful.

Whatever the reason, Doolin failed to contact the Daltons and stated that he rode on north from the Kansas line. As he topped a hill within sight of the Kansas town, he saw a horseman racing up the road toward him. The man reined to a halt in a cloud of dust as he reached Doolin, and "in excitement so great that his words tumbled incoherently," told the outlaw what had happened in the streets of Coffeyville.

There was nothing he could do now for the Daltons. His connection with the gang was known and soon a posse would be on his trail. Within a few minutes the town would know that all the gang had not been eliminated. The entire country would become aroused and an intensive search spread for him. Miles away on the banks of the Cimarron was the nearest

Dalton hideout, a haven of safety. Doolin "responded to the
instinct of self-preservation." As soon as his informant had disappeared down the road to spread the news, he whirled his
horse and headed back into the Indian Territory. The rest of
the day he rode, pausing only for two hours rest. When night
fell he rode on again, making camp at daylight in a sheltered
ravine twenty-five miles north of Tulsa. There he waited
until darkness fell again. That night he rode until he reached
the Dalton cave on Hell's Fringe.[1]

He was safe now. He could have escaped out of the country
then, gone to the ranges of the North and West and returned
to an honest life. The fate of the Daltons should have presented
more terrors than he was willing to face. But he had "tasted the
fruits of victory in gun fights, he had known the glow and
excitement that came in bank and train robberies and he
thirsted for the life." Hidden in the dugout that so many times
had sheltered him, he was "all outlaw" and began to lay plans
for the organization of a new band.[2]

Bill Doolin was the son of Mack Doolin, a poverty-stricken
Arkansas cotton farmer. He had no education, could hardly
read or write. When he reached manhood, Bill drifted west
into the Indian country. Oscar Halsell, a Texas cattleman, had
just established his HX Bar ranch on the Cimarron, thirteen
miles northeast of Guthrie, and he hired the lanky, backwoods
youth who was so handy with an axe to cut out logs for his
corrals and cabins. In a few years, Doolin learned to rope, ride,
and shoot, and became a top hand.

He was a slow, deliberate fellow, six feet two, with tousled
red hair, drooping mustaches, and gander-blue eyes that gave
him a woebegone look. He grinned little, talked less, but was
a droll, drawling rangeland comedian once he got started. A
long-barreled six-shooter was a toy in his big fist. Soon the toy

---

[1] Statement of Bill Doolin to Deputy Marshals Tilghman, Kelley, Thomas,
and Hale in Marshal Nix's office at Guthrie, January 25, 1896, following his
capture at Eureka Springs, Arkansas. Also Nix, *op. cit.*, pp. 52-53; Newsom,
op. cit., pp. 168-169.

[2] Tilghman, *op. cit.*, p. 50.

became a deadly weapon and his good nature gave way to the streak of wildness in him. He had no wrongs to avenge, no persecutions that drove him to a life of crime. The hard, rough work of the range lost its appeal to him. When the opportunity came to join the Daltons, he had followed his wild urge. For eight years, from the time he joined the wild bunch, he made a record for the longest criminal career of any outlaw in Oklahoma and his gang figured in more sensational and bloody escapades than any other outlaw band before them.

First to enroll in the new organization was Bill Dalton. Acquitted in the Alila train robbery, he had never looked with disfavor upon the criminal activity of his outlaw brothers. But he was living the life of a respected citizen, had even gained strong political favor and served at least one term in the state legislature.[3] A few days before the Coffeyville raid, he had

3 "[Bill Dalton] married a daughter of Mr. Cyrus Blivens at Livingston, Merced County, California, in the early '80's; perhaps in '83 or '84, or maybe a year earlier.

"His father in law was a wealthy wheat grower, having moved from Stanislous county, California, to Merced county. Dalton worked in the harvest field for Mr. Blivens, and becoming acquainted with his eldest daughter, they were married, though at the time much opposition to the union was offered by the Blivens. After his marriage Dalton ran a ranch on his own account, living on a place owned by John Mitchell of Turlock. As a wheat grower, Bill was never a signal success, but he had an education and knew a thing or two of politics.

"Dalton's entrance into politics was under the direct tutelage of Hon. T. W. Breckenridge, now deceased, and at the time district attorney of Merced county.

"I have no knowledge of the time he went to the legislature of California, but it must have been after 1888, or when Dalton was living in San Luis, Obispo county, in the southern portion of that state. This writer remembers when Clark Blivens, his brother in law, and Dalton, with their families moved to San Luis, Obispo, to commence growing wheat, and can safely state that Dalton's exchequer was scant indeed, as I know the mule team Bill drove away from Merced county was given him by his father in law.

"Personally acquainted with Dalton, I am glad to state that he was a whole souled genial boy. Friends he had by the score, and brilliant, he would no doubt have made his mark in an honorable calling had not revenge entered into and converted him from an accomplished gentleman to the boldest of bandits.

"As to his one time wealth, it may be well to remark, that when William Dalton and Jennie Blivens swore to love each other as husband and wife to the end, his stock in store consisted perhaps of a small amount of wage money due from the elder Blivens for harvest work and his natural push, undoubted ability and educational accomplishments.

"Mr. Blivens' family consisted of two girls, Jennie (Dalton's wife) and Susie, three boys living in 1888, of whom Clark was the eldest. The names of the other

come from California to visit his mother. When news came of the killing of Bob and Grat and the wounding of Emmett Dalton, he threw aside all pretense of respectability and sought out Doolin.

At first Doolin resented his presence. Already Doolin visualized himself in the light of a romantic hero like Bob Dalton. Too often he had watched his former leader "basking in the doubtful glory of the lurid publicity" he received "as if it were the mellow sunshine of an early spring day," and envy of the latter's "peculiar prestige" made him fear that another member of the Dalton family might jeopardize his complete control of the gang. "Bill Dalton, however, seemed to entertain a certain respect for the ability and experience of Bill Doolin—and he soon convinced Doolin that they should join hands and carry out their plans together. . . . He could lead the new organization in all its exploits. . . . Dalton would serve as an aide and endeavor to be as helpful as possible."[4]

Next to join them was George Waightman, alias Red Buck, a surly, vicious individual with a reputation as a killer and professional horse thief. In 1889, Deputy Marshal Heck Thomas had arrested him for horse stealing. He had been convicted and sentenced to prison, where he remained until October, 1892. Within a week after his release, he stole seven good saddle ponies and, thus equipped, joined Doolin and Dalton.

Doolin added George "Bitter Creek" Newcomb, handsome son of a good Fort Scott, Kansas, family. In 1883, Newcomb

two I have forgotten."—Letter to the editor, *Daily Ardmoreite*, from "J. G. W." of Thackerville, Oklahoma Territory, June 13, 1894.

"Mr. B. C. Wear, a gentleman who has lived nearly all his life in the section disgraced by Bill Dalton in California, says the story told of his affluence and influence is likely borrowed from Hon. H. C. Dalton, who was worth a quarter million dollars, and represented his county (Fresno) twice in the state legislature. In this wealthy valley, Bill Dalton's California depredations would likely lead to the identity, or rather confusion with the real worthy H. C. Dalton who was sixty years old and was accidentally killed last August. Mr. Wear's position in state politics for the last twenty years was such that he feels sure in stating that Bill Dalton was never a rich man nor honored."—*Daily Oklahoma State Capital*, June 14, 1894.

4 Nix, *op. cit.*, pp. 57-58.

had come to Oklahoma to work on the 4D ranch, but his
affinity for red lights and cards switched him to train robbery
and holding up banks as a business. He was to achieve notoriety as the sweetheart of the lady outlaw known only as "The
Rose of Cimarron."

Other worthies on the Doolin roster were Ol Yountis, a
local product with a checkered past, whose sister had settled
a claim near Orlando; Bill Raidler, alias Little Bill, a well-
educated man of good Pennsylvania-Dutch ancestry; and Dick
West, alias Little Dick, a spindle-legged, sallow-faced waif who
had washed dishes in the greasy restaurants until Oscar Halsell
picked him up on the streets of Decatur, Texas, and brought
him to his Oklahoma ranch to wrangle horses. Little Dick, too,
had a chance to live an exemplary life, but he was "full of
cussedness" and "wild as a cat." Here he worked with Doolin
and knew the Dalton boys. Their tales of adventure beyond
the pale of the law stirred the wild blood in his veins. Doolin
was his hero, and when Little Dick learned he was organizing
a new outfit, he carried his belongings to the hideout on the
Cimarron, where he quickly learned the techniques of Western banditry.

The only other member of the gang in the beginning was
Tom Daugherty, alias Jones, alias Arkansas Tom, who came
from Doolin's native state. His parents were religious people,
and his two eldest brothers had been educated for the ministry.
He had run away from home at the age of fourteen, to be a
cowboy in the Cheyenne country, but, like Doolin, he readily
gave up ranch life for the faster and more violent ways of getting rich.

Following the lesson learned from Bob Dalton, Doolin
established a second headquarters for the band in event the
old outlaw cave was discovered. The new place was known as
"Rock Fort"—a dugout with stone walls. It was built on the
Bee Dunn farm, southeast of Ingalls, a settlement in the eastern edge of Payne County, and the homes of Dunn's five
brothers and cousins along nearby Council Creek also became

convenient stopping places for members of the gang. There was much unsettled land over the line in the Creek Nation, and the wild reaches of the Pawnee and Osage country to the north and the timbered hills along the Cimarron made escape easy. And the gang knew every mile of the two territories.

Hardly had the first excitement succeeding the raid of October 5 died down than an alarming rumor swept southeastern Kansas: The Dalton gang had not been wholly exterminated; the survivors had reorganized and were coming back to wreak vengeance upon valiant Coffeyville!

John Kloehr received a letter mailed October 12 from Arkansas City:

To John Kloehr (credited with killing three of the Dalton Gang):

Dear Sir:

I take the time to tell you and the citizens of Coffeyville that all of the gang ain't dead yet by a damn sight and don't you forget it. I would have given all I ever made to have been there the 5th. There are five of the gang left, and we shall come and see you. . . . We shall have revenge for your killing of Bob and Grat and the rest. . . . You people had no cause to take arms against the gang. The bankers will not help the widows of the men that got killed there and you thought you were playing hell fire when you killed three of us but your time will soon come when you will go into the grave and pass in your checks. . . . So take warning. . . .

Yours truly,

DALTON GANG[5]

As the startling news spread through the town, irate citizens again armed themselves to defend their homes against this threatened invasion.

In a way they had been expecting it. Since the raid, Bill Dalton and many of his sympathizers had been loitering about the streets, openly condemning the manner in which the gang had met its death. Several already had been arrested and jailed,

[5] *Coffeyville Journal,* October 14, 1892; *Stillwater Gazette,* October 21, 1892.

and Bill Dalton, threatening to bring civil action against the city,[6] had departed with his mother for Independence, where Emmett Dalton's body had been removed. Nothing had been heard of him since.

The morning following the receipt of the letter by John Kloehr, Detective Dodge, of the Wells-Fargo Express, who had been in the Indian Territory searching for Doolin since the raid, wired the mayor of Coffeyville:

A large body of desperadoes has left Wharton, in the Outlet, presumably en route your city to avenge the death of the Daltons, Powers and Broadwell.

One of his men, Dodge explained, had picked up information that one of the survivors of the Dalton gang (Bill Doolin), with forty men under his command and completely armed, would ride into Coffeyville at 9 o'clock that night and "wipe out the place."

Informal meetings were held. Telegrams were sent to Parsons and Kansas City asking that Winchesters be shipped at once. Within a few hours, every man was ready for the fight. A car from the Missouri, Kansas, and Texas railroad at Parsons stood at the depot, barricaded and armed. That evening a bonfire was started on the plaza to furnish a reassuring illumination.[7]

Whether Bill Doolin scouted the situation and decided it fatal, or it was part of his strategy to draw the full attention and protection of the country to Coffeyville, is not known.

6 "A new feature in the Dalton affair is promised. . . . Will Dalton is contemplating suing the city for damages, alleging as a cause of action that while the bodies of the dead bandits were in charge of the city, unauthorized persons were allowed to rifle the pockets and extract money and valuables which have not been turned over to William or the family. . . .

"Will said that he knows one of the citizens robbed the bodies of the $900 which Emmett claims they had before coming to Coffeyville. This is in all probability the sheerest nonsense, as no one else seems to know anything about it. The chances are that it is only a bluff game, played in order to force those who took articles from the bandits' pockets and are keeping them as relics to return them. . . ."—*Coffeyville Journal*, October 26, 1892.

7 *Ibid.*, October 14, 1892.

The attack did not occur. Instead, the gang struck nineteen miles to the west, stopping the Missouri Pacific train at Caney.

Just as the train drew up to the station at 10:15 P. M., masked men, heavily armed with Winchesters and revolvers, climbed on the locomotive tender from the front of the combination baggage and express car and covered Engineer Eggleston and his fireman with their rifles. The locomotive men were ordered to pull slowly to the switch, where all was darkness and where there was no danger of molestation. This was done.

At the whistling post the outlaws ordered the engineer to stop and made the fireman uncouple the express car from the rest of the train. All this was done so quietly that no one in the coaches was disturbed. The engineer was then ordered to pull ahead with the express car and obeyed, for the Winchesters held close to his head looked unpleasantly dangerous. When a deep cut half a mile further on had been reached, the engine was halted.

Express Messenger J. N. Maxwell, who had witnessed the uncoupling had in the meantime blown out his lights, barred and barricaded the doors, and made ready for desperate resistance. The order to open up the car elicited no response and the robbers began firing into the sides of the car with their Winchesters. Maxwell answered the shots with his revolver for a few minutes, but finally received a bullet in his right arm, which disabled him and he was fain to surrender. The robbers ordered him to light his lamps and open the car door and as soon as he had done so they entered the car with the engineer in front of them as a shield. Maxwell was then forced to open the safe and deliver up his watch and personal property. The men then backed from the car and disappeared in the darkness.[8]

News of the robbery, reaching Coffeyville by courier the next morning, caused another furor of excitement. Was the gang approaching closer to the city, raiding everything in its path? They might ride into Coffeyville at any moment. . . . Women and children huddled in the homes, frightened at the prospect of another bloody encounter with the outlaws. The

[8] *Ibid.*

mayor, in an attempt to soothe their anxiety, told them the number of the attacking party obviously had been greatly magnified, that already posses were scouring the area west of the city and a matter of a few hours would result in their capture.

"You people," he added, "have shown your ability to care for yourselves."

So Coffeyville waited. Still the attack did not come.

Bill Doolin had led his gang back into the Indian Territory.

For a few days they rested in the Creek Nation cave, then rode west into the Outlet. The night of November 8, the gang appeared at the railroad station at Wharton.

A short time before the train was due, a stranger came in and bought a ticket to Orlando. His actions were such as excited suspicion but little attention was paid him. When the train ran into the station, the baggage man thrust his head out the car door when he was ordered to put it back and a shot fired to emphasize the order. The conductor saw that a holdup was on hand and remained on the platform of the coach. The bandits then began a regular fusillade to intimidate the passengers. The engineer was compelled to go back and detach the express car from the remainder of the train and run south to Cow Creek (in Oklahoma Territory) where the car door was blown open with dynamite, the entire rear of the coach being wrecked. After the robbers had secured what money they could find, they mounted their horses and headed in an easterly direction. When the report was received at Guthrie, a posse under Deputy Marshal Madsen was dispatched to Wharton to pursue the bandits. The trail was easy to follow at first because of recent rains (but soon lost in dry country).[9]

Again Doolin doubled back, leading his gang north through the Osage into Kansas. The morning of November 27, they descended upon Spearville, sixteen miles east of Dodge City, looted the First National Bank and again escaped unharmed.[10]

9 *Stillwater Gazette*, November 11, 1892.
10 Nix, *op. cit.*, p. 61; Newsom, *op. cit.*, p. 161; Tilghman, *op. cit.*, p. 39.

The gang's success undoubtedly can be credited to the generalship of Bill Doolin. Doolin had the experience of the Daltons, plus the ability to lead others. He planned each foray carefully and saw that each man did his job efficiently and effectively.

At Spearville, Little Dick West was assigned to cover the street and generally terrorize the citizens. During the robbery he strode up and down the main thoroughfare, yelping like a coyote, leaping high in the air and pouring lead into the business houses. The intimidated citizens made no resistance, and the holdup went off like clockwork. It netted the gang a total of $4,500.

Outside of town the bandits divided the loot. Then they separated to confuse the officers, scattering to the east and south to meet later at their Creek Nation rendezvous. Sheriff Chalk Beeson, of Ford County, Kansas, struck the trail of Ol Yountis, who had headed toward Oklahoma, and rode in pursuit.

All might have gone well with the outlaw had he not discovered the officer tailing him. Lacking the cold nerve of Doolin and the others, he became frantic and, in haste to put as much distance as possible between himself and his pursuer, rode his horse to exhaustion. Leading the animal, he staggered on afoot.

At the boundary of the Outlet and Oklahoma Territory, he met a farmer who kindly offered his assistance. Instead of merely robbing the man of his mount, Yountis calmly killed him, mounted the horse, and raced away. Sheriff Beeson arrived upon the scene within an hour. The dead farmer and the outlaw's exhausted animal standing nearby convinced him the murderer was the man he had trailed from Spearville.

Word of the cold-blooded murder spread and the whole community was aroused. A posse of neighbors organized and began looking everywhere for the killer. Beeson wired the marshal's office at Guthrie, and before dark, Deputies Madsen, Thomas, and Tom Houston arrived at the scene. They picked up Yountis' trail and never lost it. It led to the home of his sister, near Orlando.

The officers surrounded the place and waited. At daybreak, a man emerged from the house carrying two six-shooters buckled around his waist and a Winchester across his arm. The fact that he was heavily armed and the furtive manner in which he crossed the yard toward the barn satisfied them he was the man they were seeking. As he passed within a few feet of a stone fence that concealed Thomas, the deputy rose quickly.

"Throw up your hands, Ol!" he shouted. "You're under arrest!"

The killer snapped up his rifle and began firing. The bullets split rocks and knocked chips from the stone wall, which was all that saved Heck Thomas' life. Madsen stepped from behind the corner of the barn fifty feet away and fired one shot. The renegade fell. As he lay on the ground, writhing and moaning, the officers ran forward and disarmed him. But Yountis was beyond offering any further resistance. He was taken to Orlando and given medical attention, but by night he was dead. In the waistband of his trousers, they recovered his share of the money taken from the Spearville bank.[11]

The United States Marshal's office had chalked up its first major catch in the battle with the outlaws of Oklahoma Territory. It was to net almost one hundred deaths and more than five thousand arrests within the next few years.

It was the first nail in the coffin of Bill Doolin.

11 Nix, *op. cit.*, pp. 61-64.

CHAPTER
4

Crime Fighting Organization

During the Dalton depredations the embryo state had grown rapidly. In the spring of 1890, negotiations were completed with the Cherokee Nation for the relinquishment of their unoccupied lands (the Outlet) west of the 96th meridian, and with the Iowa, Sac and Fox, and the Pottawatomie-Shawnee, whose reservations lay just east of Old Oklahoma. In June, negotiations were completed with the Cheyenne and Arapahoes for their lands south of the Canadian River and west of the region settled in 1889. These tribes agreed to accept allotments in severalty and permit the opening of their surplus lands to white settlement.[1]

The Iowa, Sac and Fox, with the lands of the Pottawatomie and Shawnee, totaling 868,414 acres, were the first opened, September 22, 1891.[2] Although these lands were not given away, but sold in tracts of 160 acres at $1.25 per acre, this rush for homesteads was a repetition of the run of '89. Practically every acre was occupied the first day and over twenty thousand persons participated. From these lands Logan, Oklahoma, and Cleveland counties were enlarged to the east, the area of Payne County increased by adding that part lying south of the

[1] Thoburn and Wright, *op. cit.*, p. 555; Gittinger, *op. cit.*, pp. 197-198 (especially footnote 42) ; Dora Ann Stewart, *Government and Development of Oklahoma Territory*, p. 66.
[2] *U. S. Statutes at Large*, XXVII, pp. 989-993.

Cimarron River, and two more counties added to the original seven.[3]

On April 19, 1892, the Cheyenne and Arapaho country was opened by a third run.[4] This area added 3,500,562 acres to Oklahoma Territory and six more counties were formed.[5] Kingfisher and Canadian counties were also enlarged with the addition of this vast area to the west. As in the opening of 1891, county seat townsites were chosen in advance and reserved for homestead entry, and the land sold to occupants under the usual regulations at $1.50 per acre. Anyone, if he had money, could buy acreage by awaiting his turn at the land offices.

No land districts were established for either of these openings. The lands were apportioned to the Guthrie and Oklahoma City offices, to the great inconvenience of settlers, who lived long distances away, and there was much complaint of sooners taking the best lands as in the opening of '89.[6] Many failed to obtain homes, and large groups of dissatisfied settlers gathered on the borders of the Outlet, pressing for entry into this only other strip of land negotiated for in 1890.

In towns on the north side of the territory and at convenient points where fuel and water were abundant along the southern border, large camps of men approximating the number that had entered the Cheyenne country sprang up, and, in Kansas, on the north line of the Outlet, thousands more waited for homes. Led to believe the government meant to open this land at an early date, many had brought their families and were living up their means which should have

---

[3] One was designated County A and the other County B. In the general election of November, 1892, the people, by popular vote, chose the names by which they have since been known. County A was voted to be called Lincoln with the county seat at Chandler. County B chose the name Pottawatomie and Tecumseh became the county seat townsite.—Thoburn and Wright, *op. cit.*, p. 555; Stewart, *op. cit.*, pp. 61-62; Harlow, *op. cit.*, p. 266.

[4] *U. S. Statutes at Large*, XXVII, pp. 1018-1021.

[5] These were designated as counties C, D, E, F, G and H, and subsequently named Blaine, Dewey, Day (later eliminated and became part of Ellis county), Roger Mills, Custer and Washita, respectively.—Thoburn and Wright, *op. cit.*, pp. 555-556; Stewart, *op. cit.*, p. 68; Harlow, *op. cit.*, p. 266.

[6] Thoburn and Wright, *op. cit.*, p. 556.

gone into improvements on claims. Congress, in an effort to keep down expenditures of public funds until after the fall election, dictated postponement of the opening; and the settlers charged it was because the cattlemen were making their influence felt by the use of money among congressmen. In either case, the necessities of the people were ignored and begot discontent. Men in the Outlet declared they were there to stay, and this was no idle threat. The soldiers burned their buildings and drove them out, but they would return immediately and resume work.[7]

Meanwhile, the settled parts of the territory had been struggling for a start in every way. Congress had appropriated $47,000 for the destitute farmers who had arrived too late the first year to start a crop. Inability to break enough of the tough sod and lack of seed produced only a small crop the second year. By 1892, however, the farmers "got the hang of the new land" and had good crops coming on. Since no farm lands could be taxed, the territorial legislature had to depend upon taxes on personal property, and a state levy was permitted for roads and bridges and for the operation of three state universities which had been located at Norman, Edmond, and Stillwater. A common school system also had been set up, with four schools to the township and one high school to each township or city of over 500 population, and Congress had allowed $50,000 for the temporary support of such schools. In this same year the population increased to 133,100. The assessed valuation of the territory was $11,500,000, of which $3,848,000 represented town lots. There were five national banks, with deposits of $150,000 each, and fourteen private banks, with $15,000 capital each. There had been much railroad building. The Rock Island, which had built south from the Kansas line to El Reno after the first opening, was extended, in 1892, into Texas. The Choctaw Railway Company had built from El Reno to Oklahoma City, and was planning extensions both to the east and west. The school population was 31,920 and

[7] *Stillwater Gazette,* April 29, 1892.

already the districts were beginning to make provisions for permanent structures to replace the sod houses and shacks in which schools had first been held.[8]

This new frontier was "blessed" with the efforts of small groups of the better element of men "loyal and honorable to the core" and whose "good influence comprised the very fabric of each community's ideals and ethics"; they had the "backbone to enforce their own conception of right and the moral principles for which they stood," and their women approached the difficulties of the period in a "highhanded" manner. But because of the unsettled conditions, the constant opening of new lands and the constant shifting of population, lawlessness had thrived.[9]

"The bandit problem had become acute, hampering the development of legitimate business and making it almost impossible for money or merchandise to be successfully transported through the territory."[10] Trains, banks, stores, postoffices, and even the isolated farms of the settlers were objects of attack. Big eastern dailies proclaimed it a "horrible society" in which it was possible for outlaw gangs to roam at will, "interrupting the functioning of those two factors so essential to civilized progress—transportation and communication . . .[11] without the slightest chance of meeting with opposition that would discourage their predatory tendencies,"[12] and otherwise painted Oklahoma as a "precarious place to live" at a time when the territory needed "new people and new capital."[13]

The Organic Act had granted jurisdiction to the new courts of Oklahoma to try and condemn for violations of both federal and state laws committed upon any portion of the territory. The limit of their power was that these courts might not,

8 Territorial Governor's Report, 1892.
9 Nix, *op. cit.*, pp. 30-31.
10 *Ibid.*
11 *Ibid.*, pp. 64-65.
12 *Ibid.*, p. 16.
13 *Ibid.*, p. 32.

under a charge of a violation of a law of the United States, try a prisoner for the violation of a law of the territory; neither could they, upon a charge of a violation of a law of the territory, try a prisoner for a violation of the law of the United States; provided that "all offenses committed in said Territory, if committed within any organized county, shall be prosecuted and tried within said county, and if committed within territory not embraced in any organized county, shall be prosecuted and tried in the county to which such territory shall be attached for judicial purposes." But in any case, if the prisoner was properly charged with an offense either against state or federal law, the courts had power to transfer the prosecution to a county in any judicial district in the territory by change of venue.[14]

So there was plenty judicial authority in the territory. But the office of Marshal William Grimes, with only half a hundred deputies to police thousands of square miles of raw frontier, was unable to cope with the situation. The citizens grew impatient, and territorial newspapers carried such bitter comments as appeared in the *Stillwater Gazette* of July 8, 1892:

A tidal wave of criminality is sweeping over the country. There is scarcely a county that is not the scene of bloodshed, suicide, rape, robbery or gigantic thefts at the present time. About one murderer in fifty is brought to justice. The inexorable hand of Judge Lynch, in many cases, has meted out merited punishment to the despoiler of woman's virtue. Some of the thieves and highwaymen are apprehended and made to pay the penalty for their crimes. But the punishment of those who fall into the hands of the law does not prevent others from giving loose rein to passion and committing the gravest offenses against the laws of the land. . . .

The wiping out of the Dalton gang by the irate citizens of Coffeyville brought a measure of relief to every Oklahoma community. The slaying of Ol Yountis and Black-Faced

14 May 2, 1890, Sec. 10; also *In re Terrill*, 144 Federal Reporter, pp. 616-622.

Charley took some of the heat off the back of Marshal Grimes. But the formation of the Doolin gang and rumors of the forming of other, smaller bands aroused "new and dire threats against the peace and welfare of the territory"[15] and the people realized something had to be done or "bow to the will and power of the brigands."[16]

There had been a political turnover nationally, with Grover Cleveland defeating Benjamin Harrison, the Republican candidate for re-election as president, in November, 1892. Cleveland would not take office until the following March, but his return to Washington after four years absence meant a new group of territorial officials. In Guthrie, center of all activity—business, political, and otherwise—attention turned to Evett Dumas Nix for appointment as United States marshal.

Nix was born in rural Kentucky, September 19, 1861. His mother was of pioneer stock; his father, S. S. Nix, served as a lieutenant in the Confederate Army and, after the war, was for several years deputy sheriff of Calloway County, at Murray. Both were strongly religious and believed children should be taught to work. Young Nix finished common school at seventeen, working in a wagon and buggy factory to complete his education. His grandfather Nix backed him in his first venture, a grocery, hardware, and furniture business at Coldwater, which was successful and sold in 1880 at a good profit. Then he went to Paducah, Kentucky, as a traveling salesman, and two years later joined the staff of J. J. Bondurant and Company, wholesale grocers. On July 15, 1885, he married an old schoolmate, Ellen Felts.

In 1889, he caught the Western fever. Not that Kentucky had become too thickly settled by this year. His grandfathers had moved west as young men from South Carolina to acquire many slaves and vast tobacco plantations, and his wife fired his inherent urge to get a start in a new country. Nix chose this untamed land called Oklahoma.

---

15 Nix, *op. cit.*, p. 16.
16 *Ibid.*, p. 32.

At Guthrie, he entered the general merchandise business with a man named Ed Baldwin. In March, 1890, he purchased Baldwin's interest and began to search for a broader field than retail business offered. Oscar Halsell, the Texas cattleman, had come to Guthrie from his ranch on the Cimarron. He and Nix became close friends. In the fall of 1890, they entered the wholesale grocery business together under the firm name Nix and Halsell Company, and soon were supplying most of the small inland towns. For 1891, they planned a campaign of business expansion to Indian trading points over the whole territory, but, like other business men of Guthrie, found themselves faced with the hazards of transporting merchandise at great distances and safely returning with large amounts of money. They could not afford to take such chances until the outlaw problem had been solved.

In the same year, Nix was saddled with another difficulty. The Commercial Bank of Guthrie had closed its doors in the first banking failure of the territory, and he was appointed receiver, under bond of $450,000. It was a trying responsibility for a young man of thirty, but he disposed of the affairs of the ill-fated organization so satisfactorily that the people, in looking about for a man in whom they could place great confidence and with executive ability to conduct the affairs of the office of United States marshal in a businesslike manner, again called upon Nix.

While I was considerably flattered that these men should have entertained such a high opinion of me, I was flustrated at their proposal. It seemed that it would be absolutely impossible for me to consider such a thing. I had my own business to take care of— I hardly wanted to throw the burden of responsibility upon my partner. . . . I refused pointblank . . . but this group of citizens, not to be turned aside, called upon my partner and discussed the matter with him—requesting him to urge my serious consideration of the matter. Oscar Halsell came to me and said that he felt that as citizens we owed as much of our services as we were able to give to the general good of the new country and that if I would consent to apply for the appointment he would do his part by relieving me of a large share of my duties in our wholesale grocery business. His persuasion . . . caused me to tell the committee that I would accept the appointment if President-elect Cleveland desired to give it to me. . . . [They] immediately started getting indorsements from leading business men of Guthrie and the Territory, and accumulated as fine a collection of credentials as any man could hope to have. I then visited Washington, calling on President Cleveland and his Attorney General to discuss territorial conditions and my application for appointment to United States Marshal.[17]

There were twenty-three applicants filed for marshal with the President, nineteen from Oklahoma Territory and four from outside, but Nix "won the crown and wears it."[18]

[He] arrived in Guthrie Sunday afternoon and was enthusiastically received by a legion of friends. . . . This young exemplar of the young democracy of Oklahoma bears his well won honors with a modest dignity that well befits him. . . . He was as smiling as a father gazing on the first paternal triumph, and assured the *News* that he was all there. . . .[19]

The *State Capital* described him as "a man, self-made."

[He] is known for his energy, his approved honesty and because he is an agreeable gentleman. If Cleveland had searched Oklahoma with a microscope he could not have found a squarer man than E. D. Nix. He was never a politician . . . [his] persistency and good cheer got him this big plum. The "leading" democrats ridiculed the idea of his being a candidate; said he was a mere boy who had done nothing for democracy. Nix held onto the pole and finally knocked the persimmon. . . . We believe he will fill the office well.[20]

[17] *Ibid.*, pp. 66-67.
[18] *Guthrie Daily News,* June 6, 1893.
[19] *Ibid.*
[20] May 29, 1893.

His sole purpose was "to apply himself to the solution of Oklahoma's outlaw difficulties and return to civil life and the peaceful pursuit of his own business" as soon as possible.[21] "I little realized," stated Nix, "just how strenuous a life I was to live for the next few years, nor how gruesome a trail of blood my organization would be forced to leave behind in its battle to exterminate the outlaws and establish law and order."[22]

While in Washington he had discussed the problem with Department of Justice officials, who had agreed upon a force "adequate to handle the situation." When he had suggested 150 field deputies, there had been no objection, although this number was over twice that ever allowed any territorial marshal.

As a business man, he was convinced that these deputies must be honest and "never compromise the dignity and prestige of the United States government." This was no job for swashbucklers, for men who "fenced themselves round with revolvers and cartridges for show." A revolver, with the men he would appoint, would be to supplement their "cool daring and bravery" against the outlaws "they would be sent out to defeat."[23]

As chief deputy, he chose John M. Hale. A native of Virginia, Hale had come to the territory several years before and had wide experience and knowledge of the country. He was even younger than Nix, but possessed such "equilibrium and depth of character" that within a short time he was rated by the Department of Justice as "one of the most capable chief deputies in the service."[24]

To head his campaign in the field against the outlaws, Nix carefully selected such men as William M. (Bill) Tilghman,

21 Nix, *op. cit.*, p. viii.
22 *Ibid.*, p. 67.
23 *Ibid.*, p. 70; *Guthrie Daily News*, June 6, 1893.
24 *Guthrie Daily Leader*, July 2, 1893; Nix, *op. cit.*, p. 71.

Chris Madsen, and Heck Thomas, who became known as Oklahoma's "Three Guardsmen."

Tilghman grew up in the West when handling firearms and bad men was a matter of course. For fifty years he was successively scout, plainsman, buffalo hunter, Indian fighter, deputy sheriff, and United States marshal—bull's-eye in hundreds of gunfights and wounded only once before he was shot to death attempting to arrest a drunken prohibition agent at Cromwell, Oklahoma, in 1924. He was born at Fort Dodge, Iowa, July 4, 1854. When he was three, his parents moved to Atchison, Kansas, where Bill grew up. His father was a freighter, and Bill accompanied him on numerous trips across the plains. At fifteen, he had visited all the forts on the frontier, and at eighteen, was a scout for the Army, taking part in the Cheyenne-Arapaho Indian War of 1874 and the campaign against the Cheyenne chief, Dull Knife, when he and his followers escaped from the reservation at Fort Sill, where they had been held captive following the Custer Massacre on the Little Big Horn. In 1875, Tilghman settled at Dodge City and became the intimate friend of such border gunmen as Wild Bill Hickok, Wyatt Earp, and Bat Masterson, with whom he passed many hours on the back lot of the notorious Lone Star Dance Hall, practicing the finer points of "firing on the draw." Bill stayed in Dodge fourteen years, serving one term as deputy and one term as undersheriff of Ford County. For three years he was city marshal when Dodge was known far and wide as "the toughest cowtown in the West" where they "killed peace officers for breakfast," and took his job so seriously that bad men "found no profit in operating and departed for other climes." He had come to Oklahoma in 1889 to play his part in building early Guthrie and obtained a farm near Chandler in the Sac and Fox opening of 1891. One hundred and eighty pounds of bone and muscle, with kindly blue eyes and a handsome, open countenance that reflected good will and friendliness to all whom he met; soft-spoken, never overbearing, but with a reputation for having captured some of the Southwest's worst desperadoes, he was a natural for the Nix appointment.[25]

Heck Thomas was from Georgia, a man of breeding and a polished gentleman. At twelve, he served as a courier in the Thomas division of the Stonewall Jackson brigade. Following the Civil War he migrated to Texas, and despite his youth, was commissioned in the Texas Rangers. His cold nerve and keen judgment soon established him as an officer to be feared by lawbreakers. On May 1, 1885, after the Lee brothers had shot and killed Jim Guy, Jim Roff, and Andy Kuykendall, Thomas took their trail. He located the pair in a hayfield on a Texas ranch, and opened fire on them, wounding one brother, then crawled to the shelter of a haycock and got the drop on the other. Governor John Ireland, of Texas, declared the feat one of the most remarkable in the history of the Ranger forces, and Thomas was paid $5,000 reward for his single-handed capture. As his reputation spread, he resigned from the Rangers to accept an appointment as deputy United States marshal in Texas and helped wipe out the Sam Bass gang. He was soon transferred to the Indian Territory, and was working out of the federal court for the Western District of Arkansas when commissioned under Nix.[26]

Chris Madsen came to Nix from a life packed with high adventure. He was born in Schleswig, Denmark, in 1851. As a boy he heard of the Civil War in America, the Archduke Maximilian's audacious acceptance of the throne of the Montezumas, Napoleon's inept namesake in France, and the thunderings of the Iron Chancellor in Berlin. When the Franco-Prussian War flared, in 1870, young Madsen marched

[25] Zoe A. Tilghman, *Marshal of the Last Frontier*, pp. 15-185; William MacLeod Raine, *Famous Sheriffs and Western Outlaws*, pp. 212-216; Stuart Lake, *Frontier Marshal*, pp. 145, 168; Newsom, *op. cit.*, pp. 145-147; W. B. (Bat) Masterson, "Famous Gunfighters of the Western Frontier," *Human Life*, July, 1907.

[26] A biography of Heck Thomas, *Daily Oklahoman*, August 18, 1912; J. Marvin Hunter and Noah H. Rose, *The Album of Gunfighters*, pp. 65, 67; Newsom, *op. cit.*, pp. 149-150.

away in the Danish Army and was captured by the Germans. He escaped, and after several skirmishes, made his way back to a detachment whose officers had been killed and led it in a sortie against the Germans to celebrate his successful dash for freedom. After the war he went to Algiers with the French Foreign Legion, and while riding the sultry Saharan plains of Sedan, heard stories of the gold strikes and Indian fights in the United States. At the end of his enlistment, he sailed for America. He landed in New York in 1875, joined the United States Army as a scout and was soon promoted to rank of quartermaster sergeant with the "Old Fightin'" Fifth Cavalry. He possessed a keen eyesight, and uncanny alacrity with firearms, an unruffled temperament, and as his frontier experience ripened, he became one of the chief Indian scouts in Wyoming and the Southwest. He took part in campaigns against the Cheyennes and Arapahos in Western Kansas and the Indian Territory, fought the powerful Sioux in Nebraska, Dakota, and Montana, and accompanied Army expeditions against the Nez Perce, the Bannocks, and the Utes. He was a close friend of Buffalo Bill Cody, plumed knight of the Wild West epic, and saw Cody kill the Sioux chief, Yellow Hand, at Hat Creek with a knife. Hairbreadth escapes from roving bands of warriors were common experiences for Madsen until 1889. When news of the Oklahoma opening swept through the settlements, he made a gesture toward a peaceful life and settled on a farm near El Reno. But "sod-busting" held no allure for him, and he forgot all about agriculture when William Grimes offered him his first deputy marshal's commission. From that day, his lot was with the unflinching handful of men, who, wearing six-shooters and silver stars, were sent forth to roll back the rising tide of criminality.[27]

Other Nix appointees were men like Frank Lake; George Starmer, brother of Bill Starmer, who had been slain by the

---

27 "Four Score Years A Fighter" (the authentic life of Chris Madsen), *Daily Oklahoman*, November 17, 24, 1935; December 1, 8, 15, 29, 1935; also Newsom, *op. cit.*, pp. 147-148.

Dalton gang in the battle at Twin Mounds; Charles F. Colcord, of Oklahoma City, who became one of the state's most illustrious citizens; John Hixon, pioneer officer on the Kansas frontier and later sheriff of Logan County; Ed Kelley, Guthrie's first chief of police; Jim Masterson, brother of Bat Masterson; Frank Cochrane, deputy marshal for the Western District of Kansas and the Western District of Arkansas and detective on the Wichita police department until commissioned under Grimes in 1889; J. S. "Steve" Burke, who turned evangelist; Tom Houston; Dick Speed; Lafe Shadley; Frank Canton, who established a reputation as a fearless officer in the Johnson County War, in Wyoming, and was later honored with appointments as adjutant general by four Oklahoma governors; and there were many others who were to play outstanding roles in the war Marshal Nix now launched against the outlaws.

In *Oklahombres,* Nix writes:

Immediately upon the selection of my deputies, I called them together at Guthrie where we held a three-day conference, establishing our policies and laying our plans. I urged the men to never forget that they would be going up against some of the wildest characters of the frontier and to always make sure they safeguarded their own lives and the lives of respectable citizens. These things were to come first. . . . I wanted my men to have the drop on the other fellow before they commanded him to hold up his hands and consider himself under arrest, because this order was invariably disregarded by the bad men, provoking a lightning attempt to murder the officer. I wanted to make sure my men should shoot first. . . . My officers were especially urged to thoroughly examine their prisoners for firearms and other weapons. . . . An overlooked gun or knife has caused the death of many an officer who failed to properly disarm their prisoner.

In addition to laying down the policies we would always follow in our dealings with criminals, I reminded them of their very definite obligation to deal fairly and honorably with everyone— citizen or outlaw. . . . I considered lack of courtesy and gentle-

manly bearing a very serious offense. In my opinion, a man with a
smile was more to be feared when it came to a test of real nerve
than the would-be man-eater. Promising that I would communi-
cate regularly each week with every deputy on my staff, informing
them of all our office had learned that might increase the effective-
ness of their work . . . my men dispersed to their assigned positions to take up the campaign.[28]

Meanwhile, the Doolin gang staged two of the boldest robberies of their career. On June 11, 1893, they held up the California express on the Santa Fe, a half mile west of Cimarron,
Kansas, and shot the express messenger; took $1,000 in silver
and the contents of the way safe and escaped.[29] On their return
south across the Cherokee Outlet, they pulled a double train
robbery at Wharton by taking charge of the southbound passenger train and guarding its crew until the arrival of the train
going north. Within a few minutes they looted both trains of
several hundred dollars, a quantity of registered mail, and valuables of the surprised passengers, and headed for their Creek
Nation hideout.[30]

Bill Doolin had picked the opportune moment to exalt the
power and success of his band and his own generalship, for
Nix was too busy organizing his new force to give hot pursuit,
and no sooner had the new marshal completed his appointments and assignments of deputies than the government thrust
upon his office the great responsibility of policing the Cherokee Outlet, together with the surplus lands of the Pawnee
and Tonkawa reservations, which President Cleveland suddenly proclaimed would be opened to the homesteaders for
settlement at high noon, September 16.

No proclamation issued ever caused more excitement. It
made headlines in every state paper. This long-coveted land,
six million acres of rich grass, stretching for sixty miles south

28 Nix, *op. cit.*, pp. 83-85.
29 *Daily Oklahoma State Capital*, June 12, 1893.
30 Nix, *op. cit.*, pp. 89-90.

from the Kansas line, nearly 10,000 square miles divided into 35,163 claims, was to be broken under the plow.

The machinery at Washington moved in high gear. Four land offices were established and town sites set apart with them that were to become boom towns: Wharton, on the Santa Fe; Enid, on the Rock Island; and Alva and Woodward, on the Southern Kansas railroad. To prevent "sooners" and other ineligible persons taking part in the rush, nine registration booths were established, five on the northern boundary along the Kansas line and four on the southern border between the Outlet and Old Oklahoma. At these booths, settlers were compelled to file their intentions in writing, showing their qualifications for the right to homestead entry. A certificate issued by the registry clerks and attached to the declaration made was then held by the settler as his identification when he appeared at the district land office after the opening to file his homestead claim.

From August 19, the date of the proclamation, the scenes of 1889, 1891, and 1892 were reproduced on a much larger scale. More than 100,000 registered. From Caldwell to Arkansas City at intermediate points on the Kansas border, and at Orlando, Hennessey, and intermediate points on the southern border of the Outlet, this scrambling, fighting horde gathered to await the "zero hour." [31]

Nix writes:

It would be hard for mere words to describe the circumstances and conditions that contributed to the great magnitude of the preliminary planning that must be done in order that the run might be held under perfect control and rendered as peaceful and amicable as possible. . . . I appointed one thousand special deputies to assist in the orderly handling of the tremendous crowds. . . . My men were to patrol the entire boundary between Old

[31] *Guthrie Daily Leader,* August 11-23, 1893; *Ibid.,* September 1, 1893; *Daily Oklahoma State Capital,* August 26-30, 1893; Thoburn and Wright, *op. cit.,* pp. 556-557; Gittinger, *op. cit.,* pp. 201-205.

Oklahoma and the Cherokee Outlet. Immediately upon the opening, we were to take charge of the entire area, including all new
town sites.[32]

Tilghman, assisted by Charles Colcord, already had been
assigned to the land office at Wharton, and Chris Madsen and
many of the other regular deputies sent to Enid, Alva, Woodward, and other points north and west, when Nix learned
suddenly that the Doolin gang, enjoying the fruits of their last
raids in Kansas and at Wharton, was celebrating three or four
nights a week at Ingalls, on the border of Hell's Fringe.

[32] *Op. cit.*, 88-89 (Also letter of suggestions to President Cleveland from
Governor Renfrow, United States Attorney Horace Speed, and Marshal Nix,
dated at Guthrie, July 15, 1893) .

The Ingalls Invasion

Ingalls lay thirty-five miles northeast of Guthrie and eleven miles east of Stillwater. Far from a railroad and not even on a beaten trail, there seemed no excuse for it having been given birth.

Doctor A. G. McMurtry and a farmer named Robert Beal had released from their original quarter sections forty acres to be used as a town site and the government had surveyed and platted the town in 1889. McMurtry constructed a building and started a drug store. Beal became the first grocer. A. J. Light put in a blacksmith shop, where the road from the west entered the town limits, and down the street, a block south, J. W. "Preacher" Perry established a dry goods store and J. D. Ramsey opened a hardware.

Fall City, two miles southeast, had a post office that had served the country for miles around since before the opening and, even after Ingalls was platted, people had to get their mail at Fall City or Stillwater, until McMurtry obtained a grant for a post office which he set up in one corner of his drug store. This was soon taken over by J. W. Ellsworth, a minister and notary public, and within a few months transferred to William Selph, who opened another grocery next door to the Ramsey hardware and built his home a block south of his store. Delegations representing six other towns had gone to Guthrie to present claims for the community trading point to be placed elsewhere, but now stores from all the places that had cried for the location moved to Ingalls.

A saloon, run by a man named Vaughan, a cotton gin, flour mill, another blacksmith shop, owned by William Wagner, two restaurants, a barber shop, and shoe shop did good business. Doctor D. R. Pickering opened an office in his home, and Doctors Briggs, D. H. Selph, and W. R. Call assisted in caring for the sick, "not leaving out secret visits from the outlaws."[1] Between Light's blacksmith shop and Briggs' drug store, Pierce and Hostetter operated a livery stable. West of the Ramsey hardware, across the street and beyond the public well, George Ransom and Old Man Murray established another saloon with a gambling hall, and opened another livery barn next door south. The only two-story building in town was the City Hotel in the block east, run by Mary Pierce, who "always kept three or four girls around and spent all her waking hours planning new diversions for her guests."[2]

In his frequent visits to the Rock Fort on the Dunn place, Bitter Creek had met Rosa Dunn, slim, dark, fifteen-year-old sister of the Dunn brothers who had settled along Council Creek in 1889. She is alleged to have fallen in love with the handsome, dashing young outlaw, who nicknamed her "The Rose of Cimarron," and joined him when the Doolin gang was in town on their nights to howl.[3] Here, too, from the Pawnee country north, came sixteen-year-old Annie McDoulet and fifteen-year-old Jennie Stevens to "make love" with other members of the gang and join their "wild parties." In the months to follow they became notorious as "Cattle Annie"

1 On March 1, 1893, the *Oklahoma Hawk* described Ingalls as "one of the most prosperous and thriving trading points in Payne County . . . located in one of the most prosperous agricultural sections of Oklahoma . . . built on a site with just enough slope for drainage which is so essential to good health . . . surrounded by rolling prairie and plenty of bottom land." Council Creek was two miles northeast, the Cimarron River six miles southeast, the Little Stillwater three miles west. "Most of this land will produce from 50 to 75 bushels of corn per acre. . . . Its natural resources have been its only support and it is a town because there is a demand for one where it is located."

2 Nix, *op. cit.*, pp. 103-104.

3 James D. Horan, *Desperate Women*, pp. 246-247; Melvin Harrel in "The Outlaw Was A Lady," *Northfork Sparks and Flashes*, July, 1951, claims she was Rose O'Leary, daughter of a Georgia family who settled on Hackberry Creek in old Day County, near the Cherokee Outlet.

and "Little Breeches" and rode for the Doolin gang, delivering messages, stealing horses, bootlegging whiskey, and watching the trails for the marshals. Doolin himself met and courted Edith Ellsworth, daughter of the town minister and former postmaster.

These "facilities" and the close proximity of Ingalls to both the Rock Fort and Creek Nation hideouts made it a "natural pop-off valve" for the outlaws. They spent their stolen money for provisions, ammunition, and whiskey and found residents in sympathy with them, sheltering them for their trade, lending every assistance in the way of information whenever officers came into the neighborhood, and even contributing their bit to the periodic festivities. Those who might have informed the officers of the presence of the outlaws were so "terrorized by the gang that they kept silent."[4] Only by accident did Nix learn that the band was making the place its headquarters.

One night in August, while the gang was playing poker at the Ransom and Murray Saloon, Deputy Sheriff Bob Andrews, of Payne County, walked in to arrest a small-time thief named "Ragged Bill," who had knocked an old man in the head at Stillwater and robbed him of $40. Ragged Bill immediately pleaded with the men at the table not to let the deputy take him back to stand trial. Addressing the tall, red-headed leader as Doolin, he explained that he had come to join his gang.

The sweating Andrews, realizing he was at the mercy of the most dangerous band in the territory, explained why he had come after Ragged Bill, and Doolin is credited with saying: "Anybody who would knock an old man in the head for $40 couldn't carry water for our bunch." He told the deputy to handcuff his man, then ordered Bitter Creek to get their horses, and the two outlaws rode out a short distance with the deputy and his prisoner.

As they parted, Doolin said, "Andrews, I'm taking your word you won't double cross me. If you do, we'll meet again sometime."

4 *Guthrie Daily Leader,* September 5, 1893.

$5,000.⁰⁰

REWARD

FOR CAPTURE

DEAD OR ALIVE

OF

BILL DOOLIN

NOTORIOUS ROBBER OF TRAINS AND BANKS

ABOUT 6 FOOT 2 INCHES TALL, LT. BROWN HAIR, DANGEROUS, ALWAYS HEAVILY ARMED.

IMMEDIATELY CONTACT THE

U.S. MARSHAL'S OFFICE, GUTHRIE, OKLAHOMA TER.

Then the four men parted, Doolin and Bitter Creek going back to Ingalls and Andrews going on to Stillwater with his prisoner. It was a rather strange situation, Doolin with a $5,000 reward on his head dictating to an officer of the law. But Andrews, true to his promise, never mentioned his meeting with the gang.[5]

Ragged Bill, however, cursed Bill Doolin in jail; and details of his capture soon were in the hands of Marshal Nix. On the night of August 31, two white-topped covered wagons left Guthrie for Ingalls. Each wagon boasted a single driver, but carefully concealed beneath their flapping canvas were a cargo of arms and ammunition and thirteen United States deputies.[6]

Many cattle outfits were on the move since the announced opening of the Outlet; everywhere homeseekers in covered wagons crossed the country for the promised land, so they attracted little attention. On the morning of September 1, they camped in a ravine southwest of Ingalls, and two scouts were sent ahead to study the lay of the town. Shortly before ten o'clock they were back with the report that seven outlaws had just ridden in, placed their horses in the Ransom livery barn and separated, one going to the hotel, the other six entering the saloon. Hixon, who was in charge of the expedition, dispatched a message to Chief Deputy Hale, who was attending court at Stillwater. Hale gathered a posse and started for Ingalls at once.

Meanwhile, Hixon assigned his men to positions about the town to cut off all avenues of escape.[7] One wagon, carrying Deputies Masterson, W. C. Roberts, Henry Keller, Hi Thompson, George Cox, H. A. Janson, and Lafe Shadley, circled the town, coming into Ingalls from the south and stopping in a grove of trees north of the residence of Doctor

[5] Lon R. Stansbery, "Cops and Robbers: Famous Battle of Ingalls in 1893," *Tulsa World*, March, 1937.

[6] *Daily Oklahoma State Capital*, September 2, 1893.

[7] *Guthrie Daily Leader*, September 2 and 5, 1893; *Daily Oklahoma State Capital*, September 2, 1893.

Pickering. Dick Speed drove the second wagon in from the west. As it approached the town, Deputies Hixon, Houston, Burke, Red Lucas, and Ike Steel, carrying Winchesters and heavily armed with six-shooters and ammunition, dropped from under the canvas and scattered through the timber and brush to the south to take up positions behind buildings, fences, and trees. Speed turned the empty vehicle down main street past Light's blacksmith shop and stopped in front of the livery stable of Pierce and Hostetter.

The outlaws were playing poker in the saloon. They had seen the wagon from the south disappear in the grove near Pickering's, but gave it no thought since it was a favorite camping spot for travelers passing through. When the second wagon lumbered into town from the west and stopped up the street, Bitter Creek grew nervous and left the game to investigate.

Deputy Speed had climbed down from the wagon with his Winchester and entered the livery stable, covering its only two occupants and informing them there was going to be a raid and if they left the barn or attempted to warn the outlaws, they would be slain. As he stepped back to the open doorway, he saw Bitter Creek mount a horse in front of the saloon and start walking it up the street toward the wagon. At that moment a boy left Light's blacksmith shop and Speed called him to the doorway and inquired the name of "that rider down there."

The incredulous youth, later identified as Dell Simmons, exclaimed: "Why, that's Bitter Creek Newcomb!" and Bitter Creek saw the boy point his direction.

The outlaw jerked his horse to a halt behind the well and reached for his Winchester. Speed whipped his rifle to his shoulder and fired, and it was he, Deputy Speed, who fired the opening shot of the famous battle.[8]

Speed's bullet shattered the magazine on Bitter Creek's Winchester and drove part of it into his leg.[9] The outlaw

[8] Stansbery, *op. cit.*
[9] *Ibid.; Perkins Journal,* September 7, 1893.

flinched with pain as he fired, and his shot went wild. His rifle wouldn't work for a second shot, and, as he wheeled his horse in an effort to escape, Speed stepped from the doorway to kill him.

Arkansas Tom was in a room on the second floor of the hotel. He heard the first shot and ran to the rear window. As Speed stepped from the livery stable, he fired at the officer, hitting him in the shoulder. Speed started back to the stable door, then turned around and tried to reach the shelter of the wagon, when Arkansas Tom fired again, killing him instantly.[10]

This shooting forced the other officers into the fight before they had gained their positions.[11] They began shooting at Bitter Creek as he rode south out of town. Doolin, Dalton, Tulsa Jack, Dynamite Dick, and Red Buck opened fire from the saloon, covering Bitter Creek's escape. The air was thick with flying lead. The youth who had identified Bitter Creek to Deputy Speed was shot dead by the outlaws as he fled down the street, a citizen named N. A. Walker was shot through the lungs, and a horse that had broken loose from a hitching post in front of the Selph store and post office was killed by a stray bullet before Bitter Creek disappeared in the timber along the creek and the first burst of firing ceased.

The Hixon party in the draw on the west side of the street began moving behind the stores and other buildings to concentrate their fire on the saloon, from the side and rear. Masterson and his party spread from the grove north of Pickering's and advanced through the brush west of the hotel and south across the street behind the homes of Doctors McMurtry, Selph, and Call, covering the front of the saloon and the livery stable where the gang had left their horses. After several minutes Hixon sent word to Doolin that the gang was surrounded and had no chance to escape, and Doolin replied with an oath: "Go to hell!"

10 *Ibid.*
11 *Guthrie Daily Leader,* September 5, 1893.

The marshals opened a withering barrage on the building. Bullets ripped into the saloon from both sides, the front, and rear. Ransom was hit in the leg and his partner, Murray, received a wound in the left side and a broken arm.[12] The fight grew so hot the outlaws decided to make a run to the livery stable for their horses.[13]

Doolin left the saloon first, the others covering him with a shower of lead. As he reached the stable, he opened fire on the marshals, and Dalton and Red Buck dodged down the

[12] *Ibid.*, September 2, 1893.

[13] The legend is that Bitter Creek did not escape from Ingalls at the beginning of the battle, but was shot from his horse, and at this stage of the fight was lying, helpless from his wounds and bleeding badly, behind the well; that Rose of Cimarron, observing his plight, remembered he had left his Winchester (six-shooters?) and belts of ammunition in the hotel room. Anxious for the safety of her lover, she grabbed up the belts and weapon and leaped (or slid down a rope made of torn bedclothes) from the upper-story window and carried them through the fire of the outlaws and marshals to her lover. The officers stopped shooting at the sight of Rose, and the Doolin gang, one of them helping Rose drag the wounded Bitter Creek, ran from the saloon into the livery stable, mounted their horses, and made their escape.

This story first appeared in Richard S. Graves' paper-backed pamphlet *Oklahoma Outlaws,* which sold for a few cents in conjunction with a road show attraction entitled, "The Passing of the Oklahoma Outlaws," produced in 1915. The story was retold in Newsom's book, *op. cit.,* pp. 173-174 (1923), and in Zoe A. Tilghman's *Outlaw Days,* pp. 62-64 (1926); and obviously these sources were relied on by MacDonald and Sutton in *Hands Up!,* p. 195 (1927); Edwin L. Sabin, *Wild Men of the Wild West,* pp. 314-315 (1929); and Nix and Hines in *Oklahombres,* pp. 107-108 (1929). The tale has been included in every article written about this battle since. The most recent version, in considerable detail and greatly expanded, appears in Horan, *op. cit.,* pp. 253-254 (1952), and this writer depended on these sources for his chapter "Battle on Hell's Fringe," in *Toughest of Them All,* pp. 117-130 (1953). Recent affidavits of surviving eyewitnesses, given this writer, state that Rosa was not present during the fight; that she was not in Ingalls until some time later, and first-hand accounts of the battle appearing in the *Guthrie Daily Leader, Daily Oklahoma State Capital, Perkins Journal,* and *Stillwater Gazette,* quoted herein, make no mention of the incident. It didn't happen.

The legend continues that Rosa tried to get Bitter Creek to reform, and when he refused, she continued to ride with the Doolin gang to be near him until, years afterwards, she was captured by the marshals and sentenced to the Federal reformatory at Farmington, Massachusetts. This didn't happen either. Bitter Creek was "enamored" with a "woman of the world" who plied her profession in a building near the Pierce hotel. Rosa gave her love to Charles Noble, a young blacksmith at Lawson, northeast of Ingalls, and on December 5, 1897, she and Charles were married by S. T. Peague, Minister of The Gospel in Payne County.

street into the doorway. They joined Doolin, and the three opened a second fusillade while Dynamite Dick and Tulsa Jack, their own guns blazing, rushed from the saloon and gained the stable entrance.

This series of surprising, daring moves made it necessary that the Hixon party shift positions in order to effectively cover the stable. Deputy Houston moved around the corner of a granary back of Perry's store to fire at the rear door. At the hotel, Arkansas Tom, no longer able to assist his comrades from the rear second-story window, had crawled up a ladder into the attic and poked a hole in the west roof with the muzzle of his Winchester. He thrust the barrel through as Houston left the granary and shot the deputy twice in the left side and bowels.[14]

Deputy Shadley ran from cover east of the hotel and dropped behind the carcass of the dead horse in the street. From this point he poured a close, accurate fire into the stable and drove the outlaws back from the doorway.

Inside the barn, Doolin and Dynamite Dick bridled the horses. Then the two mounted and rode out the rear door and down the draw. Dalton, Red Buck, and Tulsa Jack rode out the front door. Hixon, guarding this avenue of escape, shot Bill Dalton's horse in the jaw. The horse stopped. Dalton put spurs to his mount, but before he rode another dozen yards, Shadley, shifting his position from behind the dead horse to the corner of the hardware store, fired and broke the horse's leg.[15]

As the animal went down, Dalton leaped clear and ran toward the other outlaws who had stopped at a wire fence. Too late Dalton realized the only pair of wire cutters were on his saddle, and he started back to his injured horse. Shadley left the hardware store, running for the cover of a storm cave

14 *Territory of Oklahoma v. Tom Jones,* Case Number 323, District Court, Payne County, May 17-21, 1894.

15 *Stillwater Gazette,* September 1, 1893; *Daily Oklahoma State Capital,* September 4, 1893; *Guthrie Daily Leader,* September 5, 1893.

east of the Selph residence. The wire fence ran east of the cave, and as the deputy tried to crawl under it, Dalton fired three bullets into his body "so close together they could be covered with one hand." [16]

The other outlaws kept shooting at the officers until Dalton obtained the wire cutters. The United States men were firing at long range now, which gave Dalton a chance to cut the fence. Then Doolin lifted Dalton up behind him, and the five outlaws, on four horses, rode through. At the top of the hill they turned and fired several more shots back at the marshals. The fourteen-year-old son of Doctor Briggs had run to the corner in front of Pickering's to see which way they had fled and was shot in the shoulder as the outlaws disappeared into the timber.[17]

Arkansas Tom remained behind in the hotel attic. He knocked a hole in the east roof, which gave him command of the whole town. The marshals surrounded the hotel, ordering all occupants out. When all had left the building except Arkansas Tom, they began a continuous firing into the roof and upstairs until it was virtually riddled with bullets. It was a miracle how the outlaw survived, but at eleven o'clock, one hour after the shot that began the battle was fired, Arkansas Tom "still pumped lead down at the besieging party . . . and seemed to have an inexhaustible supply of ammunition."[18]

Doctors Selph and Pickering gave first aid to Houston and Shadley. Chief Deputy Hale had arrived from Stillwater, and his posse of eleven men rode in pursuit of the outlaws who had escaped. Hale joined the marshals who had surrounded the hotel and again warned Arkansas Tom to come out.

"If I come out," the outlaw replied, "I'll come out shooting!"

Jim Masterson produced two sticks of dynamite which he had brought along for just such an emergency and told the

16 Stansbery, *op. cit.; Stillwater Gazette,* September 8, 1893.
17 *Daily Oklahoma State Capital,* September 2, 1893.
18 *Ibid.*

outlaw he would "blow the house into the middle of next week." Within a few minutes Arkansas Tom strode from the hotel, unarmed, and surrendered.[19]

Hale, Steel, and Roberts returned to Guthrie with the prisoner, several witnesses to the battle, and three citizens whom they arrested and later charged with harboring the outlaws. Steel led Bitter Creek's horse, which the outlaw had left in the livery stable, and Roberts carried Bill Dalton's saddle.[20] Hixon accompanied the dead body of Dick Speed and the wounded Houston and Shadley to Stillwater. "His arrival in this city, together with a report of the fight, caused the most intense excitement, and men in large numbers left immediately for Ingalls; the court room was vacated at once, lawyers, jurors, and witnesses joining in the stampede to the scene of carnage, making it necessary for Judge Green to adjourn court. . . ."[21] Other posses spread through the hills on the trail of the outlaws. "Another battle may be looked for, and if it comes . . . from the temper of the people . . . it will be a war of extermination."[22]

One group went in the direction taken by Bitter Creek. At the creek crossing they found a bloody pool of water where he had stopped to bathe his wound and a spot in a cornfield where he had rested.[23] The trail led to Fall City, where J. D. Vickery reported the outlaw had approached his blacksmith

19 (The legend is that the marshals began piling brush against the hotel to set fire to the building and Mary Pierce pleaded with them to spare her place; that it was her only livelihood and contained everything she owned; that if they wouldn't burn the hotel she would make Arkansas Tom surrender. She then called out to the outlaw and went up in the attic, where he lay wounded and bleeding, and after a few minutes, appeared at the window and told the officers that if Arkansas Tom was promised protection from mob violence and not placed in chains he would give himself up; that he had eighty rounds of ammunition left and could kill at least seven men whom he had range on at the moment, and the marshals readily agreed to the outlaw's proposition. "This story is not true."—*Daily Oklahoma State Capital*, September 4, 1893; *Perkins Journal*, September 7, 1893) .

20 *Perkins Journal*, September 7, 1893.

21 *Guthrie Daily Leader*, September 2, 1893.

22 *Ibid.*

23 *Ibid.*

shop, still riding his borrowed horse and looking very pale, and demanded a bucket of water. Vickery had poured the water on the wound and stopped the bleeding.[24] The outlaw had ridden east from Fall City, where the posse lost his trail. The rest of the gang were traced to the Cimarron. After crossing the river, their trail vanished in the Creek Nation.[25]

At Stillwater, Houston and Shadley, surrounded by family and friends, suffered through the night and died. In its issue of September 8, 1893, the *Stillwater Gazette* lamented:

Dick Speed, Tom Houston and Lafe Shadley were three as brave and fearless officers as ever operated in support of law and order. They were cut down in the prime of life by assassins, while in defense of our homes and firesides. They are no more, but their memories will live forever. Their labors and deaths will form a page in the history of Oklahoma which will shine all the brighter and read the better when outlawry and organized bands of marauders are completely wiped out of existence.

In the *Guthrie Daily Leader* of the same date appeared this biting editorial:

There is nothing which should appeal more strongly to an outraged sense of justice than a murder of a man in the discharge of his duty. . . . It is a matter of vital necessity that those men shall be caught and made to pay the penalty of their crimes, and it is time that the false glamor surrounding such dastardly deeds be dispelled. . . . Nothing will do this but the killing of the scoundrels as one kills a wild beast. . . .

On the evening of September 12, with hundreds of Guthrie's citizens already having departed for the opening of the Outlet, a startling rumor swept the city: The Doolin gang, in rendezvous in the Creek Nation, nursing their battle wounds and gathering reinforcements, proposed to raid

24 *Daily Oklahoma State Capital,* September 7, 1893.
25 *Guthrie Daily Leader,* September 5, 1893.

Guthrie, headquarters of the marshals, in revenge for the Ingalls invasion, and liberate Arkansas Tom!

A report received by Colonel Dick Reaves, of the Guthrie cavalry, described "a band of men numbering thirty-five, armed to the teeth . . . camped twenty-two miles northeast of here. . . ." Although it was not certain "that they are the bandits or another party gathered for the opening . . . it behooves the people who remain in Guthrie to be on the lookout. . . ." The banks of the city closed at once, "the time locking having been set and cannot be opened until Monday." Two squads of forty men were organized under Deputy Marshals Hixon and Heck Thomas. It was Thomas' opinion that if the gang entered the city they would "come in separately and concentrate about the jail," and he advised his men to parade the town with their Winchesters and arrest all suspicious persons who could give no satisfactory account of themselves. Scores of other armed citizens joined the marshals and promised a repetition of the Coffeyville affair if the outlaws appeared.[26]

They guarded the city three days and three nights, but nothing happened. A report from Orlando stated the gang had passed that place, headed west. Another report claimed the outlaws were camped on the famous Dalton farm, near Kingfisher, and members of the Dalton family were refusing to allow strangers to come near the place. In the federal jail, Arkansas Tom laughed over the scare as the effort of some prankster to confuse the "little army," as he styled Nix's force of deputies, and said Guthrie people "made him weary."[27]

[26] *Ibid.*, September 13 and 16, 1893; *Daily Oklahoma State Capital*, September 16, 1893.

[27] *Guthrie Daily Leader*, September 22, 1893.

Cherokee Strip

Many versions have been given of the race for homes in the Outlet. As the years have passed, stories told and retold often fail to add up, and historians have overlooked, or deliberately chosen to disregard, the bold facts.

The last day at the booths in the one-hundred-foot neutral strip around its borders, with thousands of newcomers still pouring in, the crush was tremendous. Passenger trains, with crowded seats, aisles, and platforms, rolled into the border cities and were sidetracked; wagon roads teemed with prairie schooners; cavalcades of horsemen in tens, twenties, and fifties rode like an army, until there were "eight persons for every 160 acres, not to mention town lots," and the registration points unable to accommodate them.[1]

Men and women huddled in lines like swine, with the burning sun beating down on their heads. No rain had fallen in weeks. The ground was baked and the tall prairie grass dry as tinder. Soldiers had set fire to huge tracts in forcing removal of the last grazing herds and to locate sooners, and hot winds sweeping across the plains filled the air with sooty dust which settled on perspiring persons. Water unfit for a horse to drink sold for ten cents a cup, and food, poor food that caused much illness, retailed at enormous prices, while "thieves and thugs plied their vocations with zeal for the sheckles they could

1 *Daily Oklahoma State Capital,* September 7-9, 1893; *Guthrie Daily Leader,* September 6 and 14, 1893.

extract from the purse of the honest settler." Hundreds of "professional boomers" were on the grounds, holding places in the lines and selling when they had worked to the front at five and twenty-five dollars. The plan of the government to obviate "sooner trouble" by requiring registration proved impracticable. Many certificates were bought and sold and, as time grew precious, the lines became "solid walls." Men and women ate and slept in their places; some died; scores were carried away, prostrated with the heat, dirt, and exhaustion.[2]

At eleven o'clock the opening day everybody was jamming the starting line. Struggling, pushing, cursing men clambered over each other, and women vied with men; clothes were torn off, regardless of sex; pedestrians were knocked down and trampled. As the hour approached, the anxiety on their faces was painful. When the bugles blew and the signal shots were fired the sight was at once sublime, exciting, and appalling.[3]

It was a race for blood and homes.

Soon the vast prairie was dotted with farms. Cities sprang up within a few hours. Seven new counties were added to Oklahoma Territory.[4]

[2] *Daily Oklahoma State Capital,* September 12-13, 1893; *Guthrie Daily Leader,* September 16, 1893.

[3] "The mob plunged forward as if some great force had impelled them from behind. The whole line swayed and pushed and roared and cursed and then broke asunder as it were, and then began gradually to scatter into fragments of life, while the dust and sand rose up in dense, mighty clouds. Men knocked each other down as they rushed onward. Women shrieked and fell, fainting, only to be trampled upon and killed. Horsemen tumbled into the dust from excitement; men, weary of the race, turned back bleeding and fainting to the line from which they started, broken hearted. . . . Vehicles of all kinds were smashed and made useless. . . . Men, women and horses were lying all over the prairie. Here and there men were fighting to the death over claims which each maintained he was first to reach. Knives and guns were drawn. . . . It was a terrible and exciting scene; no pen can do it justice."—*Weekly Oklahoma State Capital,* September 23, 1893.

[4] The counties were designated "K," "L," "M," "N," "O," "P" and "Q," and subsequently named Kay, Grant, Woods, Woodward, Garfield, Noble, and Pawnee, with county seats at Newkirk, Medford, Alva, Woodward, Enid, Perry, and Pawnee. By nightfall the opening day, Enid had 12,000 people encamped on eighty acres. Twenty-five thousand slept in Perry (formerly Wharton). There were 8,000 at Pond Creek. Other places of promise were Kildare, Blackwell, and Cross (now Ponca City).

But for hundreds who rushed in, full of hope and confidence, there was bitter disappointment.

Small white flags bearing the words "This claim is taken" were more than a bit of irony. Many were placed so thickly they presaged bitter fights in land office proceedings.

And violence against sooners was repeated. All over the land men cursed and fought and pulled up stakes, and several instances of lynching, robbery, and murder were recorded.[5]

One army lieutenant said: "There was bloodshed enough to satisfy the very worst of bad men. . . ."[6] In *Hands Up!* Fred Sutton confesses that nine-tenths of the settlers in the Cherokee Strip won their homesteads and lots with a six-shooter.[7]

Those who failed to obtain claims—beaten men and women with clothing in tatters, their faces torn and bloody, and hearts filled with deep and burning disappointment—drifted about the Outlet, "talking loudly and cursing violently . . . the administration and everybody concerned," blaming their failure on the government's planning of this "excruciating game of devilish and ingenious sport for devils" and the Secretary of Interior as "responsible for the sick, the wounded and the robbed . . . and the graves his registering system dug."[8] They never considered the damage and injury done the result of their own selfishness and greed rather than the method.

Town sites had troubles, too. On many, vice was rampant, and Governor Renfrow ordered that elections be held and town governments organized immediately. Perry was so tough it gained the title "Hell's Acre," and so many complaints reached the chief executive, of numerous robberies and homicides taking place in and around the gambling houses, that wholesale raids were conducted until "known wheels of fortune, faro layouts, and chuck-a-luck tables were piled in

<hr />

5 *Guthrie Daily Leader*, September 18 and 20, October 7, and November 6, 1893; *Weekly Oklahoma State Capital*, November 4 and 18, 1893; *Daily Oklahoma State Capital*, September 20 and November 13 and 23, 1893.

6 *Perkins Journal*, December 14, 1893.

7 MacDonald, *op. cit.*, p. 182.

8 *Weekly Oklahoma State Capital*, September 23, 1893.

innocuous desuetude on the outside of the principal resorts
. . . and the most prominent of these looked like deserted
tabernacles. . . ."[9]

Enid also furnished its quota of sensations. It was a "poor
day" when something did not occur to "vary the monotony."

A riot and probable lynching was checked in its incipiency
yesterday afternoon. A gang of desperadoes from South Enid . . .
rode into town with drawn revolvers. They proceeded to the
Cherokee allotments on the east side of the track and jumped the
land. Houses were torn down and women and children terrorized.
Mrs. Darragh, owner of the City Hotel, was driven from her place
and the desperadoes took possession. The citizens turned out and
held the outlaws in check until the sheriff and a posse could be
summoned, when the entire gang was arrested and taken to the
county jail.[10]

Enid suffered an additional conflict in the form of a com-
petitive town site, and the same situation existed at Pond
Creek. The Rock Island had established its station at North
Enid, a company town site in which the railroad was interested, and refused to stop trains at "government Enid," hoping to draw population to "railroad Enid." At Pond Creek,
a petition bearing 3,667 names asked Governor Renfrow to
declare it a city of the first class, and a committee went to
Topeka to interview the Rock Island officials about stopping
trains a mile and a half north at the "railroad site" of the city.
Wrangling went on for months until railroad officials agreed
to stop trains at South Enid if paid $3,500. One thousand
dollars brought a "stop" order from the railroad which reserved the right to refund the money and discontinue service
if the balance was not paid. Cash was hard to get. The railroad
refused paper securities, and precipitated a war that was to
end in bloodshed and much damage to public and private
property.[11]

9 *Daily Oklahoma State Capital*, October 3, 1893.
10 *Guthrie Daily Leader*, November 10, 1893.
11 *Daily Oklahoma State Capital*, September 20, 25, and 30, 1893.

Marshal Nix and his deputies lent every effort to help clear up such matters and control the mobs until local government could take over.[12] To facilitate the establishment of law and order in this new section, the 53rd Congress, by an act approved December 21, 1893, added two territorial justices.[13] President Cleveland appointed Andrew G. C. Bierer and John L. McAtee to these positions. The membership of the supreme court for Oklahoma Territory thus increased to five and the judicial districts likewise increased to that number. Judge Bierer was assigned the fourth district, covering the eastern half of the Outlet with headquarters at Perry, and Judge McAtee was in charge of the fifth district, comprising Kingfisher, Grant, and Garfield counties, with headquarters at Enid. When Judge Seay resigned in 1891 to become territorial governor, John H. Burford, of Indiana, had been appointed to the vacancy. In May, 1893, Frank Dale, of Kansas, had succeeded Judge Green in the first judicial district, at Guthrie and Stillwater, and Henry W. Scott succeeded Judge Clark, at Oklahoma City and Norman. Of these first men on the bench in Oklahoma, Judge Burford remained longer than any and retired only when statehood eliminated the territorial courts. His jurisdiction included the extreme western counties, "where settlers were few and cattle range ideals and customs still prevailed,"[14] and his dockets particularly were replete with cases which dealt with killings.

With the organization of new courts and local governments, Marshal Nix found it necessary to reassign a number of his field deputies in order to work in close co-operation with the new federal judges and United States attorneys. He stationed Jack Love at Woodward, Gus Hadwinger and E. W. Snoddy at Alva, W. A. "Pat" Murphy at Pond Creek, Frank Lake at Pawnee, left Tilghman at Perry, and sent others to remote sections of the districts to assist in the proper service

12 Nix, *op. cit.*, pp. 97-98.
13 *U. S. Statutes at Large*, XXVIII, p. 20.
14 Thoburn and Wright, *op. cit.*, p. 722.

of papers, the accumulation of evidence, and maintenance of order.[15]

Nix's office had formerly taken care of train robberies committed in the Outlet, but with the strip now organized under territorial laws, such cases no longer came under his jurisdiction and he was charged only with the investigation of crimes against the laws of the United States, such as cutting timber on government land, violation of revenue and postal laws, and selling whiskey to Indians. For such crimes as robbery and murder, his jurisdiction lay in the Osage, Comanche, Kiowa, and other Indian reservations not ceded for settlement. Otherwise these crimes belonged to the sheriffs of the counties in which they were committed. Unless the reward was tempting enough to make a posse for it alone, the marshals received no pay for going after train robbers. In the general attempt to apprehend and punish these criminals, however, Nix assured the sheriffs all possible assistance, and many of his deputy marshals were sheriffs, and officers in other capacities.[16]

The depredations of the Doolin gang had lulled. So much that the *Guthrie Daily Leader* observed, in its issue of December 9, 1893, that the territory was "rapidly growing law-abiding," and commented:

This is not only due to the steady march of civilization but also the . . . vigilance and sincere work of United States Marshal Nix and his corps of deputies. Some of the most courageous men that ever strapped a cartridge belt about their loins or drew a six-shooter are on his force . . . and they rarely miss the game they go after.

While much praise was due the marshals, and it was the general belief that, although only one member of his band had been captured and another badly wounded, the desperate

---

15 Nix, *op. cit.*, p. 98.
16 For instance, Jack Love was elected sheriff at Woodward; Frank Lake became sheriff at Pawnee; and Bill Tilghman was city marshal at Perry.

battle at Ingalls had broken the back of Doolin's power, Nix read into this non-activity "a lull before the storm," and realized that safety for citizens and property could never be achieved until the last member of the gang was dead or behind prison bars. Early in January, 1894, he made a special trip to Washington to make arrangements for the government to offer a $2,000 reward for the members of the gang, and asked the people of the territory to increase the government reward from other sources.[17]

Many of the bandits from the two territories, believing they could operate with more freedom among new settlers, not acquainted with them, had moved into the Outlet.[18] Fugitives from justice from Texas, Kansas, and Arkansas, and some of the worst outlaws in Montana, who had been driven out by Granville Stuart in 1879, had made the run for homes with the thousands of good men and women.[19] Doolin had made two formidable additions to his band—a pair of seasoned Pawnee country renegades, Charlie Pierce and Tulsa Jack Blake.

It was estimated there were "a dozen or fourteen in the gang, all heavily armed," and that they were undoubtedly preparing to make a wholesale raid upon the new banks in the Outlet or rob some train on the Santa Fe or Rock Island roads. "Four times within a week have they made public appearance in towns near the Cherokee Strip, only each time to again disappear for a day and reappear at some other point."[20]

The afternoon of January 23, the citizens of Pawnee were startled by the discharge of two volleys from firearms. At the same moment three horses "went tearing down the hill northwest toward the Black Bear." Two of the horses each bore one rider. On the third horse, in addition to the man in the saddle, rode Cashier Berry of the Farmers' and Citizens' Bank.

17 *Daily Oklahoma State Capital,* January 19, 1894.
18 Nix, *op. cit.,* p. 98.
19 Frank Canton, *Frontier Trails,* pp. 107-108.
20 *Pawnee Scout,* January 26, 1894.

A few minutes after three o'clock, while Berry was waiting on a customer, Bill Doolin entered the bank with a revolver and demanded: "Hands up!" He was followed immediately by another armed robber, later identified as Tulsa Jack, who stood guard on the customer while Doolin stepped behind the counter. Doolin placed the muzzle of his gun against Berry's head and ordered him to open the vault. The time lock on the large safe was set for four o'clock, when daily balances were made, but Berry turned the dial. When it did not open, Doolin remarked: "Fail on that again, and I'll blow your brains out!" Berry made a second attempt, explaining that the safe could not be opened for half an hour. Finally Doolin put his ear to the safe and, hearing the timepiece running, seemed satisfied. Raking $300 off the counter, he marched Berry out the door and around the corner of the hotel, where Bitter Creek waited with the horses. They mounted, Doolin taking Berry up behind him, and as they rode from town, fired two volleys into Bolton's meat market, where the bank customer had fled to spread the alarm. Outside of town, Doolin ordered Berry to "pile off," which the cashier did "without ceremony" and walked back to town. Posses were quickly organized by the sheriff and deputy marshals. At the crossing on Black Bear they found signs where the trio had been joined by other members of the gang, but the trail vanished at Gray Horse ford.[21]

At one o'clock the morning of March 13, two men entered the railroad hotel at Woodward and went upstairs to the room of the station agent, George W. Rourke. They awakened him with their six-shooters and told him to dress quietly, then marched him downstairs to the depot. As they approached the station, they noticed a youth, named Sam Peters, lounging near the baggage room and ordered him to "fall in and throw up his hands." Inside the office they forced Rourke to open the safe and sack up $6,540 in currency consigned to the army paymaster at nearby Fort Supply; then they made Rourke and

21 *Daily Oklahoma State Capital*, January 24, 1894; *Pawnee Scout*, January 26, 1894; *Pawnee Times*, January 26, 1894.

Peters carry the route safe a quarter mile east of the depot, where they broke it open and left it empty on the ground. The robbers proceeded to the stockyards a half mile from the depot. Here they left their captives, mounted their horses and rode southeast with the loot. The victims were discovered at daybreak, and a posse under Sheriff Jack Love took the trail of the bandits. Colonel Parker, commanding Fort Supply, detailed Lieutenant Kirby Walker, with twenty cavalrymen, for the hunt and called into service Amos Chapman, veteran Indian scout of the Canadian.[22]

Full descriptions of the robbers were telegraphed Marshal Nix: The leader, "thirty years old, five feet ten inches tall, weight 170 pounds, closely built, moustache, dark brown shirt, dark slouch hat, rather heavy voice," was identified as Bill Doolin. The other, "twenty-five years old, five feet seven inches tall, weight 150 pounds, two weeks' growth of beard, slouch hat with high crown and crease in top, pants in boots, checkered handkerchief about his neck, dark suit, sack coat, dark complexion," was identified as Bill Dalton. Both had been riding "red bay" horses.[23]

Nix sent "a strong squad" to the scene at once. "Undoubtedly eight men were concerned" in the robbery, for there were indications that six other riders had joined the pair a short distance from town. Great excitement swept the Outlet. A courier from Ochiltree brought word to Canadian that men answering the description of the bandits had been seen traveling west. Sheriff Love and his posse, with Marshal Nix's depu-

22 *Guthrie Daily Leader,* March 14, 1894; *Daily Oklahoma State Capital,* March 14, 1894.

23 Telegram to U. S. Marshal Nix from D. H. Rhoads, Superintendent of the Santa Fe, Woodward, O. T., March 13, 1894. (The legend is that Little Bill Raidler and Bitter Creek Newcomb pulled the Woodward robbery and spent their "accumulated" wealth in "riotous living" at the Worlds' Columbian Exposition in Chicago. The Exposition closed October 30, 1893, five months before the Woodward affair, and during September and October of that year, Bitter Creek was recovering from the leg wound he had received in the Ingalls battle.)

ties, headed for Lipscomb, on South Wolf Creek, obtained fresh horses at Mose Zeigler's ranch, and continued in hot pursuit, but the outlaws had vanished in the badlands of the Cheyenne country.[24]

24 *Daily Oklahoma State Capital*, March 14, 1894; *Guthrie Daily Leader*, March 14 and 15, 1894.

CHAPTER
7

Hands Up!

☆ The methods used in the Pawnee and Woodward robberies indicated both Doolin and Dalton realized it was no longer safe to travel in a large band "nor conduct their escapades with the wild abandon that had characterized their earlier depredations."[1] At a rendezvous of the gang, which may have occurred near Edmond the night of March 27,[2] the loot from the Woodward raid was split among the members and it was agreed the band would scatter, yet keep in touch with each other and share the fruits of their "toil" at meetings to be held at frequent intervals.

On the night of March 29, three members of the gang appeared at Todd, in Blaine County, eighteen miles west of Hennessey, and held up the general store and post office operated by E. H. Townsend, lecturer of the Masonic Grand Lodge of the territory. Townsend seized an iron bar and threw his weight against the front door to prevent them entering, and one of the robbers drew a revolver and fired, disabling his left wrist. With the bar in his right hand, the merchant knocked the outlaw down. With "tremendous oaths" the remaining pair broke open the door, firing two more shots, one

---

[1] Nix, *op. cit.*, p. 187.

[2] On March 28, Tom Sebring, a farmer near Edmond, arrived in Guthrie and reported that the gang had camped on his place the night before. While he was driving in his cattle, a band of fourteen begrimed men rode up and demanded that he feed them. They ate with "keen appetites," and when the meal was finished, a young man of medium height asked Sebring for his bill. An amount was agreed upon by Sebring and his wife, which was promptly paid. Then the band retired to a small grove a hundred yards from the house, built

entering the merchant's breast and the other his head just above the mouth and to the left of the nose. While his wife and children huddled in fear for their lives, the robbers kicked over the lamp and stove, looted the place, and rode off.[3]

T. H. Carr was one of the oldest deputy marshals in the territory, he had worked out of the federal courts at Fort Smith, Arkansas; Wichita, Kansas; and Paris, Texas, when all Oklahoma was still the Nations. He still held several commissions but operated a store at Sacred Heart on the border of the Seminole country. At eight o'clock the evening of April 1, Bill Dalton and a companion—thought to have been Bitter Creek, but tentatively identified as "George Thorne"[4]—entered his store to buy corn for their horses. Carr was waiting on a seventeen-year-old youth named Lee Hardwick. As he glanced up, he recognized Dalton immediately and reached for his gun. Thorne cried: "I guess not," and whipped a revolver from his coat pocket. Carr and Thorne fired at the same time. Carr's bullet struck Thorne in the left shoulder, and the latter's

---

a fire and began making preparations to spend the night. When Sebring complained that their horses were "barking" his trees, the young man replied:

"Damn the trees! We'll pay you for them."

This nettled the farmer and he asked sharply: "Who are you fellows?"

"My name is Dalton," the young man said. "The others can introduce themselves."

The statement upset Sebring. In an effort to repress his excitement, he asked: "Ain't you fellows afraid of being nabbed?"

"Naw—we ain't much," replied a gruff older man, who was warming his hands at the fire. "But say, do you get the papers? Has the government offered that $2,000 apiece for us yet?"

Sebring shook his head, and the man chuckled. "I guess they're waiting for us to come in."

Afterwards the outlaws spoke few words among themselves and refused to be disturbed. When Sebring tried to make more conversation, the man at the fire told him:

"That's the graveyard, pard; we're tired tonight and need rest. Do any queer business and you'll croak."

Sebring avers he slept soundly during the night, and when he looked out the window this morning, the grove was deserted.—*Guthrie Daily Leader*, March 29, 1894.

3 *Daily Oklahoma State Capital*, March 30, 1894; *Enid Daily Wave*, March 30, 1894; *El Reno Democrat*, April 5, 1894.

4 *Oklahoma Times Journal*, April 3 and 5, 1894; *Daily Oklahoman*, April 3, 1894.

lead tore into Carr's arm above the wrist, causing him to drop his weapon. As he stooped to recover it with his left hand, Dalton drew and fired. His bullet missed Carr, slivering the floor under him. Young Hardwick grabbed a shotgun; Dalton whirled and fired three shots at him, but missed him. Carr raised from the floor and Thorne shot him through the abdomen, but he managed to stay on his feet and kept firing at the outlaws as they backed through the door and disappeared in the darkness. Next morning the pair was reported in the Seminole country, where an Indian woman dressed Thorne's shoulder and they had left, riding north.[5]

In the middle of May, Bill Doolin, with five members of the band, left Rock Fort, crossing the Creek and Cherokee nations to Southwest City, Missouri, where they had heard the bank was "easy and fit to be picked." Doolin went in alone and looked things over. On the afternoon of May 20, the gang swooped down on the town in one of the most daring raids of their career.

Little Dick did his usual chore of terrorizing the citizens while the others entered the bank. But his job didn't go off as smoothly as at Spearville. When the shooting began, citizens ran outside to learn the cause. Realizing the bank was being held up, they hastily armed themselves. When the outlaws emerged from the bank, they were met by shots from such weapons as the citizens had gathered, and had to fight their way from the city. As they swept down the street, Alf Seaborn, a bank official, and his brother, J. C. Seaborn, former state auditor and one of the town's foremost citizens, exposed themselves just as Little Bill rode past with a revolver in each hand. The outlaw sent a bullet in the direction of the two men. It passed through the body of Alf Seaborn, without serious effect, but killed his brother.[6]

Contrary to some authorities, Bill Dalton was not in the

<hr>

[5] Report of Deputy Marshal W. E. Hocker to the *Guthrie Daily Leader,* April 3, 1894.

[6] Newsom, *op. cit.,* pp. 182-183; Tilghman, *Outlaw Days,* pp. 74-75.

Missouri robbery. He had already planned a spectacular foray of his own, and while Doolin and the others were busy dodging posses on their way back through the Indian Territory, four men rode into an alley behind the First National bank at Longview, Texas. Two remained on guard with the horses, the other pair went inside. One wore a slicker and carried a Winchester concealed in its folds. He handed a note to Cashier Tom Clemmons:

Home, May 23

The First National Bank, Longview:

This will introduce to you Charles Speckelmeyer, who wants some money and is going to have it.

B and F

It was written in pencil on the back of a poster, and Clemmons, thinking it an impromptu subscription to some charity, started to donate, when the robber pointed his Winchester at him and told him to "hold up." The second robber rushed into the side wire door and ordered the other officials to put up their hands, then hurriedly emptied the vault of $2,000 in ten and twenty dollar bills, including seven unsigned Longview bank notes. Outside, the guards in the alley had been spotted. City Marshal Muckley and his deputy, Will Stevens, opened fire on them. The guards returned their fire and began shooting at everyone who appeared. George Buckingham was shot and killed. J. W. McQueen, a saloon-keeper, was shot in the body as he ran into the alley. Charles S. Leonard, who was walking through the courthouse yard, was wounded in the left hand. The robbers in the bank shoved the officials from the doorway, using them as shields. As they started for their horses, the officials broke away and fled around the corner of the building. Marshal Muckley turned to fire upon the robber in the slicker and received a bullet in the bowels. Lead was flying all around Deputy Stevens, but he stood his ground. Firing at short range, he killed one of the bandits as they rode from town.[7] Within a few minutes, a heavily armed posse was in pursuit, but the gang soon outdistanced the pursuers and vanished in a canebrake near Paris.[8]

At Longview, the bank offered $500 reward and the citizens $200 for their capture, dead or alive.[9] On May 29, deputy marshals arrested three suspects northwest of Antlers, in the Choctaw Nation, but released them when three men fitting the bandits' description stole fresh horses near Stringtown and headed west toward Coalgate.[10] On Monday, June 4, two men appeared at Duncan, on the Rock Island, in the Chickasaw Nation, and bought a new wagon with ten and twenty dollar bills. "The bills looked new, but were wet and creased."[11] A telegram to Longview giving the numbers on the bills identified them as the unsigned notes from the looted bank. Deputy marshals of the district at Ardmore began an investigation, but nothing more was learned of the robbers until June 7.

In the afternoon, a farmer named Houston Wallace, accompanied by Mrs. Wallace and a "pretty blond about twenty-seven years old," drove into Ardmore in a wagon. They purchased a supply of ammunition and a large stock of groceries amounting to over $200, for which Wallace paid cash. Known as a "worthless fellow who never had a cent," he immediately fell under suspicion, and the officers followed him. In a short time he went to the express office, presented an order signed "Hines" and was given a package. "His refusal to sign the receipt book precipitated matters and the entire party was

7 The dead bandit was identified as "a reckless fellow named George Bennett" (Thorne?) who had come to Texas a few months before and married the daughter of a respectable farmer near Longview, but had left her and gone back to the Indian Territory. He was dressed like a cowboy, with high-heeled boots and spurs and a belt full of cartridges and two double-action revolvers. His horse, which was caught later, had three hundred rounds of ammunition strapped to the saddle.

8 *Daily Oklahoman,* May 24, 1894; *Guthrie Daily Leader,* May 25, 1894.

9 *Ibid.*

10 Dispatch to Marshal Nix from the U. S. Marshal's office at Paris, Texas, June 1, 1894.

11 *Daily Oklahoma State Capital,* June 11, 1894.

arrested by Deputy Marshal S. T. Lindsay." The package contained nine quarts of whiskey. Wallace was charged with introducing and the women as accessories. The wagon was identified as the one purchased at Duncan. Then began a questioning in which Wallace admitted the whiskey was for "other people" staying at his home near Elk, a small town twenty-five miles northwest of Ardmore, and "from incautious remarks by the women," the officers concluded they had discovered the hideout of the Longview robbers.[12]

A posse consisting of Deputy Marshals Lindsay, D. E. Booker, S. Leatherman, E. Roberts, W. B. Freeman, M. Glover, Loss Hart, and two local officers named Denton and Reynolds rode to the Wallace place. They surrounded the house at seven o'clock the morning of June 8, and while they were taking positions, a man with black curly hair and goatee, clad in woolen shirt, black pants with yellow suspenders, and top boots, came out of the house and looked around. Sighting the officers on the east side of the house, he leaped back inside, grabbed a revolver and jumped from a window on the north, running for a small ravine. Deputy Marshal Hart, who was less than forty yards away, called for him to halt. Quickening his pace, the man half turned to locate the voice and raised his revolver to fire. It was "the last voluntary act of his life. A .44 bullet from the deputy's Winchester tore into his body "through the waistband of his pants near the right rear suspender button," and "with two convulsive leaps he fell. . . ." Hart raced to his side, seizing his weapon. "Who are you? Where you from?" the deputy asked. The man glared up at him. Then he smiled, as if experiencing deep satisfaction at not having been recognized, and "expired without a word."[13]

The other officers rushed the house. Inside they found only a group of frightened children, six boys and girls. A search of the premises turned up "numerous rolls of crisp

---

12 *Ibid.; Daily Oklahoman,* June 10, 1894.
13 *Daily Oklahoma State Capital,* June 9, 1894; *Guthrie Daily Leader,* June 10, 1894; *Daily Oklahoman,* June 10, 1894.

bank bills," and $275 was found concealed on the dead man. But the officers did not know "the importance of their game," and "their surprise was great" when, in questioning the children, two of them, a small girl and a boy, admitted their name was Dalton.[14]

The officers obtained a wagon and placed the body in it. With some of them on horses, some in a hack, and others guarding the corpse, they started for Ardmore.

A short distance from town they met another wagon occupied by the women who, through the efforts of two local attorneys, had been released from the charges filed the evening before. To the blonde woman, Deputy Lindsay said: "Mrs.

---

14 Newsom, *op. cit.*, p. 189, and Tilghman, *op. cit.*, p. 88, outline the events leading up to and the slaying of Dalton only briefly, but they adhere to these facts. In *Oklahombres*, pp. 215-216, Nix relates: "An Indian scout who was acquainted with Bill Dalton's wife was called into the case and assigned to watch for her at Ardmore, as it was probable that she did her trading there. Shortly after that she was seen in Ardmore and followed to her home about twelve miles away. The scout notified Colcord and his deputies and they hurried to the place. The house was surrounded and watched for several hours. On the morning of September 25th, 1895, Dalton walked out into the yard and he was commanded to throw up his hands. He quickly drew his six-shooter and Deputy Loss Hart fired upon him, fatally wounding him." This is in error. Obviously Hunter and Rose relied on the Nix version in *The Album of Gunfighters*, p. 26. A highly prejudicial account without any merit whatever is given by Emmett Dalton, *op. cit.*, pp. 308-310. He states his brother was shot while seated in a chair, bending over playing with his daughter seated at his feet, and that he was never given a chance for his life. Author Dalton was in prison at the time, so knew nothing of the details. He admits that a letter from his mother "conveyed the news." He also claims that the posse "came in for considerable public censure, and one by one they were discharged and drifted to other points." This didn't happen, either. The on-the-scene reports of Col. Clarence B. Douglas, a resident of Ardmore and valued correspondent for the *Daily Oklahoman*, are the most authentic sources to date. In a dispatch of June 14, 1894, he wrote: "When Loss Hart saw a man leap from the window of the Wallace house, pistol in hand . . . when he called to the fleeing man to halt, when he sighted carefully along the barrel of his Winchester and even when he drew the bead and pressed the trigger with his steady finger and sent a .44 caliber ball hot and stinging into the vigorous body of the suspect, his only thought was that he may have been at Longview. By the wildest stretch of imagination he could not connect the stricken fugitive with the most celebrated outlaw of three decades, and when reaching the side of the dying man he asked who he was and why he was there, not knowing that it was not some petty offender perhaps some common whiskey peddler who fell a victim to his unerring aim, but that Bill Dalton, the robber chief and leader of a hundred raids, was passing to the great unknown."

Dalton, we have your husband and on his person we found considerable money. . . ."

She glanced in the hack which had come up, and seeing nobody, replied:

"I am not Mrs. Dalton and you have not got Bill."

The wagon then approached, and when the woman looked at the dead body, she broke down completely and in a hysterical voice admitted the dead man was Bill Dalton and that she was his wife.

Back in Ardmore, she told the officers how he had left their home in Merced County, California, in 1892, to come to the Oklahoma country. "We kept up a regular correspondence, and though he requested me to address him under various names, I had no thought that he was living other than an honest life. I followed him East, arriving at the home of his mother near Kingfisher in September, 1893. He did not meet me on my arrival and I was very much surprised, and it was only when he came home the following night during a terrible storm heavily armed that a suspicion that all was not right crossed my mind. When I asked him why he wore his pistols, he laughingly replied: 'Oh, it is just for style.'

"He left in the morning at daylight without saying where he was going and after that time I only saw him at long intervals, mostly at night at the home of some of his friends. Soon his name became prominent in the papers, always connecting him with some act of desperation, and gradually I, too, became cautious of his movements, and was in constant dread of his being killed or captured.

"We came to the Wallace place six weeks ago, where he had engaged board for myself and children, and he left immediately, saying he was going to Texas, and paid Mr. Wallace $40 for our board. I heard nothing more of him until May 30. . . ."[15]

She sent two telegrams, signing her name "Jennie Dalton." The first went to her father in San Francisco and read: "My

15 *Daily Oklahoma State Capital*, June 12, 1894.

husband, Bill Dalton, lies here dead. . . . I want his remains
sent home." The other was addressed to Mrs. A. L. Dalton, at
Kingfisher: "Bill Dalton is dead, come at once if you wish to
see him."

Mrs. Dalton had "scarcely recovered from a severe siege
sickness" and shock of her son's death caused a relapse. Charles
Dalton, the elder brother, and never an offender against the
law, left his farm to come and see the body. His lip quivered
as he said: "Yes, this is Bill Dalton."

He, like many others, had expected to find his brother's
death a mistake. Every train brought eager residents from
cities throughout the territory and the roads were jammed by
hundreds who came to view the remains, and "among that
number were numerous reputable citizens who knew there
had been no mistake in the killing of the celebrated outlaw."[16]

Wrote Correspondent Douglas:

Stretched on a pine board in the rooms of Undertaker Appolis
on Caddo street, Bill Dalton . . . the terror of the Southwest, the
mention of whose name made bank cashiers from Kansas City to
the Rio Grande shudder . . . lies stiff and cold . . . a .44 Winchester hole at the pants band on the right side of the spinal
column near the hip . . . and that small piece of lead has rid the
country of the worst outlaw who ever stole a horse or shot a
man. . . .[17]

From Longview, came Sheriff Howard with the bank cashier and citizens Frank Fisher and Claude Lacy, who looked at
the body of Dalton and "unhesitatingly pronounced him to be
the man who presented the note of introduction and led the
raid." An old fisherman, near Longview, with whom the gang
had spent the day before the robbery identified the boots he
wore by a peculiar patch on the instep. At the Ardmore jail,
J. T. Harris, of Duncan, identified Houston Wallace as the

16 *Ibid.*
17 *Daily Oklahoman,* June 9, 1894.

man who had passed the unsigned bank notes for the wagon.[18] Wallace refused to name the other bandits who had returned to his place with Dalton on May 30, but identified a picture of the robber killed in the fight at Longview as his brother Jim.[19]

At Guthrie, Marshal Nix "gave no credence to the report of the killing" but dispatched Deputy Marshal Forest Halsell to Ardmore "just to make sure." Halsell wired him June 9:

THIS IS BILL DALTON. WILL REACH GUTHRIE WITH BODY AT 3:20 SUNDAY AFTERNOON.

In *Oklahombres,* Nix states: "The body was brought to Guthrie, his mother and older brother claiming it."[20] This is in error, as evidenced by the following account from the *Guthrie Daily Leader* of June 13:

The telegram from Deputy Marshal Halsell published in the *LEADER* Sunday morning . . . was the means of causing nearly 2000 people to congregate at the Santa Fe depot. When the northbound passenger train arrived, they clambered over the cars in an attempt to gain a glance at an outlaw stiff, but all were doomed to disappointment. Bill wasn't there. At the last moment, the Ardmore officers decided not to bring the body to Guthrie, owing to the fact that the embalming was imperfect and the body was in a badly decomposed state. . . .

On June 14, Jennie Dalton returned from the Wallace farm with her personal effects and two children. The body was loaded on the midnight train, and Mrs. Dalton and her children accompanied it to its last resting place in Merced County, California.[21]

In closing his report of that day, Douglas wrote:

It has often been said that when Bill Dalton died he would go to the shadowy land accompanied by a number of his pursuers and

18 *Guthrie Daily Leader,* June 13, 1894.
19 *Daily Oklahoman,* June 14, 1894.
20 Nix, *op. cit.,* p. 216.
21 *Daily Oklahoma State Capital,* June 14, 1894.

that any man who faced him in the last great duel of his life would bear him company, but he was killed like some pitiable chicken thief and the glamour of romance and daring thrown around his life by his brave and lawless deeds before the facts of his death prove once more that law and justice are supreme and must in the end be triumphant.[22]

The death of their lieutenant must have been a severe blow to the Doolin "band of border terrors." Douglas observed:

When these boys read of his death, and that he died not in a fierce hot battle where the bullets were singing, where horses were wildly plunging, where quick sharp commands were given, and where he was outnumbered a hundred to one—but that one lonesome shot fired in the quiet of a summer morning, in a peaceful vale near a pleasant cottage house—a single puff of white smoke, a single leaden messenger of justice, and a little round hole in the waistband of his pants and all was over—when they read of these things it is to be hoped the scales will fall from their eyes and they will realize the adage fully that the way of the transgressor is hard.[23]

Doolin must have wondered which of his gang would be next when he learned that Arkansas Tom, who had been removed from Guthrie to Stillwater[24] and tried in the spring term of court before Judge Frank Dale, had been convicted of the slaying of Deputy Houston, at Ingalls, and sentenced to fifty years in the territorial prison at Lansing.[25]

He must have got his answer in the dispatch to the *Enid Daily Wave* on June 20, 1894:

Eight deputy marshals trailed Bud Smith into Watonga yesterday afternoon and attempted to arrest him. He was one of the most desperate members of the Doolin gang, and when the offi-

22 *Daily Oklahoman,* June 14, 1894.
23 *Ibid.*
24 *Weekly Oklahoma State Capital,* December 2, 1893.
25 Territory of Oklahoma v. Tom Jones, *op. cit.; Daily Oklahoma State Capital,* May 22 ,1894.

cers ordered him to throw down his weapons he fired at close range, leaped on his horse and started through the town, firing indiscriminately.

One of the deputies rested his Winchester on the saddle and fired at long range at the fleeing bandit, hitting him in the back and killing him instantly. He was taken to the courthouse and an inquest was held by the coroner.

There was about $1,500 in rewards on the dead bandit's head.

CHAPTER

8

New Problems Arise

☆ Marshal Nix might have ordered an all-out search for the Doolin gang had not new problems arisen too numerous to enable his staff to concentrate on apprehending the wild bunch. Much outlawry was being carried on by the desperadoes in the Outlet. Though not connected with the Doolin gang, Doolin's influence was felt in most of the new bands organized.

"Many wild tales had been told in the territory about the enormous sums bandits were getting away with," states Nix.[1] "Bill Doolin was rated as a very rich man. . . ." Felix Young, a notorious horse and cattle thief, and Nate Sylva, familiar on the streets of almost every town in the territory as a horse trader and jockey, sentenced to the penitentiary once from Gainesville, Texas, and long suspected of disposing of stolen stock for the Dalton gang, decided to emulate Doolin. They recruited a man known only as Morgan and one Bill Rhodes, alias Pitts, notorious as an old member of the James gang, who had come from Clay County, Missouri, and taken a claim adjoining the Daltons.[2]

[1] *Op. cit.*, p. 189.
[2] *North Enid Tribune*, April 12, 1894; *Daily Oklahoma State Capital*, April 25, 1894; *El Reno Democrat*, May 17, 1894 (Nix identifies Morgan as Jim Bourland, Nate Sylva as "Henry Silva" and Rhodes as Bob Hughes, and states that a fifth member of the gang, Jim Fuller, was never apprehended. Contemporary reports do not bear him out, however; and in a letter to the *Daily Oklahoman*, dated at El Reno, May 17, 1894, Madsen wrote: "Allow me to correct some errors in your description of the fight with the train robbers, or rather the con-

On the night of April 9, two of them concealed themselves in the tender of the engine on the Rock Island express when it stopped for water at Round Pond, and, as it neared Pond Creek, a mile north, the others, stationed on the break near the track, held up the train.[3]

Guard Jake Harmon saw the men, and as they were about to hold up the engineer and fireman, blazed away with his Winchester. The train slowed up and the robbers jumped off, but one ran only a few steps and dropped dead. The men near the track began firing and literally perforated the baggage car, but Harmon and another guard named Fossett poured hot shots into the remaining robbers and drove them off. The citizens of Round Pond heard of the holdup, and a large crowd turned out and captured one of the robbers (Morgan). The dead robber (Rhodes) was taken to Pond Creek, where an inquest is now being held. The sheriff of L (Grant) county has a strong guard around Morgan to prevent lynching. . . .[4]

Morgan made a full confession, identifying Rhodes, Sylva, and Young, while Deputy Marshal Madsen, with a large posse, "scoured the country for miles around." The place chosen for the scene of the robbery was "singularly unfitted for an enterprise of the kind." The prairie extended, level and unbroken, in every direction except north, where the ground was cut by river bluffs and the "scattering timber of the Salt Fork outlined itself faintly against the sky." The only other "obstructions to screen a fugitive from pursuit" were the pine shacks of homesteaders. "Nothing but thick darkness enabled the outlaws to escape."[5]

---

nection had by other parties with them. 'Slim Jim' Hathaway [Bourland?] was in no way connected with Young and Sylva . . . and has not been arrested or charged with having any connection with their crime. . . . Neither have any of the Fullers been accused of having any connection with this matter . . . and it is but justice to those people, whose friends reside in and around Oklahoma City, that the correction be made. Respectfully, C. Madsen, Deputy U. S. Marshal."

3 *El Reno Democrat*, April 12, 1894; *North Enid Tribune*, April 12, 1894.
4 *Daily Oklahoma State Capital*, April 11, 1894.
5 *Enid Daily Wave*, April 10, 1894.

On May 12, while federal court was in session at El Reno and the town crowded with Saturday shoppers, someone recognized Young and Sylva, and the streets "miraculously filled with marshals." Deputy Eichoff surprised Sylva near the Kerfoot hotel and quietly placed him under arrest. Young stood in the street talking with a local gambler, and Madsen approached within forty yards of him before he sighted the marshal and ran for his horse. Madsen shouted an order to halt, but Young mounted, whirled, and fired twice. Madsen fired five times. One bullet struck the horse above the hock and the animal ran only a few yards and fell. Young leaped clear and fled for shelter of the depot nearby. "Several posse had come up by this time. . . . With half a dozen Winchesters turned on him, he surrendered." [6]

Madsen took both prisoners, under heavy guard, to the federal jail at Guthrie. On May 17, they were removed to Pond Creek for preliminary examination. A writ of habeas corpus brought before Judge Bierer, at Perry, failed, and they were held for the action of the grand jury of Grant County. Sylva was indicted. Young was released for lack of evidence, but immediately re-arrested and jailed on a United States warrant. [7]

While awaiting trial, both men escaped. Sylva fled to Texas, where he had been sentenced to prison before coming to the Outlet, and within a few days was captured by Texas officers and taken to the penitentiary at Huntsville. The federal government asked for his release, and he was returned to Oklahoma for trial. Meanwhile, Madsen traced Young to Colorado. The deputy went there immediately, but learned the fugitive had gone to California. Madsen trailed him to Wheatland, placed him under arrest and returned him to the territory. Both Young and Sylva were convicted and sentenced to long terms in the territorial prison.

    [6] Daily Oklahoman, May 16, 1894; El Reno Democrat, May 17, 1894; Canadian County Republican, May 18, 1894.
    [7] Daily Oklahoman, May 19 and 26, 1894; Guthrie Daily Leader, May 29, 1894.

There were more members in the gang than the four killed and captured. At least six robbers had been counted by witnesses to the Pond Creek affair. On May 21, two "suspicious looking characters" were observed by Sheriff Jackson, at El Reno. Roughly dressed in cowboy garb, dirty and unshaven, they rode into town with Winchesters strapped to their saddles, and the sheriff detailed a deputy to "discover their mission." They visited several hardware and second-hand stores, finally exchanging one of the rifles for a six-shooter. In answer to a question, they stated they were from Chickasha en route to the Outlet, and rode north toward Enid. A short distance out of town, however, they turned east toward Yukon, following the line of the Choctaw railway. Between El Reno and Yukon they met the train from Oklahoma City and made signals to a passenger on one of the coaches. When the train reached El Reno, the passenger was identified as the wife of Nate Sylva, the arrested Pond Creek robber, who was still in jail. Believing the men to be the remaining members of the gang and that arrangements were under way to "secure Sylva from the clutches of the law," Sheriff Jackson telegraphed Deputy Sam Farris, at Yukon, to apprehend and hold them for investigation.[8]

At three o'clock in the afternoon, they rode into Yukon and were entering a grocery store when Deputy Farris stepped up behind them and demanded their surrender. The man with the six-shooter broke away, drew the weapon, and shot Farris in the left side, the bullet passing through the deputy's body. Farris drew his revolver and returned the fire, and the second desperado ran from the store, opening fire on the officer with his Winchester. The deputy fired until his revolver was empty, then walked into a drug store next door and fell on the floor, weak from loss of blood. The gunmen started for their horses, but Joe Farris, brother of the wounded deputy, ran into the street and seized the one with the rifle about the waist, holding him until a crowd gathered and disarmed him. The other gun-

8 *Daily Oklahoman,* May 22, 1894; *El Reno Democrat,* May 24, 1894.

man reached the corner of a building across the street. Seeing his companion held captive, he reloaded his six-shooter and began firing at the crowd. On the sidewalk, a citizen named Ben Wilson removed a Winchester from the saddle of a horse tied at the rail and opened fire on the desperado, and the latter "paid his respects to Wilson" by "emptying his revolver at him at close range." He missed Wilson, but one bullet ricocheting from the iron seat of a mowing machine, struck a man named Snider in the forehead.[9] He then mounted his horse and left town, closely pursued by a dozen citizens.

Fourteen miles southwest of Yukon, the fugitive's mount grew jaded. One of the posse, riding a fresh, strong animal, circled ahead and shot his horse through the jaw. Two other members, approaching close behind, shot the fugitive in the right leg, and "it looked as if he must be taken, when suddenly he reached the timber and disappeared in the bottoms of the South Canadian."[10]

Darkness and a storm that came up forced the posse to abandon the hunt and return to Yukon. The captured outlaw was taken to El Reno and questioned. He refused to give his name or the identity of his companion. At eight o'clock, Deputy Farris died of his wounds, and Madsen and Eichoff had to rush the prisoner to Fort Reno to prevent a lynching. Early next morning, Madsen and Eichoff, with Captain Prather and an Indian scout named Black Coyote, and Sheriff Jackson, with his deputies Clay, Hancock, and Williams, left for the South Canadian. They picked up the killer's trail and followed him northwest of Arapaho in Custer County, where they "took him without a fight."[11]

The killers were identified as James and Victor Casey, youngest sons of Old Man Casey, who resided near Arapaho,

9 *El Reno Democrat*, May 24, 1894; *Canadian County Republican*, May 25, 1894.

10 Dispatch from Yukon, May 21 (*Canadian County Republican*, May 25, 1894) ; dispatch from El Reno, May 21 (*Daily Oklahoma State Capital*, May 22, 1894) ; *Guthrie Daily Leader*, May 23, 1894.

11 *El Reno Globe*, May 25, 1894.

and who, a few years before, with his eldest son, had been jailed at El Reno and tried for the slaying of two bachelor homesteaders to obtain their claims.[12] The brothers denied any connection with the Nate Sylva-Felix Young gang or having participated in the Pond Creek robbery, but they were indicted for the murder of Sam Farris and arraigned before Judge Burford, at El Reno. While awaiting trial, Victor Casey died of his wounds in the El Reno jail,[13] and James Casey, on a change of venue, was transferred to the jail in Oklahoma City, pending trial before Judge Scott, of the second judicial district.

Another band suspected of being connected with Bill Doolin, and who drew the attention of the marshals from the hunt for the more notorious outlaws, was the Wyatt-Black gang, noted for post office robberies and cattle and horse thefts in the northwestern part of the Outlet. Their leader was Zip Wyatt, alias Wild Charlie, alias Dick Yeager.

His full baptismal name was Nathaniel Ellsworth Wyatt. He had come from Indiana with "poor and respectable, though almost illiterate" parents, who staked a claim on Fitzgerald Creek, ten miles northeast of Guthrie, in 1889.[14] As a youth he cared nothing for school or religion. There was a wild strain in the family. His brother, notorious in the West as "Six-Shooter Jack," was slain at Texline, Texas, in 1891. By the time he was eighteen, it was young Zip's delight to "throw his long legs over a forty-pound saddle, fill up on coffin varnish and course wildly through the settlements, whooping and yelling and firing his Colt forty-fives at fences and trees."[15]

On the night of June 3, 1891, he shot up the town of Mulhall and escaped in a running gun fight, in which two citizens were seriously wounded. A warrant was issued for his arrest

12 *Daily Oklahoman*, May 27, 1894. (Both Casey and his eldest son were acquitted on insufficient evidence).

13 *El Reno Globe*, May 24, 1895.

14 Marquis James, *They Had Their Hour*, pp. 295-296.

15 "A Short Sketch of the Life of Dick Yeager" (*Daily Oklahoma State Capital*, August 9, 1894).

and placed in the hands of John Hixon, then sheriff of Logan
County, and, to avoid capture, young Wyatt fled to Kansas. At
Greensburg, on July 4, he stole some riding equipment from
a livery stable. Deputy Sheriff Andy Balfour trailed him ten
miles north to Pryor's Grove, and was slain attempting to effect
his arrest. With a $1,000 reward on his head, Wyatt fled to his
native Indiana, where he was arrested in the home of an aunt,
near Cory, and returned to Guthrie for trial by prior right of
first warrant. Kansas officers filed a requisition to return him
to Kansas to be tried for murder, and while the matter was
being argued in the territorial courts, Wyatt escaped jail.[16]

While dodging posses in the wild reaches of the Outlet, he
was identified as one of Doolin's gang in the robbery at Cimar-
ron, Kansas.[17] Many believed Wyatt and his gang, and not the
Doolin outlaws, had murdered E. H. Townsend in Blaine
County, and shot to death Fred Hoffman, treasurer of Dewey
County, during a series of robberies in Kingfisher, Dewey,
Major, and Woodward counties in the summer of 1894.[18]
Doubtless he was innocent of many crimes charged to him and
guilty of many with which he was never connected.[19]

The established facts are: His gang consisted of Ike Black,
"an outlaw of so little account as to be hardly worth the
trouble of arresting except for mileage,"[20] Black's wife, Pearl,
S. T. Watson, and Jenny Freeman, wife of a former bandit
partner of Wyatt, "but so lacking in discretion" that Freeman and Wyatt had become "estranged on her account."[21]
The women reportedly participated in the gang's banditry.[22]
For nearly three years the outfit "kept the new country in a
state of apprehension and terror,"[23] and avoided the marshals

[16] Glenn Shirley, *Toughest of Them All*, pp. 108-112; George Rainey, *The
Cherokee Strip*, pp. 246-248.

[17] *Guthrie Daily News*, June 16, 1893.

[18] "The best evidence is that Hoffman's slayer was Red Buck of the Doolin
gang." (Rainey, *Cherokee Strip*, p. 249.)

[19] *Ibid.*

[20] Marquis James, *The Cherokee Strip*, p. 27.

[21] James, *They Had Their Hour*, p. 288.

[22] Anthony Gish, *American Bandits*, p. 44.

[23] Rainey, *Cherokee Strip*, p. 248.

who tried to catch them by escaping to their hideout in the Gyp Hills, or Gloss Mountains.[24]

Meanwhile, the disagreement on town sites with the people of Pond Creek and Enid, by the Rock Island railroad, had erupted in civil war, obstructing the mails and interstate commerce.

An act of Congress, approved March 2, 1887, had granted the Rock Island charter right to cross the Indian Territory and Texas to Galveston. A junction at Herrington, Kansas, had been completed the preceding summer. The new line ran south from this point in a direction slightly west of south through Wichita and Caldwell, followed closely the old Chisholm Trail to a crossing on the North Canadian five miles below Fort Reno, thence almost due south, connecting the Oklahoma Territory towns of Pond Creek, Enid (then known as Skeleton), Hennessey, and Kingfisher with Minco, Duncan, and Terral, on Red River, in the Chickasaw Nation, by September, 1892.[25] Construction was rapidly continued to Fort Worth, and the Rock Island became the main connection between that city and Kansas City, Missouri.

Records do not reveal who dreamed up the idea of centering Rock Island depots on the town site locations of Pond Creek and Enid, with the railroad in complete control, but "the skullduggery backfired with a vengeance."[26] The ruse allegedly was planned by railroad men and a group of Indian leaders. The treaty which paved the way for opening the Outlet had allowed White Feather, the Cherokee chief, and sixty-nine tribal leaders to select allotments not to exceed eighty acres each. There was a station and water tank on the Rock Island railroad just north of the Salt Fork, called Pond Creek

24 "The Gyp Hills, rising abruptly from the plain in southeastern Dewey county, were called the Gloss Mountains because the shining rocks in the steep red slopes caught the sun and glistened. Unfit for homesteading, the hills were government owned and rarely visited except by outlaws." (James, *The Cherokee Strip*, p. 25.)

25 *Railway Review*, June 1, July 12, and October 4, 1889, and January 17, 1892; *Railroad Gazette*, September 16, 1892.

26 "Rock Island Lines Had Troubles, Too, In Early Oklahoma," *Daily Oklahoman*, March 1, 1953.

station for the creek nearby, which originally was called Round Pond Creek. The government had planned county seats for L and O counties (Grant and Garfield) at Pond Creek in L and Enid in O, but kept the plans secret. The railroad men and Indians learned of the plans, however, and made some of their own. The Indians were to select lands adjoining the depots, then sell out to the railroad for whatever the Rock Island was willing to pay for a chance to speculate in townsites. When Secretary of Interior Hoke Smith learned of the deal, he announced that no county seat should be located within three miles of an Indian allotment. Pond Creek and Enid would be located on the railroad as planned, but three miles south of each Rock Island depot.[27]

When the Outlet was opened and the towns mushroomed into thriving municipalities, the necessity for having depots in the county seat towns, which bore the names of the stations to the north, became increasingly apparent to the business men. Balked in its scheme to control the townsites, the railroad refused to move either depot or stop its trains at the government sites.[28] It promoted sites of its own, selling the Indian allot-

[27] G. E. Lemon, "Reminiscences of Pioneer Days in the Cherokee Strip," *Chronicles of Oklahoma*, Vol. XXII, No. 4, Winter, 1944-45. (In *The Chisholm Trail*, pp. 546-547, author Sam Ridings, early day attorney and one of the legal advisors of the Rock Island Townsite Company, states: "The allotments were selected at these points on account of the proximity of the townsites"; that the Rock Island was not interested in the allotments and property other than depots and right-of-ways on the townsites; that although the townsite company operating at the Pond Creek station was named the Rock Island Townsite Company; that "it was incorporated prior to the opening . . . and this name was selected simply because its holdings were on the line of the Rock Island Railway. The incorporators were citizens of Wichita, Caldwell, and other towns along the railway in Kansas and Oklahoma.")

[28] Ridings, *op. cit.*, pp. 546-548, gives the railroad's side of the "argument" as follows: "The Rock Island considered the moving of the towns to points where they had no depots unwarranted. . . . They had selected (their right of way) to accommodate conditions at the points where the stations were built. In order to comply with the requests of the new towns the Railway Company was not only called upon to erect new improvements at the new locations only a few miles away from their regularly established depots, but these new locations lacked the facilities for operating a depot, and improvements connected therewith. It also not only rendered the old location practically useless, but if they retained the same it added the extra expense of operating another station and the stopping of trains at intervals only a few miles apart."

ments to settlers with the understanding that it would not recognize the county seat towns and would force them to move to
the stations. The people in the north towns took sides with the
Rock Island, while those in the south towns took sides with
the government. These were the grounds for the bitter controversy as both sides prepared to fight it out.

All four towns petitioned for post offices—two in O County
under the name of Enid and two in L County under the name
of Pond Creek. Enid was given the post office. It already had
the land office and was the county seat, and it appeared now
that it had all the advantage. But the north town had the depot
and the south town had to transport all passengers, freight,
and mail the distance of three miles. When south town people
went after passengers, their rigs were upset and their harness
cut. It was dangerous to obtain freight left at the north town
until the merchants decided to get their supplies regardless
and furnished every mule freight with an armed guard. A
regular stage was sent to meet the passenger trains, and the
drivers carried Winchesters.[29] Both towns claimed the name
Enid. South town called the north town North Enid and north
town called the south town South Enid. While the north town
people made it as difficult as possible for south town citizens,
the south town citizens jeered the north town folk when they
came after their mail.

Finally the government gave North Enid a post office, and
ordered the railroad to leave mail at both towns. The railroad
erected a mail crane at the south town, and changed the mail
bags without so much as slowing down, often tearing the
pouches and scattering the mail along the right of way.[30] J. L.
Isenberg, editor of the *Enid Wave,* called it "The Snubbing
Post" and stirred the wrath of north town citizens by referring
to North Enid as "the Tank." "A broad smile perambulates
the faces of the Enid passengers on the Rock Island trains as
they approach this point," he wrote. "The train porter always
yells out, 'The next station is Enid; the first stop is at the

29 James, *The Cherokee Strip,* p. 13.
30 Lemon, *op. cit.*

tank.' The announcement is as true as Holy Writ, the first and only stop is at the Tank; the infernal trains don't stop at Enid, nor do they slow up unless someone expectorates on the track." Again, he served notice to the world that: "There is but one ENID. The post office address of this city is simply Enid. The post office in the addition is called North Enid, but this is positively not South Enid. You uneducated scapegoats, can't you understand that?"

Meanwhile, similar trouble was brewing in L (Grant) County. Pond Creek citizens began to take a hand in forcing the Rock Island to stop there as well as at Round Pond, or Sandy Hook, as the depot at the north town was called. A small shack loaded on a wagon was conveniently stalled across the track. A man ran down the track some distance with a flag to signal the south-bound freight. But the engineer pulled the throttle wide open and scattered the obstruction in kindling wood over the adjacent townsite. The *Pond Creek Voice*, reporting the incident, stated: "The wagon tongue stuck in the Milky Way and the kingbolt hit the man in the moon."

But the angry citizens were not so easily thwarted. The moment the train had passed spikes began to fly and ties and rails were torn up for two blocks and piled high to be seen afar by an engineer. Again a man ran down the track to flag a north-bound freight loaded with Texas cattle, but his frantic signal was disregarded. When the engineer saw the track piled up, he opened the throttle wide and jumped. The engine and cars left the track and piled up in a terrible crash, killing and crippling hundreds of cattle. The others, escaping from bursted cars, fled bellowing and galloping promiscuously through the streets and over the surrounding country.[31]

This was the first train that stopped in Pond Creek, and it brought official interference from the attorney general. In response to a telegram, United States Marshal Nix proceeded to Pond Creek with warrants for eighty citizens.

[31] Ridings, *op. cit.*, p. 549; George Rainey, *The Cherokee Strip*, pp. 383-384.

Through his deputy, Pat Murphy, at Pond Creek, Nix had made every effort to "adjust the matter," and Grant County Attorney C. C. Daniels, while in sympathy with the position of the people, had joined Deputy Murphy in the attempt to "convince them of the futility of destructive tactics" and interference with interstate commerce and the mails. "The government would naturally have sided with the people on the government townsites," states Nix, but this "rash conduct" caused the Department of Justice to order him to the two towns at once and "place them under martial law, if necessary, to quell the disturbance."[32]

Nix relates the action he took as follows:

Being closer to the situation than the government at Washington, I realized the fact that diplomacy and not a show of force would be necessary. . . . Feeling in Enid and Pond Creek had become such that any trifling incident might have turned the situation into a bloody battle with great loss of life. . . . I was convinced that if I gave out information to newspapers and set out with a trainload of men to enforce my authority, I would probably precipitate a bloody fight. I went into consultation with United States Attorney Roy Hoffman, Justice Frank Dale and my chief deputy, John M. Hale, and we agreed that it would be better for me to take three or four trusted men and go to make an appeal to the better instincts of the citizens of Pond Creek, where the feeling was most critical. . . . I gave out no news concerning the trip, but proceeded to the town as quietly as possible. Deputy Murphy met us, telling us that the townspeople were prepared for battle. It seems that the railroad had intercepted the Attorney General's telegram and informed the people I was coming to place them under martial law. Murphy's life had been threatened . . . because the people were convinced the government was taking an unfair attitude toward them and discriminating in favor of the railroad company.

I decided to go up town alone. . . . I found a hundred citizens lined up with Winchesters and shotguns in hand, awaiting what they thought would be an attack by a large group of deputy mar-

[32] Pp. 159-160.

shals. . . . Drawing near them I recognized S. L. Bradley, the county clerk and recorder, whom I knew quite well. . . . Notwithstanding that he was a county official, he stood with his fellow citizens ready to fight. . . .

I motioned to Bradley and he . . . came forward to meet me. County Attorney Daniels joined us in our discussion of the situation. (They) took the position that the government should force the railroads to stop at the townsites. I agreed . . . but explained they were going at the matter the wrong way, thereby forcing the government to take action to protect interstate commerce and the mails. I showed them the telegram and explained that unless some amicable understanding could be reached I would be forced to carry out the government's order and that there would probably be useless bloodshed. I explained I had not attempted to embarrass the Pond Creek people by giving out publicity regarding the situation but that I had come to them in a quiet, respectful way, hoping to be able to adjust conditions without being forced to the martial law order the government had given.

Bradley turned and made a short talk to the men who were lined up for battle, after which I was asked to talk to them. County Attorney Daniels followed my remarks, urging that the people follow my suggestion and give the government time to adjust their differences with the railroad company. The crowd, much to their own credit, fell into the spirit of the agreement. . . .

I then told the citizens that I had warrants for about eighty of their people on charges of having to do with obstructing the mails and interstate commerce. I told them I had no desire to embarrass anyone and that if they would have their citizens appear before me as their names were called, I would check the warrants and allow each one to go on his own recognizance to appear before the United States Commissioner at Kingfisher at a set time. They agreed to this and I immediately sent a runner for my deputies to join me and take charge of the work. . . . Word had gone on to Deputy W. A. Ramsey at Enid as to what had been done and when I arrived there late in the evening he had a large crowd of Enid citizens gathered in the public auditorium to meet me . . . and they were handled in the same way. . . .[33]

[33] *Op. cit.*, pp. 160-163.

Although a potential riot had been averted, the hearings at Kingfisher were unsuccessful. One after another, the prisoners were released for "lack of evidence," and two days later all returned home.

The railroad employed guards to patrol its tracks through and near the towns. One night two citizens concealed themselves in the grass along the right of way. As one of the guards approached, one of the men whispered to the other, "Watch me snuff that lantern." His rifle cracked, the lantern globe exploded in bits, and the frightened guards fled through the darkness toward Kansas.[34]

Marquis James adds this incident:

A committee of South Town citizens had to throw a hint in the direction of Mr. Nat Campbell. Mr. Campbell was a lawyer. The word got around that he was a secret agent of North Town. When the committee called on Mr. Campbell he shut himself in the shack which served as his office and residence. The citizens pulled down the shack. They had a rope and I have heard Mr. W. O. Cromwell, another lawyer, say that one end of the rope was around Mr. Campbell's neck. Others who were present don't remember that part so well. Pretty soon Mr. Cromwell came to the conclusion that the committee might get worked up and do something to hurt the name of South Town as a peace-loving community. He asked the citizens to let Mr. Campbell go. When they refused, Mr. Cromwell got a dry-goods box from Meibergen & Godschalk's and climbed on it. Pulling a paper from his pocket, he began making out to read the names of the citizens who were interviewing Mr. Campbell. Mr. Cromwell said that already he had started a copy of the list on the way to Guthrie, and if Mr. Campbell wasn't turned loose somebody would go to the pen as sure as shooting. They turned Mr. Campbell loose.[35]

The trains kept whistling through the south towns without stopping. "Red lanterns and dynamite caps on the tracks failed to stop them. Bullets failed to stop them; conductors would

34 Rainey, *op. cit.*, pp. 378-379.
35 James, *The Cherokee Strip*, pp. 13-14.

draw the window blinds and tell passengers to scrooch down away from the glass."[36] The situation grew critical.

Enid passed an ordinance making it a violation for a train to pass through the city without stopping. But it was impossible to arrest a railroad conductor within the city limits traveling at fifty miles an hour.[37] A south-bound freight came roaring into the city. Through some act of providence the coupling pin connecting the caboose came out and the caboose ran a short distance to a stop. City officers ran from every direction to place the train crew under arrest. As they approached, the conductor, brakeman, and several other railroad men "resisted their efforts," and a "general scramble" took place, "coupling pins, clubs and revolvers being freely used." The engineer backed up to the detached caboose and a coupling was quickly made. Then he threw the throttle wide open and "with a great jerk" the train went "tearing away," carrying the three officers. It didn't stop until it reached Hennessey, where the unfortunate officers, "overpowered, bruised and beaten," were put off, and the train proceeded on its way.[38]

Enraged Enid declared itself "a city of the first class, duly chartered according to the laws of the territory, with the power to make and enforce such laws as it should deem proper for the government and control of all human conduct within its confines," and charged the Rock Island, in resisting the efforts of its officers "are no better than anarchists," and should be treated as such. "Our officers are determined to do their duty if they are compelled to deputize every man in the city . . . and the great Rock Island company will find a squad of one thousand or more officers surrounding their soulless agents to put a stop to such lawless practice."[39]

Petitions demanding legislation to compel the railroad to recognize county seat towns had been sent to Congress. As

36 Ibid., p. 14.
37 Rainey, op. cit., pp. 379-380.
38 Daily Oklahoman, May 22, 1894.
39 Ibid.

early as January, 1894, Mayor Moore and Councilman Gregg, of Enid, had gone to Washington as delegates to work for passage of a bill.[40] A bill introduced in the House had passed almost unanimously, but met fiery opposition in the Senate. Senator James K. Berry, of Arkansas, advocated and championed the cause, while Senator Breckenridge, of Kentucky, and his forces fought for its defeat. A Senate committee visited the Outlet. It reported that Enid showed every promise of becoming a real city and was in dire need of depot facilities. But no further action was taken.

A writ of mandamus was brought to compel the Rock Island to put in a depot and side tracks at Enid or show cause why not. On June 18, the supreme court convened at Guthrie with Judges Dale and Bierer on the bench to hear the case, but Rock Island attorneys demanded a full bench before answering the writ or making an argument. The hearing was delayed pending the appearance of Judge Scott, who was holding court in Pottawatomie County. With Judge Scott on the bench, the railroad company did not file an answer until June 21, and then asked that the case be quashed. The motion was overruled, and the railroad attorneys refused to argue the case until the arrival of Judge McAtee.[41] When the supreme court met again July 9, the Rock Island asked for a continuance, claiming they could not get witnesses in time for the session, and asked for a jury. The court agreed to continue the case until its next setting in August.[42]

"Nothing more than a dodge to gain time," charged the editor of the *Wave*.[43] In a scorching editorial on July 12, he wrote: "The machinery of justice has slipped a cog . . . and when August comes . . . a half dozen cogs will slip and the court will conclude that it is too hot to try the case anyhow. . . . Where is that half carload of giant powder shipped to Enid a few weeks ago?"

40 *Enid Daily Wave,* January 15, 1894.
41 *Ibid.,* June 23, 1894.
42 *Ibid.,* July 11, 1894.
43 *Ibid.*

The trains still sped through the south town, irritating and annoying its citizens, until a group of daring men assembled pledged to eclipse anything their Pond Creek brethren had done.[44]

Just before dawn the morning of July 13, a Rock Island freight thundered onto the creek bridge a mile south of the city. The engineer felt the structure give under the weight of the engine and instantly threw the throttle wide open. The engine and three cars passed to safety. The remaining twelve, consisting of two oil tanks, six cars loaded with wheat, three with lumber, and one with beer kegs, were derailed as the bridge collapsed and piled along the high grade on the south approach for a hundred yards and in the creek bed in a scattered heap. Beer kegs were strewn down the slope, the carloads of lumber smashed in splinters, the oil tanks "fearfully warped out of shape for business," and fine new wheat was knee deep all about the wreckage. The cause was "quite visible." Five posts of the center truss had been sawed obliquely so that the weight of anything crossing the bridge would have crushed it down. Two outside posts of the adjoining trusses north and south had been sawed so that the structure, with its burden, would swing to the west, and "that was the way she swung and tumbled."[45]

Other incidents occurred in quick succession. A train from the north ran into a nest of dynamite bombs which derailed several cars and sent passengers screaming in terror. Early the following morning, two small bridges were burned four miles south of Pond Creek. At Kremlin, two train loads of cattle were side-tracked, and the telegraph wires between Kremlin and the depot north of Pond Creek were spliced with broom wire to prevent messages going through.[46] Large crowds organized at Enid, loudly proclaiming they would destroy with dynamite any train passing through town without stopping.

[44] Rainey, *op. cit.*, p. 381.
[45] *Enid Daily Wave*, July 13, 1894.
[46] *Ibid.*, July 16, 1894.

At Pond Creek, Mayor C. B. Franke wired Governor Renfrow that city authorities proposed to put in effect its ordinance requiring trains to stop, even if it met bloodshed.

Soldiers rushed to Enid from Fort Reno to preserve order. County officials were called to Guthrie to answer for their failure to keep the situation under control. In Washington, Attorney General Olney again ordered the arrest of all parties connected with the reported outrages. Marshal Nix dispatched Deputy Madsen to Pond Creek with full authority to employ all deputies needed to effect such arrests, but with orders to take only such action necessary to prevent destruction of life or property. In a wire to President R. R. Carle, of the Rock Island, in Chicago, Governor Renfrow proposed to offer a $500 reward for the arrest and conviction of any party engaged in burning bridges or other railway property on condition that the company comply with the ordinances of the cities and construct depots "commensurate with their requirements."[47]

President Carle was adamant. Such an agreement, he replied, could be of no profit to anyone "so long as prevailing violence exercised against railroad property continued." He promised to consider the matter "only if order is restored and the law properly vindicated."[48]

Governor Renfrow visited the leading citizens and business men of Enid at once. For two hours he talked with them, calmly and earnestly, regarding their trouble. He assured them they had many friends in public positions and promised that the territorial officers would do everything in their power to secure a depot for their city if they obeyed the law and used every influence to suppress lawlessness.[49] With the pledge of these people to prevent further hostilities, he left for Chicago to present his appeal in person.[50]

President Carle listened to Governor Renfrow and realized

47 *El Reno Democrat,* July 19, 1894.
48 *Enid Daily Wave,* July 21, 1894.
49 *Ibid.,* July 25, 1894.
50 *Ibid.,* July 26, 1894.

that further refusal on his part would result in open war. He also faced a great loss of business on this line of the Rock Island. Already people were refusing to take passage or ship freight on trains passing through the Outlet. The great Texas cattle business going northward was shifting to the Santa Fe.

He dictated a telegram to his general counsellor, Vice President M. A. Low, at Topeka, advising him to withdraw immediately all opposition to the railroad bill before Congress. Turning again to Governor Renfrow, he said: "Tell these people the Rock Island will respect and obey any law the government may enact, but it will never surrender to a mob."

On August 1, 1894, the bill became a law. The bitter controversy ended, and Marshal Nix turned back to hunting outlaws.

In May, 1894, his deputies working the southern district, at Tecumseh, broke up the "most remarkable organization of horse thieves ever known." Twenty-seven horses were recovered, seventeen prominent citizens arrested, and sufficient evidence unearthed for a federal grand jury to return thirty indictments. The organization extended from Arkansas to Arizona, and "all along the route the thieves had caves and other places in which to seclude themselves and stock from pursuers."[51] Of the total indicted, seven pleaded guilty, one, released on bond, left the territory and was never seen again, and three escaped and were never apprehended.

In a dispatch from El Reno to the Guthrie *Daily Leader,* November 28, 1894:

A package purporting to contain $25,000 was expressed from Kansas City to George Isaacs, a wealthy Chickasaw cattleman at Canadian, Texas, arriving at that point Saturday evening last. When the train pulled into Canadian station, a gang of bandits held up the express car, opening a general fusillade on the train. Sheriff McGee, of that county, was standing by and took a hand at the shooting in the protection of the express company, and was

51 *El Reno Democrat,* May 31, 1894.

killed by the robbers, being literally shot to pieces, and several others were fatally wounded in the engagement, among them being some of the robbers, who were carried away by their pals. The robbers were frightened off without securing anything, and were chased into the Wichita Mountains and the Butte lands of the Wichita country . . . and a large force of officers are out from these points looking for the bandits. Isaacs, who shipped the money, was arrested on suspicion of complicity and taken to Texas. The scheme is supposed to be shipment of money that was to be stolen, and the express company made to disgorge and proceeds to be divided. A number of wealthy cattlemen of the Chickasaw Indian nation probably furnished the capital of $25,000 to begin business on. . . .[52]

And newspapers were replete with such items as these:[53]

Deputy U. S. Marshals Stone, McCoy and J. W. Miller took twelve prisoners to Perry yesterday morning. They were Fun Miller, charged with cutting timber on government land; Lee Hutchinson, charged with killing another man's steer in the Osage country, and ten Osage whiskey-runners. Two of the Mudd boys, Little-green-back-bullfrog, and Dick "Hack-a-way" Davis were among the bad ones.

Deputy Hawkins was up from Oklahoma City yesterday and committed three sinners to the federal inn.

Lewis Courtright was taken to Fort Smith yesterday by deputy marshals to answer two charges—one for impersonating a federal marshal and one for highway robbery. For the past year he has been systematically arresting people in the Creek and Seminole

---

[52] In *Outlaw Days*, pp. 76-78, and again in *Marshal of the Last Frontier*, p. 210, Zoe A. Tilghman credits the Doolin gang with this robbery and the killing of Sheriff McGee. Nix makes no such connection in *Oklahombres*, and Bill Tilghman himself, in listing to Fred Sutton (MacDonald, *op. cit.*, pp. 191-192) the amounts the Doolin gang obtained in their largest robberies, did not include the Canadian, Texas, affair. In November, 1895, George Isaacs was tried as an accessory to the murder of Sheriff McGee, found guilty and sentenced to life imprisonment.—*El Reno Globe*, November 8, 1895.

[53] *Guthrie Daily Leader*, November 25, 1894.

country. Bringing them on this side of the line, he would take their personal effects and then turn the victims free. In most cases the victims were poor, ignorant parties or Indians. This work has been giving the deputies of the territory considerable trouble and only a short time ago a Creek Indian was arrested and robbed of his horse, saddle, Winchester and $10, after bringing him on this side of the line and holding him until night.

Eight timber men were released from the federal inn yesterday after doing a short term to square things with Judge Burford's court.

Again,[54]

Deputy Marshals W. A. Murphy and O. C. Scoverly came over yesterday from Pond Creek with I. J. Allen and John D. Herbert and committed them to the federal jail on a charge of conspiracy. Land contest trouble.

Deputies William Banks and John W. Clanton came over yesterday from El Reno with six prisoners for the federal jail. They were George Coon, charged with selling whiskey to Indians, sentenced to thirty days; John Garrison, charged with grand larceny, sentenced to ninety days; Mexican Bill, alias Wm. Moore, horse stealing, sentence withheld; Charley Adams, a Caddo Indian, and W. C. Shelton, charged with larceny, cases continued; John Craig, accessory to assault, case continued; Craig remanded to jail.

Of chief concern to the government was a band of counterfeiters operating out of the territory in conjunction with counterfeiters in Indiana and Missouri. "Merchants were getting hold of counterfeit silver dollars," writes Nix.[55] "They were being passed among the Osage Indians and several thousand of them had already been placed in circulation. The government sent out notices to banks and merchants warning them against the spurious coins and we were beginning intensive

---

54 *Guthrie Daily Leader,* December 14, 1894.
55 *Op. cit.,* pp. 144-145.

work in an attempt to solve the mystery. Deputy Marshal Starmer was assigned to the job and he succeeded in finding a number of small operators who were quickly convicted, but the principal source of the counterfeit money continued to pour its stream of coins. . . ."

A dispatch from Guthrie to the *Daily Oklahoman,* December 12, 1894, describes how the ring was broken:

A chance word uttered by a member of the gang while intoxicated led to a raid and the subsequent lodging in the United States jail of the following leaders of the gang: Guy Harper, L. Crawford, Joseph Tillery, Jess and Sam Lockett.

After shadowing these men three months and two days, all of which time spurious coins running in denominations from ten cents to one dollar were circulated, the outlaws unwittingly led their captors to an underground cave a few miles east of Perkins.

The deputies organized and armed themselves to the teeth. At 2 o'clock yesterday morning the officers descended into the cavern, and after traversing a subterranean passage for 100 yards, quickly burst in a door and found twenty-five men at work. The counterfeiters had been trapped so adroitly and were so taken by surprise that they failed to show fight and scattered like rats through hidden exits. All escaped save those named, but it developed that the prisoners were the leaders and the spurious money makers and the others were only "shovers," their work being to float the spurious coin.

With the prisoners the officers gathered three buckets full of counterfeit dollars and two tubsful of dimes, quarters and nickels, besides a splendid and costly assortment of moulds and other queer paraphernalia. The underground cavern was elaborately furnished, containing folding beds, works of art, divans, fine Brussels carpet and a safe. The men had been operating in the cave nearly eight months, and much of the spurious coin was boxed and expressed to pals in other states to be placed in circulation.

Cave of Death

Marshal Nix had managed to keep several deputies hunting the Doolin gang. Bill Tilghman and Heck Thomas spearheaded the search for the band's hideouts in Payne County and the Creek Nation, assisted by marshals from the federal court at Fort Smith. In the spring of 1894, they raided a farm house where the outlaws were "supposed to be stopping." They captured two men, who proved to be only "sympathizers of the gang."[1]

They surrounded a dugout between Ingalls and Jennings a few weeks later, and called for the occupants to surrender. When they refused, the deputies blew off the roof with two sticks of dynamite. Eight men appeared with their hands in the air, all wanted on various charges, but none of them was the "important" outlaws they were after.[2]

In *Frontier Trails,*[3] an autobiography, Frank Canton describes the difficulty faced by the marshals:

Bill Doolin had many friends among the settlers south of Pawnee along the Cimarron river, and along the line of Pawnee county. There is no doubt Doolin furnished many of them money to buy groceries to live on when they first settled in that country and had a hard struggle for existence. They appreciated his kindness even though he was an outlaw with a price on his head, and

[1] *El Reno Democrat*, April 26, 1894.
[2] Tilghman, *Marshal of the Last Frontier*, p. 209.
[3] P. 113.

there were plenty of people who would get up at the hour of midnight if necessary to ride to Bill Doolin to warn him of the approach of officers when they were seen in that vicinity. For this reason it was almost impossible for a party of officers to travel together through that country without being seen by some friend of the outlaws who would give the alarm in time for the criminals to escape.

In *The Life and Practice of the Wild and Modern Indian,*[4] J. A. Newsom recounts how they met a girl on the trail in the eastern part of Payne County. Questioned as to the "passing of strange men," she gave "evasive" and "unsatisfactory" answers. "Although it was not known to the marshals at the time, the girl was Cattle Annie," who "sent messages at once to the hiding place of the gang."

An appeal by the press for citizens of the area to support Marshal Nix in his efforts to "rid the territory of this band of thieves and murderers," met with little favor.[5] And Canton[6] explains:

In addition to the regular outlaws . . . there were about twenty-five or thirty members of this gang scattered over Pawnee and Payne counties, who worked under cover, and acted as a "fence" for the Wild Bunch in disposing of stolen cattle and horses, and giving information to the active members of the gang relative to the movement of the officers. The most prominent and dangerous of this class were the Dunn boys. . . .

Bill Dunn appeared to be the leader. . . . He was a dead shot, and I think . . . the quickest man with a revolver I ever met. He and Chris Bolton owned a meat market in Pawnee where they disposed of stolen cattle. . . . Chris Bolton attended the butcher shop while Bill Dunn rode the range and furnished the stolen beef (until) Sheriff Lake and I . . . finally received sufficient evidence against Chris Bolton to send him to the pen. . . .

4 (Chapter X, "Outlaws of Oklahoma and Indian Territory") pp. 180-181. This story is repeated by Tilghman, *Outlaw Days,* p. 72.

5 *El Reno Democrat,* April 26, 1894.

6 *Op. cit.,* pp. 110-111.

In January, 1895, Marshal Nix ordered his deputies to start arresting people known to be harboring the Doolin outlaws. Bill Tilghman, with Assistant Deputy Neal Brown, an old friend of his Dodge City days, and Charlie Bearclaw, a former United States Army scout, as guide, left Guthrie with their saddle horses tied behind a covered wagon, camping equipment, and supplies to last a month. The second day out the weather turned bitter cold. A cutting wind shrilled and whipped snow and sleet across the Oklahoma prairies. Sodden clouds brought darkness by mid-afternoon.

The covered wagon rumbled over the frozen ground; the grim-faced Bearclaw sat on the seat and urged the hungry, shivering horses over the dim trail; Tilghman and Brown rode behind the Indian, partly sheltered by the flapping canvas. Smoke curled from the chimney of a dugout in a ravine. Tilghman decided to seek shelter for the night.

He left his rifle in the wagon. As he walked through the snow to the door, he noted that no men or horses were in sight. When he knocked, no answer came, and he pushed the door open and went inside.

A fire of blackjack logs roared in a wide fireplace at the end of the room. A man sat in its light with a Winchester across his knees. He looked up without speaking.

As Tilghman moved toward the fire, he observed a tier of bunks on each side of the room, hung with curtains of quilt. He could not tell if they were occupied. To keep an eye on them, he turned his back to the fire and put his hands behind him to thaw the cold. Instantly every muscle in his body grew rigid.

From each of the eight bunks, poking around the edge of the curtains the muzzle of a rifle stared him in the face!

Tilghman's brain worked lightning fast. To indicate he was aware of his danger meant sudden death. Without a twitch of an eyelid or a quaver in his voice, he began talking quietly to the man at the fire. He stated his destination as Pawnee, that it was imperative his party ford the Cimarron before the storm increased, and asked casually:

"Which is the best way out of here?"

"The same damned way you got in," the man replied surlily.

"I reckon," said Tilghman, keeping his tone agreeable. He stamped his feet, rubbed his ears as if to restore circulation, then strode to the door, said a careless "So long," and stepped outside.

He kept an even pace until he reached the wagon. Climbing under the canvas, he gave quiet orders: "Drive ahead, Charlie, not too fast, and don't look around." To Brown: "Neal, that dugout is full of outlaws."[7]

Though Tilghman did not know it at the time, he had discovered Rock Fort. In that room were Bill Doolin, Tulsa Jack, Dynamite Dick, Little Bill, Bitter Creek, Red Buck, Charlie Pierce, Little Dick West, and Bill Dunn, and only his display of cold nerve had saved his life.

He hurried to Pawnee, where Chief Deputy John Hale was attending court. A large posse headed for the scene at once. They neared the place early the next morning. Searching the landscape with field glasses, they discovered a man watching the dugout from a knoll a quarter mile above. The moment he sighted the officers, Bill Dunn rode to them and informed them the outlaws had left his place in the night; that he had waited on the knoll to "avoid being shot" and in fear that his place might be "bombarded" by the officers.[8]

From Dunn, Tilghman learned the names of the outlaws who had been hiding there, and how Bill Doolin had saved

[7] Several versions of Tilghman's experience in the outlaw den appear in Newsom, *op. cit.,* pp. 186-188; Tilghman, *Outlaw Days,* pp. 82-84; Nix, *op. cit.,* pp. 165-168; MacDonald, *op. cit.,* pp. 200-201; and Colonel T. Edwin Mootz, "Rose of Cimarron," *The Pony Express,* Placerville, California, December, 1945. More reliable accounts seem to be Tilghman, *Marshal of the Last Frontier,* pp. 211-212, and Raine, *op. cit.,* 202-204 ("The Greatest of the Sheriffs," *Empire Magazine,* May 3, 1953) .

[8] Nix, *op. cit.,* pp. 168-169.

him from being killed by Red Buck Waightman. Dunn's version, according to Zoe A. Tilghman:[9]

Every one of them knew Bill Tilghman. They recognized him when he drove up, and since they could not leave the dugout without meeting him face to face, they hurriedly hung up the quilts and hid. They trained their guns on him, waiting for some move. But they saw no sign of discovery, no sign of fear. They waited.

When Bill passed the door, Red Buck leaped out in a fury, to shoot him. Bill Doolin and Dunn seized and held him, with a lively tussle.

"Tilghman's too good a man to shoot in the back," said Doolin.

"We don't want any killing here," protested Dunn.

"If you kill Bill Tilghman, there'll be a hundred men here before morning, and they'd dynamite this place off the earth."

Bill (Tilghman) by this time was safely away. Red Buck scored by reminding them that he would likely be back with a posse, and they'd better move. It was no pleasant prospect setting out in that weather for another long, cold ride. But they went.

It is doubtful Dunn's story is authentic. It has served as basis for many writers painting Bill Doolin with an honor as rigid as the ten commandments—who never took an advantage he wouldn't give another. It would seem, however, after the slaying of three deputy marshals at Ingalls, he had no scruples against Red Buck killing another officer. Canton and Sheriff Lake wanted Bill Dunn and his brother, Bee, for cattle rustling. Bill Dunn now faced a charge of harboring federal fugitives. It is logical that he decided to elicit sympathy from the marshals, and rather than go to jail, made a deal with them to help trap the Doolin gang.

Zoe A. Tilghman claims:[10]

[9] *Marshal of the Last Frontier*, pp. 212-213 (Reprinted by permission of the publishers, The Arthur H. Clark Company, Glendale, California).
[10] *Ibid.*, p. 214.

Bill [Tilghman] rode back to Guthrie where he conferred with the marshal and the U. S. attorney. These gentlemen were dismayed.

"First," said Bill, "I want that cattle stealing charge against the Dunns dismissed . . . and I want deputy's commissions for Bill and Bee Dunn."

They protested, argued. Bill won his point. Thenceforward, these men were on the side of the law, and the help they had given failed the outlaws.

Canton gives this version: [11]

Sheriff Lake and I arranged for a conference with Bill Dunn and one of his brothers at Pawnee. . . . We gave the Dunn boys to understand plainly that . . . so far as we were personally concerned, we would not prosecute them any further and use our influence with United States Marshal Nix to have him promise the same thing, provided they (agreed) to sever all relations with Doolin and other outlaws, obey the laws of the country and made good citizens. . . . That the first time the (Doolin) gang came into that part of the country, (they) should immediately bring word to Sheriff Lake and myself. . . .

We did not ask them to assist in the capture, nor did we expect them to do so. All that we expected was positive information as to the time of the arrival of the outlaws, and the place they were stopping. . . . In the event we captured any and all of the gang, we would have United States Marshal Nix collect the rewards . . . and turn all the money over to the Dunn boys, with the exception of a sufficient amount to be paid Sheriff Lake and myself to cover our actual expenses.

The brothers accepted the proposition and were taken to Guthrie, where Marshal Nix agreed to its terms. After promising to report to Sheriff Lake and Canton at intervals, they were allowed to return to their homes.[12]

11 *Frontier Trails*, p. 112.
12 *Ibid.*, pp. 112-113.

We now realized that it was a waiting game. We also knew that we were taking our lives into our hands, for we knew that the Dunn boys had no love for us, and that it would be an easy matter for them to lead us into a trap where we would not even have a fighting chance. . . . But we figured that they would not play the game that way, because if they had us killed, there would be no money in it for them, and every officer in the territory would be in the field hunting them down. On the other hand, if they played fair with us, and we succeeded in the capture, they would get a good reward, so we decided that under the circumstances they would do what they had promised.

Nothing happened for about a week. . . .[13]

It was reported that Doolin and Zip Wyatt again had joined forces and that both gangs were hiding in the Gloss Mountains. The people in the Outlet were alerted to expect "another raid of some kind at any time."[14]

13 *Ibid.*, p. 115.
14 *Enid Daily Wave*, April 4, 1895.

CHAPTER
10

The Dunn Ranch Affair

It came the night of April 3, 1895. At 11:45, the Rock Island train, made up of the usual mail and baggage cars and five coaches, consisting of a smoker, day coach, chair car, sleeper filled with passengers, and a tourist car occupied by "a party of ladies and gentlemen" en route to California, pulled into Dover, with Engineer Gallagher at the throttle. Silently two men boarded the tender. As the train left Dover, they covered the engineer and fireman with Winchesters.

A mile south of town they ordered the train stopped in a cut in a sandy desert spotted with scrubby blackjack timber. The passengers, peering from the windows into the moonlight, "were terrified at the sight of five heavily armed men on the tops of the embankments." A few shots, coupled with the gruff order of one rifleman to "get your damned heads back inside or we'll blow them off!" made them realize they were at the mercy of a band of train robbers.

As the bandits approached the express car, Messenger Jones closed and locked the door, and they opened fire. "More than twenty shots perforated its windows and wooden sides," wounding Jones in the left leg and shattering his right arm and wrist, before he opened the door and surrendered.

They opened the way safe, but found no money. They then ordered Jones to open the through safe, reported to contain $50,000 to pay United States troops in Texas. Jones explained that the safe had been locked in Kansas City and could be opened only by the express agent at Fort Worth. They ordered the engineer and fireman to drill into the safe and open it. The men worked for half an hour, "but they succeeded in boring less than half an inch and broke so many drills the robbers became disgusted and abandoned the project."

Meanwhile, the two bandits on the train "pressed the colored porter into service with a bag in his hands," visiting the coaches. One walked close behind the porter, "bulldozing" and "searching," while the second robber followed him, walking backward in order that he might guard against attack from the rear.

Former United States Marshal William Grimes was a passenger in the chair car. One of the bandits, whom Grimes afterwards identified as Zip Wyatt, recognized him with the remark:

"Ah, there, partner, we meet again. Guess I've got you this time. Come out with your dough."

Grimes had managed to slide his expensive gold watch under the stove. He tossed $1.40 in small coins into the bag, stating it was all he had, and Wyatt warned him: "You'd better be well supplied next time."

Across the aisle, a salesman for a grocery firm donated $4.05, while the bandits overlooked a $500 roll he had thrust under the seat cushion.

Two farmers from Iowa were the heavy losers, one handing over $80 and the other $85.

Despite the "mad scramble to get money and valuables out of sight when the alarm was first given," the "haul" was "over $400 cash, six gold watches and several silver ones, besides a large number of diamond studs, rings and other jewelry amounting to a thousand dollars."

Before leaving the train, Wyatt paused again before ex-Marshal Grimes. "Give my compliments to Chris Madsen," he jested.

The robbers ordered the engineer back into his cab and instructed him to wait until he heard the report of a gun from the southeast; then they rode from sight behind the cut. "In a few minutes the report came, and Gallagher pulled out for Kingfisher, where he gave the alarm and a posse started in pursuit."[1]

A dispatch was sent to Deputy Madsen's office at El Reno, and "when the 3 o'clock train pulled north, it had twelve marshals on board . . . with their horses in a box car hooked to the regular passenger train." They arrived in Dover at daylight, unloaded their horses and picked up the trail.[2]

It led west several miles, then northwest to Hoil Creek, near Ames, in Major County. Here the gang had stopped at a farmhouse for breakfast. They had made no effort to cover their tracks. "The fact was that they had been hunted so much that they wanted the marshals to follow them. They planned to bushwhack them. They went into camp . . . in the sand hills, leaving Tulsa Jack on guard. The others went to sleep."[3]

Meanwhile, Madsen and his deputies reached the farmhouse where the outlaws had eaten. Dividing his men into two posses, Madsen took his group and circled west along the Cimarron. The second squad, under Deputy William Banks, kept the trail. At 2:00 P. M., while tracking the gang through the sandhills, they rode suddenly over a knoll and saw the outlaws' horses with one man guarding them and the rest of the gang asleep in a small grove of trees. Tulsa Jack sighted them at the same moment and gave the alarm, and Deputy Banks, leveling his Winchester, fired, killing him instantly. The other outlaws, leaping to their feet, "met the marshals with a volley of rifle lead." The posse left their horses. Lying flat on the ground, they pumped shot after shot at the robbers while bullets kicked sand all around them. "No less than 200

---

[1] These details of the robbery appear in the *Kingfisher Free Press*, April 4, 1895; *Enid Daily Wave*, April 4, 1895; *Hennessey Clipper*, April 4, 1895; *Daily Oklahoma State Capital*, April 5, 1895; *Guthrie Daily Leader*, April 6, 1895.

[2] *El Reno Globe*, April 5, 1895.

[3] Barnard, *op. cit.*, p. 209.

shots were exchanged. None of the posse were injured. Three of the outlaws had their horses killed. After a forty minute running fire, they mounted, four of them on two horses, and rode rapidly away, leaving their dead companion where he fell."[4]

Banks and his men returned to Hennessey with the corpse of Tulsa Jack,[5] and Madsen's posse continued in pursuit of the outlaws. "The trail of five horses got down to four and another horse was found dead. The back of the animal was full of blood where the rider had leaned on it." It was described as the horse on which Doolin himself had escaped, and there was much speculation as to how badly he was wounded.[6] Madsen stayed on the trail all night and, the morning of April 6, reached the farmhouse of an aged preacher named Godfrey, who had been murdered by the gang when he refused to give up his team and wagon.[7]

Zoe A. Tilghman[8] and Fred Sutton[9] credit Red Buck with the slaying. And Nix,[10] eulogizing Doolin, relates how the cold-blooded murder of the old man made such an impression on the bandit leader that he ordered Bitter Creek to bring the saddle bags in which the loot was being carried and, without a word, divided the money, handing Red Buck his full share, telling him: "Drag your lousy, cowardly carcass out of my

[4] *Hennessey Clipper,* April 4, 1895; *El Reno Globe,* April 5, 1895; *Guthrie Daily Leader,* April 6, 1895; *Oklahoma Daily Star,* April 7-9, 1895.

[5] "They reached Hennessey with the dead man at eleven o'clock that night, but no one could identify him, and Banks and Captain Prather took the body to El Reno. He was placed in Perry's undertaking parlor and viewed by five hundred people the next day, but no one could identify him. The following morning he was removed to Oklahoma City, and here identified as Tulsa Jack by H. R. Whitset, a ranchman for whom he had worked near Sterling, Rice County, Kansas, in 1891. Whitset stated he had worked on the railroad near that town several months and then went to work for him on the ranch. Rewards for the outlaw, dead or alive, aggregated $3,000." (*Guthrie Daily Leader,* April 10, 1895; *El Reno Globe,* April 12, 1895.)

[6] *Daily Oklahoma State Capital,* April 9, 1895.

[7] Dispatch from Madsen to Marshal Nix, April 6, 1895.

[8] *Outlaw Days,* p. 88-89.

[9] MacDonald, *op. cit.,* pp. 214-215.

[10] *Op. cit.,* pp. 181-185.

sight! If I ever see you again I'll kill you! You could have taken
that outfit without harming a hair on that old man's head.
You are too damn low to associate with a high class gang
of train robbers. . . ." And the gang rode away, leaving Red
Buck standing in the trail, disarmed and "mouth agape in his
surprise."

Evan G. Barnard[11] charges Bitter Creek with the killing:

The bandits . . . two on one horse . . . rode west for several
miles to an old preacher's place. They told him what had happened and said they were going to take his team.

"No, you can't have it, boys," he said.

"Old man, we don't want to hurt you, but we sure are going
to take the team," they insisted.

[Bitter Creek] told Charlie Pierce to get the horses. Charlie
started. The old man picked up a shotgun and instantly Bitter
Creek shot him dead. They took the team and traveled west toward
Cantonment. . . .

This, perhaps, is the authentic version, for it was Bitter
Creek, with his share of the loot, who immediately separated
from the gang, Charlie Pierce riding with him. Madsen lost
the trail of the outlaws in the foothills of the Gloss Mountains,
where tracking was almost impossible, and Bitter Creek and
Pierce headed for the Dunn place in Payne County.

Frank Canton writes: [12]

The Dunns reported that the Rock Island train had been held
up at Dover . . . and that they were looking for the gang to show
up . . . to get fresh horses and rest a few days.

They [had learned] that Bitter Creek and Charlie Pierce were
now riding together and . . . were likely to drop in any time,
for they said that they owed Bitter Creek one thousand dollars
and he would come in to get his money if for no other reason. . . .

[Sheriff Lake and I] kept close watch and remained in camp
. . . in the neighborhood . . . for several days. One evening we

11 Op. cit., p. 210.
12 Op. cit., pp. 114-119.

rode over to George McElroy's ranch, six or eight miles from the Dunn place. We notified the Dunn boys where they would find us in case we were needed, and that we expected to stay all night at McElroy's. We fed our saddle horses and cared for them for the night. The next morning we found that our horses had broken out of the corral . . . and left us afoot. We struck their trail, but had a long tramp before we found them. We saw one of the Dunn boys that day, and he told us that the night we stopped at McElroy's ranch . . . Pierce and Bitter Creek had come to their place and stopped all night, and had left early the next morning. The Dunns said that they had hunted for us to report, but could not find us. Whether this was true or not we never knew. The next we heard of the outlaws . . . I received a telegram from the United States Marshal's office [and Sheriff Lake and I] went immediately to Guthrie. . . .

Shortly after two o'clock that afternoon of May 2, a covered wagon drawn by two half-starved horses pulled up on the east side of the water tower on Capital Hill. Two men, "armed with Winchesters and furtive glances," got down quickly and one of them ran to Marshal Nix's office. Within a few minutes, Spengel's undertaking barouche went speeding toward the hill, and two dead bodies were taken from the wagon and hauled to the undertaking parlor. Rumor swept the city "regarding dead outlaws" and the "pressure of a curious crowd gathered at Spengel's" soon became so great that the undertaker had to "throw open his doors and allow the public mind to be satisfied."

For three hours, a stream of people passed through the rooms, viewing the bodies. Meanwhile, the dead men were fully identified as Bitter Creek Newcomb and Charlie Pierce "by all the deputy marshals and man killers in the capital," and a photo was taken of the outlaws stretched on embalming boards.

Both men wore blue overalls, calico shirts, and string ties . . . aside from the myriad of bullet punctures the clothes were in good condition. The regulation high-heeled boots, with broncho spurs attached, were on their feet. Around their loins were cartridge belts, half filled. In Pierce's pockets were found a dirk and a common knife, a few coins, a rabbit's foot and twenty-six Winchester cartridges. Newcomb's pockets also contained a knife, cards, a small hand-mirror, smoking tobacco, sixteen books of cigarette paper and two dozen .45 Colt's and Winchester cartridges. Near the bodies were deposited the saddles and blankets of the dead men which upon being opened were found well supplied with cartridges, tobacco and other articles necessary for a bandit excursion. In the pockets of Newcomb's saddle were found an empty Wells Fargo money bag and three pocket knives. On the pile lay two black slouch hats, the one worn by Newcomb being mutilated and covered with blood. Two Winchesters, one shattered at the stock, and two .45 Colt's revolvers made up the collection. Pierce's body, upon being stripped, was found literally riddled with bullets, almost any one of which would have proved fatal. All had entered the front of the body and ranged backward, the holes covering a space from the sole of his feet to the top of his head. Newcomb's body showed but five bullet wounds, four of these in the head and neck; one shot had torn away a part of his forehead, exposing the brain. One arm was stiffened and raised as though warding off a blow; Pierce's eyes were still open and a sardonic grin was on his lower features.[13]

Marshal Nix wired ex-Marshal Grimes and the other witnesses who had been on the train during the robbery at Dover to come to Guthrie at once. He wired the United States Attorney General the disposition of the dead bandits, then "repaired to a private room with the two deputies who had brought them in" and a reporter for the *Guthrie Daily Leader* to hear how they had "laid to rest" the outlaws in one of the "most sensational and ferocious gun battles ever recorded in the annals of territorial history."

The story appearing in the *Leader* of May 3, 1895, reads more like a Beadle serial than actual history:

13 *Guthrie Daily Leader*, May 3, 1895.

While Madsen's posse was scouring the Gloss Mountains for the fleeing bandits, Marshal Nix had dispatched Deputy Sam Shaffer and three unnamed possemen to the "weather-beaten house owned and occupied by the Dunn family" in Payne county. They learned that Newcomb and Pierce had arrived there the night of April 25, but had immediately departed.

Shaffer and his men did not try to follow them. "Intuition told the deputies the bandits would return, and they did—reaching the Dunn farm at ten o'clock the night of May 1." At two o'clock the morning of May 2, the posse surrounded the house. "The bandits, and one or two women, were in the house in a drunken, boistrous frolic," and as the officers advanced on the building, "the sound of drunken revelry grew louder, and through the open windows the bandits could be plainly seen."

At a given signal, the deputies, who had separated at intervals of one hundred yards, fired one shot each. There was a wild commotion in the house and the lights were extinguished. In a moment, a door opened and the moonlight revealed the figure of Charlie Pierce with a rifle in his hand. As the door opened a female voice cried, "Don't go Charlie!" Pierce could not see the posse, but his figure in the moonlight "afforded a bullseye target for the officers, and in three seconds his breast was transformed into a lead mine." He fell back into the room "while the leaden hail continued, bullets being planted in his arms, legs and even the soles of his feet."

Newcomb was trying to climb out of a window, firing his Winchester as he mounted the sill. "The blaze of his rifle showed the marshals where to shoot, and in an instant, three bullets had pierced his skull, and he fell back into the room with the bullets from the marshals' guns pouring a constant volley through the window."

The remaining occupants were ordered outside. "The Dunn brothers had escaped, and only a woman . . . who is supposed to be Pierce's sweetheart" came out of the house.

They loaded the dead bodies in the wagon. Leaving part of the posse to "watch the place for other outlaws," Shaffer and one of his deputies brought the dead men to Guthrie.

"To Marshal Nix belongs the credit," concluded the *Leader*. "He spent his own money and personally directed the movement of deputies in furthering the good work."

In *Oklahombres*,[14] Nix makes no mention of a deputy named "Sam Shaffer" and credits the killing to Heck Thomas and Bill Tilghman:

We received word from Will [Bill] Dunn that these outlaws had met at the ranch of his brother Bee and would return in a few days. Tilghman and Thomas [with] a substantial posse, started immediately for Will Dunn's ranch. They found him in the dug-out and were told that the outlaws were expected to reach the home of his brother Bee during the next twenty-four hours. The officers, accompanied by Will Dunn, rode to the home of the other Dunn . . . and took places in the house where they could cover all entrances. The long wait began. . . .

On the evening of the third day, just as night was falling, Bitter Creek Newcomb and Charlie Pierce rode toward the house from the north. The officers were ready and the outlaws were sighted while yet some distance away. The deputies had no idea how many men there might be, as the gathering darkness made the figures of the riders indistinct and it was impossible to tell if there were other members of their party a short distance behind.

As the two bandits neared the house, Heck Thomas called out . . . "Throw up your hands, you are surrounded."

The two shadowy figures leaped from their horses and drew their guns. . . . Thomas and posse aimed at the running shadows . . . and the two outlaws fell, fatally wounded.

The bodies were placed in a wagon and two possemen set out on the long drive to Guthrie, the other officers remaining to attempt to capture the remainder of the gang.

Mootz[15] also credits Tilghman and Thomas:

14 Pp. 195-197.
15 *Op. cit.*

Bitter Creek took time out to spend a little while with his sweetheart, Rose of Cimarron. . . . He met Charlie Pierce and the two reined up near a ranch on the river. They had just swung out of the saddle when a voice shouted: "Throw up your hands!"

The voice was Bill Tilghman's. He and Heck Thomas had been in the ranch house three days.

Pierce and Bitter Creek tried to shoot their way out, but it was their last fight.

Barnard[16] says they were killed by the Dunn brothers:

A reward of ten thousand dollars was offered for them, dead or alive, and the Dunns wanted a share of that reward. That night, when they were all in bed, the house was surrounded by marshals from Guthrie. The Dunns gave the signal, and slipped out of bed with guns in their hands. . . . They went to the room where [Bitter Creek and Pierce] were quietly sleeping, fired at them and killed them. . . .

And Zoe A. Tilghman writes:[17]

Charlie Pierce and Bitter Creek met tragic deaths at the hands of the Dunn brothers whom they trusted. Marshal Tilghman and Heck Thomas had arranged with the ranchmen to inform them when the desperadoes were to be at the Rock Fort. . . . The officers were there at twilight, but went away (just before) Pierce and Bitter Creek returned. . . .

The two outlaws had come expecting to find shelter at Rock Fort. They put their horses in the stable and walked toward the gate, unsuspecting and not on guard. On each side of the gate stood a ranchman with a shotgun in his hands. As the bandits approached, the ranchmen fired, and Pierce and Bitter Creek were killed instantly. A second shot went through the soles of their shoes as they lay dead on the ground.

The territorial newspapers picked up the *Leader's* "first-hand account" of the affair and carried it almost verbatim.

16 *Op. cit.,* p. 212.
17 *Outlaw Days,* pp. 89-91.

The *El Reno Globe* merely commented: "We have not the particulars on the fight and have not learned what deputy did the shooting, but everybody will be glad to know that the dead robbers have been brought in and identified."[18]

The *Pawnee Times-Democrat*[19] repeated the *Leader's* story, but, in the same issue, claimed that Deputy Canton directed the movement of the men who had ended the careers of the two principal members of the Doolin gang:

The history of how the killing came about dates back to about the 1st of last December.

On account of this section of Oklahoma being the favorite rendezvous of outlaws, Marshal Nix decided that a good man was needed for special detective work in this region and about the first of last December, Deputy Marshal F. M. Canton was quite certain that Bill Doolin, Tulsa Jack, Bitter Creek and other outlaws had their haunts in the vicinity of Ingalls and made several exploits in that direction looking for them; and although certain of their hiding places he was always unsuccessful in his efforts to come in contact with them. The reason of this was, Mr. Canton and the horses he rides are well known to almost everybody in this section of Oklahoma and friends of the outlaws would put them on guard when Canton was in the neighborhood. One time he suspected Bill Doolin of being in a house and searched the premises and did not find him, but afterwards learned he was secreted in a cellar under the house.

To further his efforts in capturing the gang Mr. Canton employed Sam Shaffer and three other good men and placed them in the neighborhood in Payne county where the Dunn boys reside. Shaffer and his men had orders to watch their maneuvers, and also to keep Mr. Canton instructed and act under his orders. After considerable length of time they located the outlaws and were about to make a raid on them when the band suddenly left the country and went to Dover where they robbed the Rock Island passenger train. Shaffer and his men were not long in getting on their trail and followed it until the outlaws again returned to the

[18] May 3, 1895.
[19] May 10, 1895.

Dunn neighborhood. On May 1st, Shaffer found two horses hob-
bled near Dell Dunn's and suspected they belonged to outlaws
who were secreted nearby. To keep the Dunn boys from rendering
the outlaws any assistance, Shaffer and his men went to the home
of John Dunn and placed him and a brother under arrest, leaving
one of the officers to guard them. He then went to Dell Dunn's
place and arrested Dell and his brother George and locked them
up in a cave. Shaffer then took the two men he had with him and
hid on the inside of a stone fence that surrounded the premises
and awaited the arrival of the outlaws. They did not have long
to wait, for about 12 o'clock that night Bitter Creek and Charlie
Pierce rode up to the gate, dismounted and were about to come
inside the gate when the officers commanded them to halt. The
outlaws refused to obey the command to surrender but opened
fire on the officers who returned the compliment as fast as they
could pour the lead into them. Newcomb, or Bitter Creek, fired
three shots and then fell dead at the gate riddled with bullets;
but before Pierce was killed he had got about half way across the
yard and had emptied both Winchester and pistol.

The bodies of the two outlaws, together with two of the Dunn
boys were taken to Guthrie where the dead bodies were turned
over to Marshal Nix and the Dunns placed under bond for aiding
and abetting outlaws. Yesterday, Deputy Canton brought Bee
Dunn before Commissioner Wrightsman on the charge of aiding
outlaws. He waived examination and gave bond for his appearance at the next term of district court. . . . Mr. Canton is a
shrewd and fearless officer and Mr. Nix made a wise choice when
he selected him to perform the detective work in this matter. . . .

In its issue of May 14, 1895, the *Leader* confessed that
"Canton Deserves the Credit."

Canton[20] makes no mention that any officer was present
and states that the slaying was entirely the work of the Dunns:

[When Sheriff Lake and I reached Guthrie] we found Dal [Dell]
Dunn and John . . . and the dead bodies of Charlie Pierce and
Bitter Creek. Pierce had been killed with a shotgun loaded with

[20] *Op. cit.*, pp. 119-121.

buckshot, and had several bad wounds in his body, and was shot in the bottom of the feet with buckshot, which proved that he must have been shot while lying down.

It was the general opinion that they were shot while asleep. The body of Pierce was badly swollen. He appeared to have been dead for some time, but the body of Bitter Creek looked perfectly natural, and looked as though he had not been dead very long.

The story that Dal Dunn told John Hale, Chief Deputy United States Marshal . . . was that Bitter Creek and Charlie Pierce came to Dal Dunn's place the night before, and that Bill, Dal, and John Dunn were there waiting for them. When the outlaws dismounted and came into the yard, the Dunn boys shot them down. Bitter Creek was shot in the arm and also in the head, and they supposed that he was shot square through the head. The Dunn boys then hitched up a team to a wagon, spread out a tarpaulin, in the bottom of the wagon bed, put the bodies of the outlaws in the wagon with all their guns and covered them up. Then Dal and John Dunn started to drive the outfit across the country to Guthrie to deliver the dead bodies and claim the reward. Bill Dunn remained at the rendezvous to obliterate all trace of the blood in the yard where the outlaws were shot down. During that day Bill Tilghman and Heck Thomas rode up to Dunn's place with a posse of men. When they learned that Bitter Creek and Pierce had been killed, and their bodies taken to Guthrie, they all came in.

When Dal Dunn and John were driving across the country at night with the bodies of the outlaws, somewhere between Stillwater and Guthrie, they noticed that the tarpaulin under which the bodies lay was moving. Dal raised the canvas and found that Bitter Creek was alive, and was trying to put a cartridge into a revolver that he held in his hand. The outlaw begged Dunn for "God's sake to spare his life." As they were just passing a house at the side of the road, Dunn did not care to raise an alarm, but struck Bitter Creek a blow with his revolver, and knocked him senseless. As soon as they passed the house Dal Dunn shot the outlaw through the head.

I presume that accounts for the fact that the body of Bitter Creek was not swollen and looked natural when they brought the bodies into Guthrie. It appears that when the outlaws were first shot at Dunn's place, a bullet struck Bitter Creek in the side of the head and glanced off. It made a bloody wound and the Dunn boys thought he was dead. It must have been an awful awakening to him when he regained consciousness and found himself soaked in the blood of his dead partner who was lying by his side in the wagon bed.

There was bitter feeling against the Dunns in Payne County. Efforts of the marshals to take upon themselves the glory of the capture of the outlaws and put in claims for the large rewards offered for their heads were in vain. Newcomb and Pierce had been betrayed by supposed friends. The Dunns had "taken them into their home, got them drunk, then riddled them with bullets while they slept," because they had been "promised large sums of money by the officers who claimed the rewards." Friends of Newcomb and Pierce "openly swore revenge," and the Dunns "barricaded their place, secured arms and ammunition, and made their ranch a veritable arsenal" for months before "their strict vigilance relaxed" and they felt "free of molestation."[21]

There was at least one report that on one Sunday night a body of heavily armed men rode to the Dunn farm, seized John, Calvin, and Will Dunn and took them into the hills and lynched them.[22] The facts are: the Dunns grew more and more unpopular, new warrants were issued for them for cattle stealing in Pawnee County, and eventually they left the country.[23]

Bee Dunn blamed their plight on Deputy Canton, and his pending trial for aiding outlaws rankled him. On November 7, he rode into Pawnee, swearing to kill Canton on sight.[24]

Canton[25] describes what happened:

Judge Bierer was holding a session of district court. I was busy about town serving summons on jurors. I had just stepped out of

---

21 *Daily Oklahoma State Capital,* May 16, 1895.
22 *Ibid.*
23 Canton, *op. cit.,* pp. 137-141.
24 *Daily Oklahoma State Capital,* November 7, 1896.
25 *Op. cit.,* pp. 136-137.

a restaurant where I had been serving subpoenas, and started to walk up the plank sidewalk in the direction of the courthouse. Ten or twelve men were standing about on the street, the weather was a little chilly, and I had both hands in my trousers pockets. As I started up the street, Dunn stepped in front of me. I had not seen him until he spoke.

He says, "Frank Canton, God damn you, I've got it in for you."

He had his hand on his revolver, but had not drawn it yet. When I glanced at his face I saw murder in his eyes, and I knew that he intended to kill me. I drew my revolver instantly and fired. The bullet struck him almost square in the forehead. As he dropped he pulled his revolver, which fell on the sidewalk near his body. As he lay on his back dying, he was working the trigger finger of his right hand.

Cattle Annie and
Little Breeches

☆ During this period the Christian gang, composed of several "small time outlaws" and led by two brothers, Bob and Bill Christian, sprang up in the Pottawatomie country. They "pulled a number of robberies, stole horses and peddled whiskey to the Indians."[1] The morning of April 27, they shot and killed Deputy Marshal Will Turner, at Violet Springs, as the latter attempted to arrest Bob Christian on a warrant charging grand larceny. The Christian brothers were tried in the third judicial district court and convicted of manslaughter, and, on June 10, transferred to the Oklahoma City jail to await transportation to the territorial prison to serve sentences of eight and ten years.[2] They joined forces with James Casey, still waiting trial for the murder of Deputy Farris, at Yukon, and immediately the trio made plans to escape.

They were aided by a member of the gang, John Reeves, and an attractive, sixteen-year-old girl named Jessie Finley, the sweetheart of Bill Christian. At least three revolvers were smuggled into jail by the pair during weekly visits to bring the prisoners tobacco, food, and delicacies.[3]

[1] *Daily Oklahoma State Capital*, April 20, 1895; *Oklahoma Daily Star*, May 4, 1895; Newsom, *op. cit.*, pp. 210-214.
[2] *Daily Oklahoma State Capital*, July 1, 1895.
[3] *Reeves v. Territory*, Supreme Court of Oklahoma, June 30, 1900, 61 Pacific Reporter 828; Nix, *op. cit.*, p. 128.

There was a stove in the jail back of the cell block. The outlaws unjointed the pipe above the damper, packed it with a piece of blanket to hold the guns on top of the damper, and replaced the pipe. On Sunday afternoon, June 30, while being allowed the freedom of the corridor, the trio again unjointed the stove pipe and each armed himself with a six-shooter.[4]

At 6 o'clock, Jailer Garver entered the corridor to place the prisoners in their cells. As he opened the door, Bill Christian knocked him down and grappled him. Casey and Bob Christian leaped past them into the office. Mrs. Garver, who was in the office, ran to aid her husband, and Bill Christian "slammed the jailer into one corner, put his gun on Mrs. Garver and threatened to kill her" before making his escape from the building. He mounted a horse standing at a hitching rail outside and "rode off with lead flying all about him."[5]

Casey and Bob Christian had fled south through an alley to Grand Avenue. Gus White, a carpenter, was driving west on Grand in a buggy. Christian leaped into the front of the buggy and Casey jumped in the rear. Christian began "whipping up the horse and endeavoring to take the lines from White, who refused to give them up and pulled on them to stop the horse."

City Marshal Milt Jones, who was standing near the corner of Grand and Broadway, sighted the men and ran into the street with a revolver in his hand, shouting for them to halt. White stopped the horse in the center of the intersection, and as Jones approached within eight feet of the buggy, Casey turned and fired. The bullet struck the marshal in the base of the neck ranging downward. He staggered from the street and fell dead on the sidewalk.

Policemen Stafford and Jackson came running up the street and opened fire on the occupants of the buggy. Casey, struck in the head and the neck just under the chin, sank into the back of the buggy, dying almost instantly. Two stray shots hit

[4] *Reeves v. Territory, op. cit.*
[5] *Daily Oklahoma State Capital,* July 1, 1895.

White in the right leg and stomach, neither taking serious effect.

Bob Christian, also wounded in the head and bleeding badly, leaped from the buggy and ran back down Grand Avenue. Near the Santa Fe freight house he met Frank Berg, the blacksmith, riding in a cart. He stuck his revolver under Berg's nose, and the latter tumbled from the vehicle at once. Christian gathered up the lines and started the horse on east at a gallop.

Sheriff C. H. DeFord, of Oklahoma County, and his posse found the cart abandoned in the brush three miles southeast of the city and the fugitive's tracks leading toward the North Canadian. Deputy Marshal Frank Cochrane joined the hunt with bloodhounds and trailed him through the thickets to the north bank of the river. Marks on the bank indicated he had entered the water, but for several miles below there was no sign that he had come out, and it was the "prevailing belief" that, owing to his wound and weakened condition from loss of blood and the high stage of the river due to recent rains, he had drowned in the torrent.[6]

Sheriff DeFord "left no stone unturned" to recapture the killers. Out of his own pocket he paid the expenses of a large number of deputies and "proposed to spend a thousand dollars if it took that to recapture the murderers."[7] Little by little he pieced together the puzzle. He recalled how, on Saturday before the break, John Reeves had obtained entrance to the jail to talk with the brothers, and learned that on Sunday evening he had ridden to a point south of the river with two Winchesters and leading two saddle horses from the Christian ranch. Sheriff DeFord obtained a warrant and placed him under arrest.[8] But Reeves furnished no information on the whereabouts of the Christians.

---

6 Newsom, *op. cit.*, p. 217, states that Bob Christian swam the river and escaped, and a few days later he talked with him and his brother Bill, who had made his getaway on the stolen horse, in the hills of the Seminole Nation.

7 *Daily Oklahoma State Capital*, July 22, 1895.

8 *Ibid.; Reeves v. Territory, op. cit.*

There were numerous reports. On July 7, they went into a pasture near Violet Springs and stole four horses.[9] A dispatch to Oklahoma City on July 11 stated "they have reached an old hideout on Little River and are collecting a band that will rival the Dalton gang in its palmiest days."[10] Another claimed they had "connected themselves with the Wyatt-Black outlaws,"[11] and a dispatch on July 13 reported "they are now at the head of one of the most desperate gangs that has ever cursed Oklahoma and Indian territories, and if their plans are not nipped in the bud, the desperate deeds of the Daltons will fade into insignificance. . . ."[12]

The most reliable tip came from Paoli, in the Chickasaw country, where the brothers had been seen at the homes of their sweethearts Jessie Finley and Emma Johnson,[13] and on the night of July 12, Deputy Marshal Bud Logue wired Sheriff DeFord he had Jessie Finley in custody.[14] The others had escaped, headed east again into the Seminole Nation.

Logue boarded the midnight train at Purcell with his prisoner for Oklahoma City. When captured, the girl "was changing into male attire and had cut her hair short with evident intentions of riding with the gang." She confessed the Christians were desperate and "planned to hold up a train to make a stake and leave the country." The Santa Fe railroad was notified. Trainmen and express messengers were instructed to be especially watchful, and, for days, all passenger trains passing through the Seminole Nation were heavily guarded.[15]

John Reeves was tried and convicted as an accessory in the murder of Milt Jones and sentenced to life imprisonment at hard labor.[16] The records do not show what happened to Jessie Finley. "Her career has been too short to show its effects upon

[9] *Daily Oklahoma State Capital*, July 13, 1895.
[10] *Stillwater Populist*, July 11, 1895.
[11] *Ibid.*
[12] *Daily Oklahoma State Capital*, July 13, 1895.
[13] *Ibid.;* Newsom, *op. cit.*, pp. 217-218.
[14] *Daily Oklahoma State Capital*, July 13, 1895.
[15] *Ibid.*
[16] *Reeves v. Territory, op. cit.*

her face," said the *Daily Oklahoman* on July 18, and on July 22, the *State Capital* reported: "She endures her imprisonment with equanimity and is as happy as a lark. Last evening when an *Oklahoman* representative called at the jail, she was playing the organ and singing like a bird." Nix[17] states that "she paid the penalty for her part in the jail break."

The search for Bob and Bill Christian continued. On July 23, Deputy Marshal Owens and his posse reported an encounter with the gang near Violet Springs, in which "eighty shots were fired and the outlaws escaped."[18] Deputy Marshal W. H. Springfield and his posse came upon a band of outlaws in camp five miles south of Wilburton the night of August 11, and, in a running gun fight which followed, claimed they had "killed Bob Christian." He admitted, however, it had been too dark to positively identify the dead man, whom the gang "carried away."[19] And, on August 24, it was reported that Deputy Marshal Jake Hocker had been wounded in a fight with the gang six miles west of Purcell.[20]

The trail of Bob and Bill Christian ends here. Nix[21] writes: "The last they were heard of they had joined the Cuban Army, remaining there until after the Spanish-American War. From there it was stated they located somewhere in Mexico." And Newsom[22] says: "The boys passed out of the knowledge of anyone . . . no one has ever heard of them, and it cannot be truthfully said by one who knew them, whether or not they are dead or alive."

For several months, Cattle Annie and Little Breeches had taken "keen delight" in helping the Doolin gang evade the law by giving false information to posses. Even after meeting Cattle Annie on the trail, near Ingalls, while searching for the Rock Fort hideout in the spring of 1894, the marshals had

---

17 *Op. cit.*, p. 130.
18 Dispatch from Guthrie to Sheriff DeFord, July 27, 1895.
19 *Guthrie Daily Leader*, August 11, 1895.
20 *Ibid.*, August 25, 1895.
21 *Op. cit.*, p. 130.
22 *Op. cit.*, p. 210.

failed to connect the girls with the outlaws. Following the discovery of the hideout on the Dunn ranch, the Doolin gang had been in hiding most of the time, and the girls were not able to see their "sweethearts" as often as they wished.

In the spring of 1895, Little Breeches married a man named Midkiff, from Newkirk. In a short time, he learned that she was allowing men to "visit her room" during his absence. This caused "the worst of trouble" and he moved her to Osage City, but she "acted no better" there. Finally Midkiff returned her to her father's home, near Pawnee, and "almost the next day she went back to her dishonorable rides up and down the Arkansas River, keeping the lowest company."[23]

She met a "rounder from Pawnee" who "thought he had struck a bonanza." He conceived the idea of a partnership—he would bring the whiskey into the country and she would sell it to the Indians. "She worked as a domestic through the day, and at night would don male attire and sail forth, returning toward morning with her trouser pockets bulging and all the Indians guessing who the ki-shin-ka[24] was," until her identity was discovered and she was arrested by Deputy Marshal Canton.[25] She was taken to jail at Guthrie and charged with selling whiskey in the Osage Nation, but she immediately made bond and returned to her home near Pawnee.

She rejoined Cattle Annie in a horse-stealing venture, in which the stock was sold to unscrupulous traders wandering over the territory. Marshal Nix began to receive reports implicating the pair, but there was never enough evidence to warrant their arrest until they were recognized stealing some horses near Perry.

Bill Tilghman had been apprized of their exploits and warned that they were "going heavily armed with pistols and Winchesters . . . and were pretty accurate shots."[26] He and

23 "Midkiff's Manifesto," *Pawnee Times-Democrat*, September 13, 1895.
24 Meaning "a boy."
25 *Daily Oklahoma State Capital*, July 6, 1895; *Guthrie Daily Leader*, July 7, 1895.
26 Nix, *op. cit.*, p. 132.

Deputy Burke were on another assignment in the Osage country when they learned the two girls had been seen at an old farmhouse near Pawnee.

The officers headed there at once. As they approached the shack, the girls tried to escape. Cattle Annie leaped from a window—into the arms of Burke. She tried to draw a revolver, and he knocked the gun from her hand. Little Breeches, taking advantage of the confusion, leaped on her horse and spurred away, with Tilghman in close pursuit. She fired several erratic shots at the marshal before he "despaired of overtaking her" and killed her horse with one shot. Little Breeches was thrown to the ground and stunned for a moment, but as Tilghman came up, she bounded to her feet, fighting like a wildcat. Tilghman's face and hands were covered with scratches before he subdued her and rejoined Burke and his prisoner.[27]

They were taken to Perry and tried before Judge A. G. C. Bierer. "To the last the girls gloried in their connection with the outlaw (Doolin) gang, and this was especially apparent during their trial."[28] They sassed the judge, called the officers "soft," and cursed the district attorney.[29] But their shouts and taunts failed to aid them. Convicted of stealing horses, Judge Bierer sentenced them to two years each in the reformatory at South Farmington, Massachusetts.

There is some disagreement as to what, finally, they made of their lives. Nix[30] believes they eventually were discharged and took up settlement work in the slums of New York. Zoe A. Tilghman[31] states that Little Breeches died in Massachusetts eighteen months after her release, and Cattle Annie returned to Oklahoma. James D. Horan,[32] obviously relying on these sources, claims both were released after serving two

27 Tilghman, *Outlaw Days*, p. 80; Nix, *op. cit.*, pp. 132-134.
28 Tilghman, *Outlaw Days*, p. 81.
29 "Outlaw Girls Sassed the Judge," *Guthrie Daily Leader*, April 16, 1939.
30 *Op. cit.*, p. 135.
31 *Outlaw Days*, p. 81.
32 *Op. cit.*, p. 266.

years; that Cattle Annie, "older and wiser," married and settled down near Pawnee, and Little Breeches, after working
as a domestic for several months in Boston, went to New
York to do settlement work and died two years later, of
consumption.

It seems that Cattle Annie died of consumption, and Little
Breeches returned to Oklahoma. On November 12, 1896, the
Blackwell Times-Record carried the following story:

A few days ago a young lady passenger arrived in Perry and was
driven to the Pacific hotel. In her healthful appearance, graceful
bearing and pleasing countenance no one recognized the once
female outlaw, Jennie Metcalf (Midkiff), known among the various bands of outlaws, with whom she formerly associated as "Little
Breeches." . . . Two years ago she was arrested . . . and sentenced by Judge Bierer to two years in the reformatory . . . where
she remained one year, her father and relatives having secured a
commutation of her sentence. A gentleman who lives in Perry,
to whom she spoke freely of her former life and expressed deep
regret for her waywardness, says she further stated she was completely reformed and under the good treatment and discipline of
the reformatory, had been led to denounce her former reckless life.
She has returned to her father's home near Sinnett, in Pawnee
county, where she intends to begin a new life.[33]

[33] See also *El Reno News,* November 13, 1896.

Gathering Them In

Following the Dover robbery and the killing of Tulsa Jack, there had been no "cessation in efforts" to apprehend the Doolin and Wyatt gangs. The "shooting of innocent men" like the aged preacher, Godfrey, "robbing farmers and committing all sorts of deviltry . . . demanded that these cowardly, ruffianly, brutal and inhuman outlaws be wiped from the face of the earth," and "pursuit and annihilation" of these gangs became a "matter of absolute necessity."[1]

Chris Madsen had remained in the field with his posse. Marshal Nix had sent Deputy Halsell to assist Jack Love, at Woodward, and Hadwinger and Snoddy, at Alva, in Woods County, with orders to "stay on the job" until they had "run down" these outlaws.[2] And there had not been a moment that some well-organized group of citizens was not scouring the country with the marshals, sheriffs, and railroad detectives. The outlaws were being "hunted and hounded more than any jungle of wild beasts in history," but they seemed able to "defy these angered people"[3] until they held up the store and post office at Oxley, the night of June 12, and escaped with a quantity of cash, tobacco, groceries, and registered letters. Officers received information that the robbers had been seen

1 *Kingfisher Free Press,* August 8, 1895.
2 Nix, *op. cit.,* p. 204.
3 *Enid Weekly Wave,* August 8, 1895.

camped in a pasture in the hills between Okeene and Watonga.[4]

Sheriff Clay McGrath, of Wood County, and Deputy Marshals Hadwinger, J. K. Runnels, and Marion Hildreth, "armed to the teeth," rode to the location. They surprised the outlaws in camp, capturing two horses, saddles and bridles, and the entire camp outfit, "including two females Jennie Freeman and Mrs. Ike Black." The fight "kept up one whole day" during which the marshals "killed one horse, shot Dick Yeager (Zip Wyatt) through the left arm and Ike Black in the left side." The outlaws fled up a canyon "where it is impossible to get to them . . . and are still in the hills."[5]

The women had in their possession the letters taken in the robbery of the Oxley post office. They were arraigned before United States Commissioner Bickel, who ordered them held for trial, and transferred to Guthrie to the federal jail.[6]

Neither are good looking nor attractive. The Black woman is small, heavy set, with dark hair and blue eyes; the Freeman woman is rather tall, very slim build, of light complexion and has her hair shingled close. When searched at the jail, the Black woman had the photograph of the dead bandit, Tulsa Jack, and also the photos

[4] *Hennessey Clipper,* August 1, 1895.

[5] *Weekly Oklahoma State Capital,* June 15, 1895; *Kingfisher Free Press,* June 27, 1895. (Nix, *op. cit.,* pp. 204-205, credits the encounter and capture to a posse led by Halsell. As they neared the hideout they heard a wagon leaving over the stony trail and concealed themselves and waited. When the wagon appeared, S. T. Watson was driving with the two women in the back. Black sat in the rear of the wagon with his legs dangling over the edge, and Wyatt followed the procession on a stolen horse. Halsell fired at Black. Black cried out, clutching one foot, then jumped from the wagon and dashed into the sand hills. The other officers fired at the horses, wounding both animals, but Watson whipped them into a run. Halsell and some of the posse started after Black. The others pursued Wyatt and the wagon. It was late afternoon. A storm had been gathering. Within twenty minutes rain was pouring down in torrents and in the heavy darkness the fugitives escaped. The officers picked up their trail the next morning. Black had succeeded in re-joining his companions, and all had crossed the Cimarron. The marshals came upon them again in a deep canyon on a little creek, and in another gun battle with the gang, Wyatt, Black, and Watson again escaped, but the women were captured.) (Gish, obviously relying on the Nix version, repeats this story in *American Bandits,* p. 44) .

[6] *Weekly Oklahoma State Capital,* June 15, 1895.

of Deputy Marshals Prather and William Banks, concealed on her person.

The photos had been taken in a group after Tulsa Jack was placed in his coffin (with the marshals on each side) but someone had cut them separate and evidently murdered the deputies in their hearts, as the eyes of Prather had been rubbed out with a pen and the picture of Banks punctured in several places.[7]

The hunt for the rest of the gang quickened. More than two hundred armed men searched the country in every direction.[8]

The aim of Yeager (Wyatt) and Black was to escape from the Gyp Hills to the Cherokee Nation. Time and again they ventured upon the intervening prairie and fought incredible pitched battles, the two of them against whole posses. They failed to break through; but the posses failed to take them. In these fights Dick (Zip) seemed to bear a charmed life. Time and again men swore they had seen him knocked down by the impact of their bullets. On one of his captured horses was a saddle with nine holes in it. Dick (Zip) stole other horses and kept on. But always he and Black were driven back to the hills.[9]

Somehow, Watson had disappeared alone.

On August 1, a posse of eight men under Deputy Sam Campbell came upon Wyatt and Black resting near their picketed horses, in the blackjack timber on the North Canadian, near Cantonment, in Blaine County, fifty miles southwest of Enid. The outlaws sprang to their feet "with Winchesters and Colt revolvers in each hand." The posse shot Black in the head, killing him instantly. Wyatt, unable to reach his horse, leaped into the brush and began firing as fast as he could pull the trigger. He wounded one of Campbell's men, and received an ugly, though not dangerous, wound in

7 Ibid.
8 Hennessey Clipper, August 1, 1895.
9 James, The Cherokee Strip, p. 28.

the right breast. A glancing shot knocked his rifle from his hands, but he quickly recovered it, shot his way clear and escaped on foot.[10]

Eluding his pursuers in the timber, he came upon a boy driving a cart. He leaped into the seat beside him, frightening the lad half to death, and forced him to drive at top speed twenty-five miles northeast before letting him go. The following day and night, Wyatt drove eastward in the cart. News of the Cantonment fight had swept the country. Posses were searching everywhere. Fearing discovery, he headed back for the Gyp Hills.

At four o'clock Saturday afternoon, August 3, a report reached Enid that he had crossed the Rock Island tracks five miles south of the city. Garfield County Sheriff Elzie Thralls and a posse picked up his trail. Fourteen miles east, they found the cart abandoned and the horse nearly exhausted. They tracked the outlaw a short distance through a field and lost his trail again.

Meanwhile, Wyatt had reached the claim of a bachelor named John Daily. "Old man," he said, "I want a horse for two or three days to do a little business."

Daily looked at the front of his shirt covered with blood from his wounds, the three weeks' growth of beard, and the tired, worn expression on the outlaw's face.

"I have no horse to hire," he replied. "Who are you?"

"I'm Dick Yeager." Wyatt brandished his Winchester. "Where are your horses?"

Daily showed him his stock. Wyatt complained that they were a "poor lot," but chose one and ordered Daily to mount another and accompany him.

Riding a mile and a half southeast, Wyatt observed a fine roan in the pasture of a man named Will Blakely. He left Daily's horse in the pasture, took the roan, and continued southeast. At dark, he stopped at the claim of John Pierce, cut himself a length of well rope and rode on again. A few miles

10 *Enid Weekly Wave*, August 8, 1895; Rainey, *op. cit.*, p. 249.

farther, he stopped, improvised a rope bridle, and removing Daily's bridle from Blakely's horse, placed the rope bridle over its head and told Daily he was released.

"Don't give me away too soon," he told the farmer. "I think I've given them the dodge. If you see the sons of bitches, tell them that while they're getting me, I will get them."

It was now late in the night, but Daily galloped south to spread the alarm. At the home of Horton Miles, he found a group of men who had just adjourned an Anti Horse Thief Association meeting. He informed them of Wyatt's presence in the neighborhood, and plans were quickly made to capture the outlaw.

Billy Fox, Ben Vandemark, and Daily returned to the point where he had last been seen and waited until daylight to take his trail. The others dispersed and aroused the community. They followed the trail into Old Oklahoma to a point southeast of Sheridan. Here they were joined by a posse of men from the Sheridan neighborhood, and Sheriff Thralls and his posse, who had picked up the trail and followed it southeast eight miles during the night. They found Blakely's roan grazing on Skeleton Creek and footprints disappearing in a cornfield in a bend of the stream on the farm of Alvin G. Ross.

Sheriff Thralls assumed command and issued orders. Guards were thrown out until the cornfield was surrounded. Tom Smith, a Sheridan man, and two Enid deputies, S. T. Wood and Ad Poak, were detailed to follow the tracks through the field.

The tracks led down the creek and turned north, then east, then south. Deputy Woods happened to think that no one had been left with the horses. Fearing Wyatt might slip through the officers surrounding the field and steal one of their mounts, he turned back to guard them.

Almost at the same moment Deputy Poak sighted their quarry sprawled on his stomach at the edge of a hard patch of ground where the corn had failed to grow, his feet toward the possemen. Poak signaled Smith, and Smith came up to the left and a little behind him. Both men cocked their rifles and brought them to their shoulders. Then Poak yelled in a loud voice:

"Throw up your hands!"

Wyatt jerked up his head and grabbed for his guns. Poak and Smith fired at the same time. Both bullets struck the outlaw's body within inches of each other, one shattering his pelvis, the other tearing through his abdomen. He raised one hand. Poak ordered him to throw up the other, but Wyatt answered that he could not and begged them not to shoot again.

As they walked up to him and disarmed him, the outlaw inquired: "Who are you?"

"We are deputy sheriffs."

"Thank God for that," he said. "The marshals would have killed me."

He was removed from the cornfield to a small church building at Sheridan. Sunday services were just over. They removed the Sunday School blackboard from the wall and laid it on top of the benches, and the wounded outlaw was placed on it and given first aid by Doctors C. R. Jones and Frank Love.

Meanwhile, the "grand army" in pursuit gathered. A controversy arose as to who should have jurisdiction and collect the rewards offered for Wyatt's capture. He was now in Kingfisher County, where most of the men in the Sheridan posse resided. They claimed the prisoner, on grounds that they had been first in tracking him to the cornfield and surrounding him. The capture had been made in Logan County, while all the officers participating in the capture were from Garfield County. The Enid men "would not be shaken," and the Sheridan men were "ready to maintain their stand." The marshals threatened to send telegrams to Judge McAtee for orders to release the prisoner to federal authorities, and they finally agreed that he should be taken to Enid and that Daily and the Sheridan men should share in any reward paid Sheriff Thralls and his posse.[11]

Wyatt was placed in the Enid jail the evening of August 4 and charged with felonies committed in Garfield County. Local jurisdictions continued to quarrel over the right to try him, and the federal government finally took possession. But the prisoner could not be moved from his cell. The doctors said he had no chance to live. He had been virtually shot to pieces.

Thousands came to see the notorious outlaw, and Wyatt enjoyed the attention. He ate from hampers of fried chicken and fruit piled on his cot by admirers and "embar[r]assed the predictions" of physicians by "growing stronger and more lively each day." He would alternately pet the jail pup or suck a lemon, while he confessed every crime that had been committed in the Outlet since the opening, and estimated he had killed eleven men. He joshed local attorneys about importing a famous criminal lawyer from the East to defend him, then cursed them and told them they were "not worth the powder to blow them to hell."

But in the stifling cell, "fetid with gangrenous smells and hung with wet blankets to reduce the temperature," the doctors tended his wounds and waited. On August 12, his mind "seemed to leave him." For two days and nights he "imagined himself on the road again, holding up trains and going through the many lawless scenes of his life." On August 19, the *Enid Wave* reported: "He eats little, takes only liquids . . . and has no control of his bowels." His pulse quickened, signs of blood poisoning appeared around his abdominal wounds, and on August 28: "His pain at times is almost unbearable. . . . He still lives, a bunch of suffering humanity. . . . He is reduced to a mere skeleton and bed sores are beginning their

---

[11] Versions of Zip Wyatt's pursuit and capture appear in James, *They Had Their Hour*, pp. 290-293, and *The Cherokee Strip*, pp. 29-30; Nix, *op. cit.*, pp. 208-209; Barnard, *op. cit.*, pp. 196-197; and Rainey *op. cit.*, pp. 249-254. First-hand accounts appear in the *Daily Oklahoma State Capital*, July 30-August 12, 1895, and *Enid Weekly Wave*, August 8, 1895.

work." The evening of September 6, he suffered a "septic chill" and lost consciousness. At six minutes past midnight, he died.[12]

His funeral was held at eleven o'clock Sunday morning, September 8. The cortege that left the jail consisted only of a spring wagon, the driver, the grave digger who sat on the coffin, and the jail dog that followed them to the pauper's field south of the city. The outlaw's relatives did not claim his body.[13]

During the pursuit of Black and Wyatt, the officers had lost all trace of Watson. Nix[14] states:

Some time later we heard that he reached the southwestern part of Oklahoma, near Anadarko, where he had been joined by a half-breed Indian named Esceness. Deputy Sam Bartell was assigned to capture Watson and the half-breed. After two or three days of trailing, Bartell located the pair near the Clampton Ranch on the Washita River about twenty-five miles from Anadarko. Esceness was killed in the fight that ensued and Watson was chased several miles, the officers finally surrounding him and forcing his surrender. Of the Yeager (Wyatt)-Black gang, Watson was the only male member who lived to serve a prison term. The two women (Pearl Black and Jennie Freeman) were given short terms in the federal jail at Guthrie by Judge Dale.

The deaths of Tulsa Jack, Charlie Pierce, and Bitter Creek Newcomb had been telling blows to the Doolin gang. Dynamite Dick and Little Bill Raidler, who (the marshals learned later) were to have joined Pierce and Newcomb at the Dunn ranch, had "separated and fled in opposite directions."

Bill Tilghman picked up the trail of Little Bill Raidler in the Osage Nation. At the Moore Ranch, on Mission Creek, about eighteen miles south of Elgin, Kansas, he learned that the outlaw had been hiding in the timber nearby and coming

---

12 *Enid Daily Wave*, September 5-7, 1895.
13 *Ibid.*, September 10, 1895.
14 *Op. cit.*, pp. 209-210.

to the ranch only at nights to get something to eat. Tilghman concealed himself on the place and waited.

On September 6, shortly after sundown, Raidler came out of the timber, walking through the corral past the well and an unchinked log henhouse. Tilghman waited until he was completely in range of his shotgun, then stepped from the doorway of the structure in his path. Raidler recognized him even before the marshal shouted: "Hands up!" He drew his six-shooter and turned running and shooting, and only ceased when a blast from Tilghman's shotgun knocked him off his feet."[15]

He was still alive when Tilghman bent over him. He had received six wounds—one in each side, one through the neck, two in the back of the head and one through the right wrist. He begged Tilghman to let him die and said he "preferred death to captivity."[16]

But Tilghman got a bucket of water and some clean rags from Moore's wife and washed and bound up the outlaw's wounds. Moore brought up his team and wagon with some hay and quilts in the back, and the two men lifted the outlaw inside. Moore drove and Tilghman rode beside his prisoner, bathing his face with water from a jug and checking the bleeding of his wounds, until they reached Elgin, Kansas, and a doctor. A few days later the outlaw was placed on the train on a stretcher and removed to Guthrie.

Raidler slowly recovered from his wounds in the federal jail, while many jurisdictions bid for his custody. He was tried at Kingfisher for robbery of the mail train at Dover and sentenced to ten years in prison at Columbus, Ohio.[17]

15 *Daily Oklahoman*, September 11, 1895; *Fort Smith Elevator*, September 13, 1895.

16 *Fort Smith Elevator*, September 13, 1895.

17 *Kingfisher Free Press*, April 9, 1896; *Ibid.*, June 25, 1896. (While in prison, Raidler developed locomotor ataxia as a result of his wounds, and was finally paroled due to his illness. He returned to Oklahoma, but never to ride with an outlaw gang again. He remained a cripple the rest of his life and died several years later as the result of his last duel with the law in the cattle corral. —Newsom, *op. cit.*, pp. 190-191; Nix, *op. cit.*, p. 214; Tilghman, *Marshal of the Last Frontier*, p. 216.

Bill Tilghman received the $1,000 reward offered by the Rock Island railroad for Raidler's capture, and turned his efforts to the apprehension of the remaining members of the Doolin gang. It was rumored that Little Dick West and Dynamite Dick Clifton had fled to Texas. Red Buck Waightman was reported hiding somewhere in the Cheyenne-Arapaho country. Doolin's whereabouts were a mystery.

Twenty-One Buckshot

It had been reported in July, 1895, that Doolin had married a Purcell school teacher whom he had met during a train holdup in 1893; that he had made secret visits to Purcell under an assumed name, and "six months later the woman left her school and had not been heard of since."[1] The marshals knew, however, that Doolin had courted the preacher's daughter at Ingalls, while she was clerking in Mc-Murtry's drug store the winter of 1891, and married her in 1892.[2]

Probably Edith Ellsworth had no knowledge of Doolin's life before their marriage. No doubt he "courted her with all carefulness, but kept concealed from her all things pertaining to his past or his intentions for the future." She may have guessed that he was an outlaw, but "there was about him a dashing and debonair way that attracted her so much she found herself so in love with him that she could not say no when asked to become his wife."[3] Even after she realized her husband was one of the most desperate bandits in the Southwest—with Doolin being hunted everywhere, often unable to see her for months at a time and then forced to elude officers in long, dangerous rides at night to be with her only a few

1 *Stillwater Populist,* July 25, 1895.
2 *Guthrie Daily Leader,* January 26, 1896.
3 Newsom, *op. cit.,* p. 178.

hours—she "stood by her renegade mate in all his lawless deeds until the night she fell sobbing across his bullet riddled body."[4]

Likely it was that she found herself pregnant with a child. After the Ingalls fight, the Ellsworths moved to Lawson,[5] where Edith Doolin gave birth to a boy. The legend continues how, some months later, Doolin again eluded officers to see her. "She was holding their baby in her arms. . . . For the first time in the outlaw's life tears came to his eyes (and he) seemed to long for a peaceful existence."[6] Zoe A. Tilghman[7] writes: "Exposure had brought rheumatism upon him and that may have had something to do with his determination to quit the life of an outlaw." No mention is made of the fact that six of the regular members of his gang were already dead or behind prison bars. On December 26, 1895, Bill Doolin sent a message to federal officers at Perry, agreeing to give himself up, provided arrangements could be made whereby he could "atone for all his misdeeds by working out a short term in the penitentiary."[8]

His offer brought a furor of objection. "The object of criminal procedure should be to secure the punishment of criminals," said the *Daily Oklahoman*. "The majesty of the law would be little less than a majestic dead letter if it dealt in any other manner with this gang of brigands that have robbed, plundered and murdered at will." The *Eagle-Gazette* promised that "any endeavor to secure through the Department of Justice a short term in the penitentiary in return for the surrender of any of the red-handed members of this gang" would receive the "condemnation by the people of the territory it deserves." "He has lain low three of my men," added Marshal

---

4 Mootz, *op. cit.*

5 Now Quay, Oklahoma, on the Pawnee County line, eight miles northeast of Ingalls.

6 Newsom, *op. cit.*, p. 179.

7 *Outlaw Days*, p. 95.

8 *Kingfisher Free Press*, January 2, 1896; *Beaver Herald*, January 2, 1896; *The South and West*, January 2, 1896.

Nix. For more than three years Nix had run down every possible clue, investigated every rumor, and, again and again, sent his best officers upon long journeys in quest of clues or information; he had expended over $2,000 of his own money in carrying on the search. "I propose to capture him and make him pay the penalty of his crimes." On January 10, the *Edmond Sun-Democrat* commented: "Bill Doolin, the outlaw, after an unsuccessful attempt to compromise with the territorial authorities, is being pursued by armed deputies."

After the slaying of Charlie Pierce and Bitter Creek, Nix had assigned Bill Tilghman to Doolin's trail. "Fully backed and liberally supplied with funds by his chief," Tilghman had "inaugurated a still hunt." He had checked out a rumor first in Texas, then in the Indian Territory, then at a remote point in the Osage Nation. Edith Doolin and her son had left Lawson in the summer of 1895, and it was while following their wagon in a weary trip across the Osage that Tilghman picked up the lead that had enabled him to capture Little Bill Raidler. When he returned to the trail of the members of Doolin's family, it was cold. Finally, in late December, he learned that a letter received from Mrs. Doolin by relatives had been mailed at Burden, Kansas, and he went there at once.[9]

He learned that a man named Thomas Wilson, but "answering exactly Doolin's description" and "suffering from rheumatism," came into town every two weeks for provisions. He dressed in the ragged clothes of a typical "played-out"

---

[9] *Guthrie Daily Leader*, January 16, 1896. (Tilghman, *Outlaw Days*, pp. 95-96, claims the letter was written to Mary Pierce at the Ingalls hotel, where Mrs. Doolin had left a ring that Doolin had given her while they were sweethearts. She asked Mrs. Pierce to send it to her, and Tilghman learned the address to which Mary Pierce shipped a little package containing the ring. Nix, *op. cit.*, p. 217, gives this version: "We decided to try to locate the Doolins through the hotel woman at Ingalls. Tilghman went to call on Mrs. Pierce and she expressed deep appreciation for our treatment of her. She realized that we could have placed a charge against her for harboring bandits at the time of the Ingalls fight. . . . She had just received a letter from Doolin's wife, requesting that she mail a wedding ring that had been left in the hotel on her last visit. The package was to be addressed to Mrs. Will Barry at Burden, Kansas.")

Oklahoma boomer and drove a dilapidated lumber wagon hitched to a poor team managed with rope lines. In fact, he affected such poverty that, just before Christmas, a number of charitable ladies of Burden had solicited a purse of money and quantity of food for "that poor sufferin' family out there" and presented it to the astonished Mrs. Doolin.

They were living in a tent, pitched near a spring a short distance from town, and had been there three months. For six days and nights Tilghman watched the place. Mrs. Doolin and the baby were there, but the outlaw did not show. Night and day Tilghman made every train and watched the mails, but Doolin did not return to his family, and there was no communication between the couple. Then, on January 6, Mrs. Doolin and child went to Burden and boarded the train for Perry, Oklahoma. Tilghman wired Nix to have the woman shadowed, and Nix soon advised him that she had gone to her father's home, at Lawson.

The departure of the woman convinced Tilghman that Doolin would not return to Burden. He decided to try to trace him. Here is the story of the final search in Tilghman's own words:

"I found out that the last time Doolin had left Burden he had gone east, so I started on a search through most of the towns along the southern Kansas border, east of the Santa Fe. Finally, on Sunday (January 12), in a town in extreme eastern Kansas, I learned that Doolin had been there and had gone to Eureka Springs, Arkansas. I at once came to Guthrie for instructions."

He told Chief Deputy Hale of his tip on Doolin, and that he was going after him. Hale immediately furnished him the necessary papers. Marshal Nix offered him the pick of the force for assistance.

"I'm going alone," Tilghman said.

Both men protested. "Doolin's desperate. He has sworn never to be taken alive. He'll shoot you on sight."

"Not if he doesn't recognize me," Tilghman replied. "I'm

going disguised." And he looked down at Nix's long-skirted Prince Albert coat.

Quickly he had it on. It fitted perfectly. He added Deputy Hale's black derby. The two men stared in surprise. He always looked well in the rough clothes he wore while on duty in the territory, but dressed in a hat and coat of these styles, he would hardly be recognized on the street. From a local tailor, he obtained the other necessary items to complete his costume, and on Tuesday evening at five o'clock, left for Eureka Springs, "determined to bring back his man if he was there."

What followed was the quickest capture of one of the most notorious outlaws by a single officer in the history of the West. In less than twenty-four hours, Nix received the following dispatch:

Eureka Springs, Ark., Jan. 15, '96

U. S. Marshal Nix
Guthrie, Okla.

I have him. Will be there tomorrow.

TILGHMAN.

Several versions have been written of what happened at Eureka Springs in that twenty-four hours.[10] Most of these are happy hybrids of fact and folklore, and some slightly embroidered accounts bordering on the incredible. Mixing fiction with truth is bound to be more entertaining, but it is doubtful if the story has ever been better told than in the words of the man who was there and effected the capture:[11]

"I arrived in Eureka Springs at 10:30 Wednesday morning. Walking up town, one of the first men I met was Bill Doolin. He didn't see me at that time. I soon learned he was stopping

10 MacDonald, *op. cit.*, pp. 204-206; Nix, *op. cit.*, pp. 219-222; Newsom, *op. cit*, pp. 192-193; Raine, *op. cit.*, pp. 205-206; Tilghman, *Outlaw Days*, pp. 96-99, and *Marshal of the Last Frontier*, pp. 217-224; Gish, *op. cit.*, p. 55; Mootz, *op. cit.*; Fred Sutton, "Rose of Cimarron, The Passing of the Doolin Gang of Outlaws," *Daily Oklahoman*, May 8, 1921.

11 *Guthrie Daily Leader*, January 17, 1896; *Daily Oklahoman*, January, 17, 1896; *Indian Chieftain*, January 23, 1896; *Oklahoma City Times Journal*, January 24, 1896; *Weekly Oklahoma State Capital*, January 25, 1896.

at the Davy Hotel under the name of Tom Wilson, the same
name he had used at Burden.

"I went to a carpenter and ordered a box made in which I
could carry a loaded shotgun, determined to disguise and,
carrying the box under my arm, walk about until I met him
again, the box being arranged so that with a slight movement
of the thumb it would drop, leaving the gun in my hand ready
for action.

"While the carpenter was making the box, I decided to
take a bath in the mineral waters from the springs and went
to a bathhouse nearby. When I opened the door to step into
the gentleman's waiting room, whom should I see but Bill
Doolin sitting on a lounge in the far corner of the room, reading a paper. He looked up sharply as I entered and for a second
he seemed to recognize me, but I walked briskly through the
the room and into the bath rooms, calling to the clerk that I
wished to take a bath at once.

"Inside the door I turned so I could watch him. His view
of me was shut off by the stove. I noticed that for several
moments he watched the door through which I had passed,
but finally relaxed his vigilance and returned to reading his
paper.

"Now was my chance. With my gun in my hand I slipped
quietly into the room up to the stove, then jumping around
the stove to a position immediately in front of Doolin, I told
him to throw up his hands and surrender.[12]

"He got up, saying, 'What do you mean? I have done
nothing,' but I grabbed his right wrist with my left hand as
he raised it to get his gun, and with the revolver in my right
hand leveled at his head, ordered him to throw up his left

[12] Doolin tells the same story in relating the incident to a reporter of the
Weekly Oklahoma State Capital: "Since I lived so long in Kansas last summer
without being disturbed, I got careless. I had concluded that nobody would be
looking for me in a place like Eureka and the baths would be good for my
rheumatism. I didn't know Tilghman very well. I thought I had seen him somewhere, but he brushed past me so fast and in an unconcerned way that I just
went on reading my paper. The next I knew he was standing four feet away
from me, and I was looking straight into his gun."

hand. He put it up part way, then made a pass toward his gun. I told him I would shoot if he made another move.

"When I first called on Doolin to surrender the room was full of men. In half a minute we were alone. I called to the proprietor to come in and help me, that I was an officer. He came tremblingly to the door, and I finally persuaded him to come over where we were. After two or three attempts he managed to get Doolin's vest open and take his revolver from under under his arm, then wanted to hand the revolver to me notwithstanding the fact that I had both hands full. I told him to get out (of the room) with it, and he ran into the street, holding the gun at arm's length.

"When Doolin's vest was opened, he made a final effort to get loose, and even after his gun was gone, protested that he had done nothing. I then said:

" 'Now, look at me; don't you know me?'

"He looked me in the eye and said: 'Yes. You are Tilghman.'

"I then shackled him, got his gun and started for his hotel. I said, 'Bill, you know you are in the hands of no sucker. To get good treatment all you need to do is behave yourself.'

"Doolin said, 'I give you my word that if you will take these shackles off I will give you no trouble.' I told him I would take his word, and took them off, telling him that if he made a single move to escape I would drop him dead in his tracks.

"We went to the hotel, got his effects, went to the bank and got $100 he had deposited, and left on the first train, not a soul knowing who either of us were. Doolin rode in the seat in front of me and was perfectly quiet and docile, nobody knowing who we were until we got into Oklahoma."

News of the capture swept the territory. Hundreds flocked to Guthrie from Perry, Mulhall, and other surrounding towns, and half the population of Guthrie turned out to meet the "king of outlaws." At noon, fully three thousand people packed the grounds at the Santa Fe depot and the hill beyond, and half as many more were congregated at the federal jail to "see him locked in." When the train arrived at 12:25, there was a great rush, pushing, scrambling, jamming, and crowding for a glimpse of the notorious bandit leader. And when he left the coach, escorted by Deputies Tilghman and Ed Kelley, who had gone north to meet Tilghman and his prisoner at Lawrie, the people were astonished to see in place of a booted, spurred, and bearded desperado, a "tall, slender man, with mustache and pleasant blue eyes, with a smile on his face, dressed in a suit of well-worn ready-made clothes and walking with a cane."[13]

Marshal Nix, Chief Deputy Hale, and Heck Thomas were waiting with a cab. Doolin was put inside with Tilghman and Kelley; Nix and Hale, and Heck Thomas rode with the driver.

They took the prisoner to Marshal Nix's office. Here Doolin was "greeted by a large number of deputies and leading citizens and ladies, the latter remarking as they shook hands that they were very happy to meet him, and of course courtesy demanded that he made the same remark." Later, "the press of people became so great that the doors were opened and for over an hour thousands passed through in a steady stream to look at him." At two o'clock, the "most notorious outlaw in the United States" was locked behind bars in the federal jail.[14]

Bill Tilghman was the hero of the hour. He "bore his honors modestly," while his friends, by the hundreds, were "profuse with congratulations" and "spoke enviously" of the outstanding rewards aggregating $3,500 for the outlaw's arrest and conviction, and Marshal Nix "rejoiced in the capture that was but the climax of the continuously successful campaign against outlawry inaugurated at his advent to office."[15]

While Tilghman had been trailing Bill Doolin, Deputy Canton got a report that Dynamite Dick had been shot and killed in the Indian Territory, near Tulsa, but his body had not been identified. He got a second lead on the outlaw in

13 *Guthrie Daily Leader*, January 17, 1896.
14 *Ibid.*
15 *Ibid.*

Arizona, but before he could have him picked up there he murdered and robbed two Mexicans at a sheep ranch and disappeared.

Finally, he learned that the fugitive was hiding at the home of his mother, near Pauls Valley, in the Chickasaw Nation, but before Canton reached that part of the country, the outlaw had been arrested on a whiskey charge by deputy marshals from Paris, Texas, and sentenced to thirty days in jail.

When Canton went to the jail to identify him, Dynamite Dick was wearing a high celluloid collar, a derby hat, and had a four weeks' growth of beard on his face. Canton sent for a barber. The outlaw protested. He knew what the marshal was looking for. The shave revealed a scar on his neck the size of a half dollar caused from cutting out a bullet fired by Lafe Shadley, in the fight at Ingalls.

Canton went to Shep Williams, marshal for the Eastern District of Texas, produced a warrant from Oklahoma for Dan Clifton for murder, and demanded the prisoner. A few weeks after Doolin's capture, he delivered Dynamite Dick to the Guthrie jail.

A few days later, on March 5, 1896, Deputy Madsen and a posse of farmers cornered Red Buck in a dugout near Arapaho and ordered him to surrender. He came out shooting and was killed trying to escape.[16]

Little Dick West was the only member of the Doolin gang still at large. On May 2, Bill Doolin was indicted for the Ingalls murders and taken to Stillwater for trial.[17]

Doolin had agreed to plead guilty on the promise of the United States attorney that he would get only fifty years, the same sentence that had been given Arkansas Tom. But when arraigned in court, he pleaded not guilty. He was bound over for trial and ordered returned to Guthrie. On the way back to Guthrie, Tilghman asked: "Doolin, why did you go back on

16 *Ibid.*, March 7, 1896.
17 *Ibid.*, May 3, 1896.

your word?" And the outlaw replied, "Fifty years is a long time, and I believe there's a chance to beat that federal jail."[18]

Doolin had plans. Canton[19] recalls:

(When) I brought Dick into the jail, Bill Doolin's cell was in front of the main entrance, and as he saw the prisoner, he had a look of terror on his face and was very much excited. He asked me if he could speak to the prisoner. I motioned for Dynamite Dick to come up to the cell. The first words that Doolin said to Dynamite were, "For God's sake, stand pat." They talked a few minutes in a whisper, and I could not catch the words.

The heavy steel bars and eighteen-inch-thick stone walls of the federal jail were amply strong to hold the badmen of the territory. The jail was two stories high. Inside, a steel stairway led to the upper floor. There was a large steel cell in the center of the upper floor. The cell door opened into a corridor that ran across the front of the jail, with a steel box containing a combination lock on each side. Back of the cell, and running to the front corridor on either side, was the bull pen, where the prisoners were allowed their freedom in the daytime. Across the back of the bull pen and part way along each wall ran a tier of cells. It was customary for two guards to lock the prisoners in cells between eight and nine o'clock each night.

At 8:45 P. M., Sunday, July 5, Night Guard J. W. Miller removed his revolver and placed it in a box at the side of the front door. With keys in hand, he was then let through the bull pen door by Night Guard J. T. Tull, and started toward the row of cells at the rear.

To the right of the door, in the corner of the outer corridor, was set a water bucket so the prisoners could reach through the bars and get a drink. They were in the habit of filling tin cans with water to take into their cells at night, so Guard Tull

---

18 Tilghman, *Marshal of the Last Frontier,* p. 227.
19 *Op. cit.,* p. 134.

thought nothing of it when he saw George Lane, a huge half-breed desperado with a long criminal record, standing in the corner of the bull pen reaching through to the bucket.

As Miller passed through the door, the half-breed mumbled something about not being able to reach the water and thrust an arm through the door and around to the bucket. Miller was half way to the rear of the jail. For a moment Tull's gaze dropped to the water pail. In the same instant the half-breed pushed his head and shoulders through the doorway. With a mighty lurch he seized Tull and pinned his arms to his sides in a vice-like grip, while three other prisoners (Walt McLain, Lee Killian, and Bill Jones) [20] rushed upon him.

Killian tore his revolver from its holster under his arm. Jones snatched a hatchet from the table in the corridor; and Lane seized a long iron bar.

Before Miller could run the length of the bull pen, Bill Doolin leaped through the door and closed and locked it, leaving the guard helpless among the prisoners. He grabbed Miller's revolver from the box inside the door. His look of mildness had gone. "His eyes shone with the light of hell, his hair fairly bristled all over his head, and with set teeth and a grin of horror he shoved his revolver now in the guard's face, now in his stomach, now in his side, with his fingers clutching the trigger, seeming to need only the beginning of slaughter to complete his demoniacal joy." [21]

He dragged Tull to the middle of the corridor, in front of the steel cell door, and ordered him to open the combination locks, while Killian pointed his revolver at the guard's temple and Jones stood in front of him with hatchet upraised.

Bill Dean, a trusty, who was sitting at a desk in the corridor, ran to Tull's assistance. Doolin knocked him down with his revolver and the others kicked and dragged him down the

---

[20] McLain was serving six months for larceny from Pawnee County and ninety days for whiskey peddling; Killian was serving six months from Pawnee County for whiskey peddling; and Jones, of Pottawatomie County, had been charged with counterfeiting.

[21] *Guthrie Daily Leader,* July 7, 1896.

stairway into the basement. Doolin put his gun against Tull's breast and ordered him to open the locks or die. . . . When the combinations were worked, Doolin opened the cell door and eight more prisoners, led by Dynamite Dick, joined them.[22]

Jones and Killian took the key from Tull, went back to the bull pen, and invited the thirty-five prisoners there to go with them. When all refused, Jones locked Tull in a cell, and the fourteen men ran hurriedly downstairs into the darkness.

Bob Shugart, one of the prisoners who had gone into the outer corridor, but refused to escape with the others, gave the alarm. A crowd gathered at the jail, but it was several minutes before Jim Montgomery, a day guard, arrived to release Tull and Miller.

The escapees fled north up Second Street to the railroad and followed the tracks out of town. After running half a mile, Doolin's rheumatic left leg began giving him trouble, and the group sat down and rested. When they started on again, they separated, and William Beck turned back to the jail and surrendered. He reported the direction the prisoners had taken, and Heck Thomas set out in pursuit, with a posse.

At the city limits, they met W. A. Koons, a clerk in the county treasurer's office, and Winnifred Warner, a young school teacher, on the road afoot. Koons had been driving Miss Warner from her home in the country to attend a school normal in Guthrie. A mile north of town, a man had leaped from the darkness onto the side of his buggy, poked a revolver in his ribs, and ordered them to get out. Two more men came up on the other side, one armed with a hatchet, and the young couple complied with alacrity. The three fugitives had climbed into

22 Charley Montgomery, serving ten months for larceny; Jim Black, under indictment for perjury from Oklahoma County; Bill Crittenden, serving one year from Pawnee County for larceny; Ed Lawrence, charged with post office robbery in Kingfisher County; Kid Phillips, outlaw and all-around tough, sentenced from Woods County for one year for post office robbery; E. V. Hix, charged with perjury and held on bond forfeiture; and William Beck, charged with selling whiskey in the Osage Nation.

the buggy, turned the horse north, and sped away in the night. Koons and Miss Warner described Bill Doolin, Dynamite Dick, and Jones, the counterfeiter.

Telegrams describing the break ordered marshals in from every point in the territory. Deputies from the north left for the Flatiron country southeast of Pawnee, others, from the west, headed for Stillwater and the Ingalls area, and large posses from Guthrie and the south combed Cowboy Flats and the Cimarron, east to Perkins. It was the greatest manhunt conducted by marshals in the history of the territory. But Doolin and Dynamite Dick had escaped. Only two of the other prisoners were ever captured.[23]

The marshals were confident Doolin had found refuge with friends and was still in the area.[24] Mrs. Doolin, at her father's

[23] Ed Lawrence was captured by Deputy Marshal Smith at his father's home, near Enid. George Lane, the half-breed, was arrested near Greenwood, a small town thirty miles east of Kansas City, by Deputies Thomas and Madsen, after they had learned his whereabouts from a letter to his brother in the territory.

[24] May Davison Rhodes, in the life story of her husband, Eugene Manlove Rhodes, *The Hired Man On Horseback*, p. 28, states that Bill Doolin used the Rhodes ranch as an asylum. Rhodes himself, commenting on the authenticity of his novel, *The Trusty Knaves*, in a letter to Ferris Greenslet, of Houghton Mifflin Company, in 1931, wrote: "This yarn is not the imaginings of a gin-excited mind. Only a few of the events took place as recorded and in the sequence recorded, but these were flesh and blood people whose minds acted just that way—during the brief span of years when they were on their own, without families to disgrace or to be considered. Only three of those people are alive today—Jack Farr (past 80), Lithpin Tham—and myself. I was the boy the bronc bucked on—and Bill Doolin shot that luckless horse, as recorded, to keep him from killing me. If you read the story you may remember—along at the last—'Taps'? When Bill Doolin told me goodby—some forty years ago, he rode straight to his death. He was going to quit and settle down in the San Andres. Trying to get away from the Nations with his wife and baby, he was killed before his wife's eyes."

Zoe A. Tilghman, in *Marshal of the Last Frontier*, p. 229, in relating events following Doolin's escape, interprets this to mean: "Doolin, perhaps getting aid from friends and perhaps going part way on the train, had reached the New Mexico ranch of Rhodes. Here he stayed for several weeks, recuperating, making plans to bring his wife and baby here and start a new life"; that very soon after he saved his host from being killed by a vicious horse, he returned to Oklahoma to get his wife.

It is the belief of this writer that Doolin's visit to the Rhodes ranch, in New Mexico, occurred in the summer of 1895, after the separation of the gang

home in Lawson, was watched closely. On August 23, she brought a team to the blacksmith shop of Tom and Charlie Noble to have them shod. Most horses went unshod in that country. This meant a journey. A messenger rode through the night. Heck Thomas received the word and headed for Lawson with a posse.

The evening of August 25, they saw a covered wagon loaded and made ready to take Mrs. Doolin and her baby out of the country. Doolin and his wife talked together in a sod and hay shed that served as a stable behind the post office building in which Reverend Ellsworth ran his grocery store. Doolin told his wife to drive down the road to the west, where he would join her and the baby at a spring two miles away. Edith went back to the wagon and Doolin led his saddled horse from the stable.

Thomas and his men concealed themselves in two groups in a cane patch on the south side of the trail, where Doolin would pass. He walked down the lane in the moonlight with the reins of his horse on one arm and the other holding a Winchester. When he was within firing range, Heck Thomas called to him through the clear, still night: "Halt, Bill!" Surprised, Doolin raised his Winchester and fired one shot in the direction of the voice, at random. Up the trail, the posse almost at the side of Doolin cried: "Stop; throw up your hands!" He whirled to fire his Winchester in their direction. A shot from Heck Thomas' rifle and the blasts of two sawed-off shotguns knocked him off his feet. Mrs. Doolin, hearing the shooting, leaped from the wagon, screaming: "Oh, my God, they have killed him!" Down the road her husband lay dead, with a rifle

---

following the Dover robbery; that Doolin returned for his wife and child and started to New Mexico by a northern route, daring not to cross western Oklahoma, where the marshals, sheriffs, and railroad detectives were searching for him; that by the time he reached Burden, Kansas, he was suffering such great pain from the rheumatism in his left leg that he decided to go to Eureka Springs and pick up his family later; that after his escape at Guthrie he hid out on the Cimarron and in the Creek Nation, for when he was killed by Heck Thomas' posse, *he wore a six-weeks' growth of beard and had on the same clothes he wore in the federal jail.*

bullet through his right side and his breast riddled with twenty-one buckshot.[25]

The body was placed in a wagon and taken to Guthrie, where "thousands viewed it in the morgue and speculated as to what realm the soul of Doolin had lodged in."[26] The reticence of Thomas and his posse about the details of the slaying started a rumor on the streets that Bill Doolin had "died a natural death and was then set up against a tree and filled with buckshot to make believe he was killed. . . ."[27]

The escape and death of the desperado "gave the express companies a chance to crawl out of their reward propositions"; Deputy Tilghman, who had risked his life so often and worked so hard in capturing the outlaw, never received a cent.[28] The Wells Fargo Express Company, in Kansas City, finally paid a

[25] This account is taken from facts related by Marshal Heck Thomas to the *Daily Oklahoma State Capital* and *Guthrie Daily Leader*, August 26, 1896, and an affidavit given this writer July 13, 1953, by Harry Hoke, a Lawson resident, who witnessed the circumstances surrounding and the death of Doolin. Other versions appear in Newsom, *op. cit.*, p. 194; Tilghman, *Outlaw Days*, pp. 101-103, and *Marshal of the Last Frontier*, pp. 229-230; Nix, *op. cit.*, pp. 229-230; Mootz, *op. cit.*

[26] *Guthrie Daily Leader*, August 27, 1896.

[27] *Daily Oklahoma State Capital*, August 25, 1896. Zoe A. Tilghman, *Marshal of the Last Frontier*, page 230, states: "The same envious story . . . slightly altered, was now and again repeated for many years. Doolin, they said, had died of consumption, and his father-in-law had made a deal with the officers for a share in the reward to be given to the daughter. Doolin's body was then set up and a charge of shot fired into it. The record of the coroner's inquest and the necessity they would have to 'fix' that official and a number of others, as well as the financial records of the governmental agencies and the firms which offered the rewards, show the falsity of this story, which pretends to trace to the authority of an uncle of Mrs. Doolin." (Reprinted by permission of the publishers, The Arthur H. Clark Company, Glendale, California). The *Guthrie Daily Leader* of August 26, 1896, reported: "Sensational stories are in circulation regarding the killing of the outlaw, but they are given no credence." And in Mr. Hoke's affidavit to this writer: "There are persons still living who will say that Bill Doolin was not killed by peace officers, but that he died of T. B. or some other natural cause, and that the officers made a deal with his widow for the body, promising to give her a share of the reward. How such a tale could get started is hard to figure out for it is a long way from the actual facts. Dead outlaws just do not walk and lead horses and fire rifles and six-shooters."

[28] *Guthrie Daily Leader*, August 27, 1896.

$500 reward for the capture of Doolin, which was divided between Heck Thomas and his posse.[29]

Bill Doolin's remains were removed to Summit View Cemetery, where a huge crowd witnessed the last rites. The *Stillwater Gazette* of August 27 commented simply: "Bill Doolin's left leg will get a rest now since he has been killed and buried."

[29] *El Reno News,* September 4, 1896.

End of the Doolin Gang

A posse had been on Dynamite Dick's trail for weeks.[1] At sunrise, December 4, 1896, they surprised the outlaw in camp in a hollow sixteen miles west of Newkirk. He was shot to death by Deputy Sheriff M. Dossi, of Kay County, and Deputy Marshal A. O. Lund, as he tried to escape.[2]

Little Dick West remained the only member of the Doolin gang not killed or behind prison bars. Except for the rumor that he had fled to Texas, the only record of his whereabouts after the Dover robbery is the statement of May Davison Rhodes[3] that he sought refuge, with Bill Doolin, on her husband's ranch in New Mexico. Mrs. Rhodes states that several outlaws hid out there for some time, and at least one of them, unknown to her husband, hid on the roughest mountain in their pasture for nearly two years. Probably Little Dick stayed in New Mexico until the summer of 1897, when he reappeared in Oklahoma, riding at the head of a new band of outlaws that became notorious as the Jennings gang. It consisted of two

[1] From Harry Hoke's affidavit to the writer: "The same night, after the shooting of Doolin, another posse of officers came to our house and said they were looking for Dynamite Dick, Doolin's partner. They went down to the place where Doolin was killed and some of them watched the Ellsworth house, but after a while they all came back and father gave them permission to sleep in the hay loft of our barn. . . ."

[2] *Daily Oklahoma State Capital,* December 4, 1896; *Guthrie Daily Leader,* December 5, 1896.

[3] *Op. cit.,* p. 28.

pairs of brothers: Al and Frank Jennings and Morris and Pat O'Malley. Except for Little Dick West, all of this gang were rank amateurs.

Al and Frank Jennings were the sons of J. D. F. Jennings, who served two terms as probate judge of Pottawatomie County at Tecumseh, 1896-1898 and 1898-1900. Before that he had held a like position in Woods County. Al Jennings had been elected county attorney of Canadian County, at El Reno, in 1892, and served from January, 1893, to January, 1895. He was defeated for re-election and went to Woodward to engage in law practice with his brothers, Ed and John.

All the brothers had learned enough law in their father's office to pass bar examinations, "but only Ed, the eldest, seemed to have the stuff in him to succeed." Al "just loafed" around town; the younger brother, Frank, "dealt cards in a gambling house for a living."[4]

One day a suit arose in Justice of Peace Miller's court between two cowmen over pasture rent. In defending the case, Ed, Al, and John Jennings incurred the displeasure of their opponent, the picturesque and fiery, long-haired gun-lawyer, Temple Houston, ex-Senator, and son of General Sam Houston, first president of the Republic of Texas. On October 8, 1895, another case came to trial in Justice Williams' court in which several young men were charged with theft of a keg of beer from the Santa Fe railroad. Houston, the company's attorney, appeared with County Attorney Smith for the prosecution, and the firm of Jennings & Jennings appeared for the defense. Houston and Ed Jennings clashed over a number of minor points during the trial, their enmity for each other growing as the case progressed. Then Houston asked a witness a question, Jennings objected, and an argument followed. "You're a liar!" Jennings shouted, and guns were drawn. Only the prompt interference of officers prevented their use. The Court rebuked both attorneys, and they apologized, but their

4 Burton Rascoe, *Belle Starr, the Bandit Queen,* (Appendix Two—The Jennings Gang: Comic Relief) pp. 268-269.

tempers were seething. Late that evening, Houston, accompanied by his intimate friend, ex-Sheriff and former United States Deputy Marshal Jack Love, entered the Cabinet Saloon. Soon after, Ed and John Jennings came in, and the quarrel was renewed. Very few words were spoken before shooting commenced, Love and Houston emptying their revolvers at the Jennings and they returning the fire. Ed Jennings was hit in the head with one of the first shots, but managed to shoot once as he staggered forward to his death. John Jennings, with his gun arm shot away, ran outside and reached his home after fainting once from the loss of blood.[5]

Houston was tried for the murder of Ed Jennings, but was acquitted on the mitigating circumstance that Ed Jennings had been shot through the head from a range to appear that his brother, who was behind him, must have fired the fatal shot.[6] Al Jennings left the room, cursing the Court and swearing vengeance for his brother's death. The next night he and Frank "got drunk and boasted around town how they were going to kill Houston," but "when they woke up the next morning with hangovers and recalled their boasts, they remembered, also, what a quick deadshot Houston was, and decided it was about time they left town."[7] They rode around the territory afterward, threatening Houston, but somehow never meeting him. Apparently they "turned their hatred into less admirable channels; from attorneys they became outlaws."[8]

Judge Jennings was living at Tecumseh by this time, and Al and Frank lived with their father, with no regular occupations. They were known to be consorting with hard characters in that region, and, while their reputations became bad among the officers, there were no warrants out for them.[9] The officers

---

[5] *Oklahoma City Times-Journal,* October 10, 1895; *Daily Oklahoman,* October 11, 1895; *Daily Oklahoma State Capital,* October 19, 1895.

[6] *Daily Oklahoman,* May 16, 1896; *South and West,* May 21, 1896.

[7] Rascoe, *op. cit.,* p. 270.

[8] Gish, *op. cit.,* p. 56.

[9] Newsom, *op. cit.,* p. 195; Tilghman, *Marshal of the Last Frontier,* p. 241.

kept track of them pretty well, and they were seen often in Tecumseh and Shawnee.[10]

There is no record of where or why Al and Frank Jennings teamed up with Little Dick West. Zoe A. Tilghman[11] thinks the gang was organized in August, 1897, at Tecumseh. Burton Rascoe,[12] states that they had been "palling around" at Woodward "with a sawed-off illiterate little moron named Richard West, alias 'Little Dick,' a survivor of the Doolin gang" and "reading too many dime novels about Jesse James with incredible identification"; that they took him along when they went down to their father's place at Tecumseh, and being "temperamentally averse to doing any work," let Little Dick "talk them and a couple of Tecumseh plow-pushers," Morris and Pat O'Malley, "into the idea of being heroic bandits and holding up a train."

At 9:00 P. M., August 16, the gang struck west from Tecumseh and held up the Santa Fe passenger train at Edmond, fourteen miles north of Oklahoma City. They concealed themselves about the water tank until the train was ready to start, then boarded the blind baggage. They climbed over the tender, covered the engineer with six-shooters, and ordered him to run the train down the track three miles south and stop where an extra man held their horses.[13]

They went back to the express car and tried to batter down the door when the messenger refused to open it. In the excite-

10 "This is the period in which, in his book, *(Beating Back)*, Al Jennings claims to have been making a tour of South America, and shining in polite society in New Orleans; in making an escape from the detectives who were after him, by the aid of a beautiful young lady who was quite tender toward him. This is absolutely false, for no warrant had been issued for him, he was not charged with any crime, so no detective or officers were after him. The tour of South America, which he alleges, could not have been made within this period, especially with transportation on a tramp steamer, and with time out for other adventures, as he says. This period, as fixed by known dates, was one year and ten months; from October 18, 1895, to August 18, 1897."—Zoe A. Tilghman, "The True Jennings Story," *Daily Oklahoman*, March 25, 1951.

11 *Outlaw Days*, p. 104.

12 Rascoe, *op. cit.*, pp. 270-271.

13 *Daily Oklahoman*, August 17, 1897; *Daily Oklahoma State Capital*, August 17, 1897.

ment, they had forgotten to capture the conductor, and this
veteran leaped off the train, holding a lantern aloft to see, and
came running toward them, demanding what was the matter.
"For all the robbers knew, he might have had a Winchester,
too."[14] They didn't wait to hear the messenger's "erroneous
answer" that the train was being robbed, but "ran like jack
rabbits, leaped on their horses and flew like bats out of hell."[15]

Edmond was only forty-five miles from Tecumseh, and the
messenger knew the Jennings brothers. "He'd have known
their voices, even if they had been dressed in a Ku Klux Klan
fool's cap and night shirt."[16] Within twenty-four hours, Bill
Tilghman had a sworn statement from the man who had held
their horses, and warrants were issued for all five of them.[17]
Thus the Jennings were first marked as bandits, "even if they
hadn't earned the label."[18]

Two weeks later the gang tried to hold up the Missouri,
Kansas, and Texas passenger train at Bond Switch, twenty-five
miles south of Muskogee, in the Indian Territory. They piled
ties on the tracks, but the engineer increased the speed of the
train and raced through the obstruction.

Having no success with trains, they decided to rob the Santa
Fe station at Purcell. All express matter was transferred at this
point—an ideal place to loot it. A night watchman making his
rounds discovered five men hiding in the yards. As he approached, they slipped under a platform and disappeared, but
he "had seen their guns and heard the jingle of their spurs"
and reported to the agent that he believed they intended to
rob the place.[19] The agent notified the city marshal, who
rushed to the station with a posse of a dozen men. But the
"would-be robbers" had fled in the darkness.

14 Newsom, *op. cit.,* p. 195.
15 Rascoe, *op. cit.,* p. 272.
16 *Ibid.*
17 Tilghman, *Marshal of the Last Frontier,* p. 241.
18 Rascoe, *op. cit.,* p. 272.
19 Newsom, *op. cit.,* pp. 195-196.

A few days later, Tilghman learned that the gang was planning to rob the bank at Minco, and wired President Campbell. Campbell organized a group of citizens to guard the bank day and night, and the plan was abandoned.

The gang was now down to its last penny. Their clothing was tattered. They had eaten only such meals as they could obtain from scattered farm houses. The railroads were running night trains under heavy guard, and the detectives and marshals were very active. Finally, in desperation, they decided to hold up a train in broad daylight.

At eleven o'clock the morning of October 1, 1897, they rode up to a section gang working on the Rock Island, eight miles north of Chickasha, and ordered them to flag the train while they hid in the brush along the tracks.

As the train stopped, one of the O'Malleys boarded the cab and covered the fireman and engineer. The other O'Malley and Frank Jennings went back to terrorize the trainmen and passengers. They ordered everybody outside and made them stand with their backs to the coaches, then went down the line, pointing their weapons and collecting contributions netting $300 cash and Conductor Dan Dacy's watch.[20]

Al Jennings and Little Dick West entered the express car. There were two safes—a small and a large one—both billed through to Fort Worth, and the messenger couldn't open them. This time Al was prepared for an emergency. He had brought along some dynamite, but had no experience in the use of it. He placed the sticks on the large safe, lifted the small safe on top of it, then lighted the fuse and leaped outside.

The explosion ripped the side out of the express car, catapulting the small safe into the grade ditch without even denting it, and leaving the large safe standing in the midst of the smoking wreckage, unharmed. The robbers went back into the express car, but found nothing of value to take along. They

20 *Daily Oklahoman,* October 2, 1897; *Daily Oklahoma State Capital,* October 2, 1897.

seized a jug of whiskey and a stalk of bananas and headed west toward the Washita Mountains.[21]

When the train reached Chickasha, a posse left immediately in pursuit of the gang. Another started south from El Reno. Believing the outlaws might double back into the Pottawatomie country, Deputy Frank Cochrane joined Marshal Stowe's posse at Purcell and hurried to Lexington, where they would have to cross the Santa Fe, and a special train from Guthrie, carrying a posse in charge of Tilghman and Heck Thomas, arrived at Chickasha, were transferred to the Choctaw line, and taken to Shawnee.[22] They scattered through the country, watching all roads and bridges day and night, but found no trace of the outlaws.

The gang had ridden west for a time, and after making a dinner of bananas and whiskey, circled north until they reached a dugout on Cottonwood Creek, southwest of Guthrie. Here they divided the loot and remained two days, a disgruntled, poorly clad, starving bunch, who had operated less than two months and netted barely $60 each and one silver watch.

"Little Dick West could not help but compare this band of battered wanderers with his former companions of the dashing Doolin-Dalton gang," writes Nix.[23] "The situation became intolerable to him. One chilly evening when the others were saddling their horses for a night's ride, he bade them good-bye and rode off to the south, without an excuse or a word of comment."

The gang, now under the leadership of Al Jennings, headed back toward the Indian Territory. Their garments were thin and the weather turned bitter cold. They reached the little town of Cushing in the middle of the night and dismounted in front of Lee Nutter's store. Al Jennings awakened the proprietor, telling him they wanted burial clothes for a man who

---

21 *Guthrie Daily Leader*, October 5, 1897.
22 *Daily Oklahoman*, October 2, 1897.
23 *Op. cit.*, p. 254.

had died. When Nutter opened the door, the gang rushed inside, covering him with six-shooters. They exchanged their tattered rags for warm workmen's clothing, helped themselves to tobacco and groceries, and took forty dollars from the cash till, then rode east into the hills.

Deputy Marshal James F. "Bud" Ledbetter, at Muskogee, received word that the gang had entered his district. They had been charged with robbing the train at Chickasha, the newspapers were full of charges of other train robberies, and heavy rewards were being offered for their apprehension. Ledbetter took a posse and started after them. He rode out thirty miles east of Checotah. He learned they had been seen on the Pittsburg & Gulf railroad at the little station of Barren Fork, and he hunted for them in that area several days. He received information that they were in the Concharty Mountains, where he hunted them for six days. The next place he picked up their trail was at a blacksmith shop eight miles north of Tulsa. He learned they had been sighted in the Cherokee Nation, where they robbed the post office at Foyil, and headed south again for the Spike S ranch, between Snake Creek and the Arkansas, traveling under assumed names and heavily armed with revolvers and Winchester saddle guns.[24]

On the night of November 29, Ledbetter and his posse of six—Paden Tolbert, Lon Lewis, John McClanahan, Jake Elliott, and Joe Thompson and his son—located the gang at the home of Mrs. Harless. One of the O'Malleys, posted as a lookout, lay in a wagon about three hundred yards from the ranch house. Ledbetter crawled up to the wagon, thrust his Winchester against the man's body and told him to climb out and keep still. They took the prisoner to the ranch barn, tied him securely, and left him in a stall.

The barn was north of the house. Close by stood a log cabin with a stone chimney. Paden Tolbert took a position at the corner of the cabin, Thompson and his son concealed them-

---

24 *Jennings v. United States*, 53 S. W. 456.

selves in a thicket to the northwest, and McClanahan and
Elliott circled southeast behind a stone wall. Ledbetter and
Lewis remained in the barn.

At dawn, Clarence Inscoe, a brother of Mrs. Harless, came
out to feed the stock. When he entered the barn, he was captured and tied. He informed Ledbetter that Al and Frank
Jennings and the other O'Malley were in the house.

Within a few minutes, the hired girl came out on the
kitchen porch and called "Breakfast!" then hurried back inside, shivering from a blast of cutting north wind.

A short time later, Mrs. Harless came to the door and called
her brother. When he did not answer, she threw a shawl about
her shoulders and ran to the barn. Ledbetter stepped behind
her as she came inside, blocking her escape.

Quietly the marshal told her his official capacity and that
he knew the three men in her house were the other members
of the Jennings gang.

"The place is surrounded and they have no chance to escape," he said. "Go to the house, tell them those facts and to
come out with their hands in the air. If they refuse to surrender, you and the hired girl must leave the house at once."

The frightened woman ran back to the house. Ledbetter
took a position behind the chimney of the cabin and waited.
He heard voices inside raised in argument, and there were
"demonstrations that preparations were being made for resistance." Suddenly the door opened and the woman and hired
girl, wrapped in heavy blankets, hurried across the yard. They
were hardly out of range before Al Jennings opened fire on
Ledbetter, spattering the chimney with lead. The officers "responded" and "from sixty to one hundred shots flew thick and
fast in both directions." [25]

Ledbetter and Tolbert, both excellent shots and with a
good range on the doors and windows, poured such a hail of
lead into the house that in five minutes the bandits "found the

---

25 *Ibid.*

place untenable" and fled out the back door and through an orchard. Elliott and McClanahan fired from behind the wall. A bullet gashed the muscles of Pat O'Malley's left leg, Al Jennings was wounded slightly in both legs above the knees, and a charge from Lon Lewis' shotgun from the barn riddled Frank Jennings' clothing with buckshot without injuring him. The three outlaws reached the timber on Snake Creek, crossed the stream and ran into the hills, where Ledbetter and his men lost them in the brush thickets.

The posse returned to the ranch and took the outlaws' horses and saddles and their prisoner to Muskogee. Meanwhile, the fugitives met two Euchee Indian boys in a wagon. They took their outfit and drove south toward Okmulgee. After hiding in the brush that night and all next day, they released the boys and drove on in the wagon.

Ledbetter got the report and hurried to Rock Creek Crossing with his posse. The trail sloped down to the stream through a deep cut. They felled a tree across the cut, making it impossible for a wagon to pass, and took positions along the high banks on each side.

The wagon carrying the bandits jolted down the frozen trail until the horses breasted the fallen tree. In the same instant the outlaws found themselves looking into the muzzle of Ledbetter's rifle and heard his command to surrender. They were trapped. Their other choice was to fight and die. All promptly climbed from the wagon and put up their hands.[26]

They were taken to Muskogee, where Al Jennings was indicted on a charge of assault with intent to kill upon the person of Marshal Ledbetter in the battle at the ranch. In the May, 1898, term of court he was tried and convicted and sentenced to five years imprisonment at Ft. Leavenworth,[27] then delivered to the marshal for the southern district of the Indian Territory and held in jail at Ardmore until February, 1899,

[26] *Guthrie Daily Leader,* December 8, 1897; *Daily Oklahoma State Capital,* December 8, 1897.

[27] *Jennings v. United States,* 53 S. W. 456.

when he went on trial for robbing the United States mail in
the train holdup at Chickasha. He was found guilty and sentenced, on February 17, 1899, to imprisonment in the Ohio
state penitentiary, at Columbus, for life.[28] The other members
of the gang, tried at a later date, received only five years each.

After his separation from the Jennings gang, Little Dick
West rode to the home of a friend in Lincoln County and hid
out there until Christmas day. On February 2, 1898, Tilghman
and Heck Thomas learned that he had been seen at the gang's
old rendezvous, on Cottonwood creek. They organized a posse
and surrounded the place, but Little Dick had left the night

---

[28] Al Jennings' first conviction was appealed to the United States court of
appeals for the Indian Territory, and the judgment and sentence of the lower
court were affirmed October 26, 1899, while he was in the penitentiary at Columbus. On June 23, 1900, through the persistent efforts of his brother John and
Judge Amos Ewing, a friend of the family at Kingfisher, President McKinley
commuted his life sentence "to imprisonment for five years, with all allowances
for good conduct." With this commutation and allowances for good behavior,
Jennings' term would have expired on June 20, 1902; but a few days prior to
this date, on an order signed by the United States attorney for the northern
district of the Indian Territory, he was taken from the Ohio prison and transported to the penitentiary at Ft. Leavenworth. On petition for a writ of habeas
corpus to the Circuit Court for the eastern district of Missouri, it was held that
the marshal for the northern district of the Indian Territory had acted without
authority of law in surrendering Jennings to the custody of the marshal of the
southern district after a judgment and sentence had been pronounced committing him to prison at Ft. Leavenworth for assault with intent to kill, thereby
postponing the execution of the first sentence indefinitely; that due to these
circumstances the prisoner had been in actual custody, undergoing imprisonment, since June 4, 1898—a part of the time in jail at Ardmore, a part of the
time in the penitentiary at Columbus, Ohio, and a small portion of the time
in the penitentiary at Ft. Leavenworth. Deducting the allowance in his favor
for good behavior at the rate of two months per year, as prescribed by federal
statute, his term would have expired prior to the time his application for a
writ of habeas corpus was filed. Jennings was ordered discharged. (*In re Jennings,* 118 Federal Reporter 479)

He was released November 13, 1902, and returned to Oklahoma. On February 2, 1907, on recommendation of the attorney general, who found that
"during the four years and three months since elapsed he has been a good citizen," President Theodore Roosevelt issued him a "citizenship pardon," which
was afterward displayed in theaters where the movie *Beating Back* was showing.
On the strength of this publicity, he sought the Democratic nomination for
governor of Oklahoma in 1914, but was sorely defeated. He retired to a peaceful
life on a chicken ranch in southern California.

before.[29] They lost his trail on Turkey Creek, in Kingfisher County.

Thinking the marshals would be looking for him miles away, the outlaw doubled back to the farm of Ed Fitzgerald, four miles south of Guthrie, to hide out until spring. Fitzgerald's neighbor was Harmon Arnett, who lived half a mile away, and Little Dick made frequent visits to his place for food. One day Mrs. Arnett remarked to another woman that a friend of her neighbor's had been visiting her husband and she was afraid he was going to get Harmon into trouble. This woman mentioned the fact to Mrs. Hart, wife of the district clerk, who told Sheriff Rinehart.[30]

On the morning of April 8, Tilghman, Heck Thomas, and Deputy Bill Fossett, with Sheriff Rinehart and possemen A. M. Thomas and Ben Miller, watched the outlaw ride up to the Arnett home, dismount and unsaddle his horse. The officers approached the house from the front and went around toward the barn.

Fossett and Rinehart were together, the possemen (with Tilghman and Thomas) going in another direction to search. When they came in sight of the barn, a man standing by a shed started to run toward the timber. The officers called to him to halt. He replied by turning and firing three shots with a revolver. One shot went dangerously near Rinehart and one by Fossett. The officers then began firing. Sheriff Rinehart fired twice with a double barrelled shotgun, and Deputy Fossett fired three shots with a Winchester. At the first shots, West turned and fired again and started reloading his revolver as he ran. The second shot from (Fossett's) Winchester struck him in the right side and the third in the right eye, just missing the nose. He fell forward and was dead when the officers reached his side.[31]

29 *Daily Oklahoma State Capital*, April 8, 1898.
30 *Guthrie Daily Leader*, April 8, 1898.
31 *Daily Oklahoma State Capital*, April 8, 1898.

CHAPTER
15

The Last Outlaw

The death of Little Dick West ended the Doolin trail. It was not, however, the end of organized banditry in Oklahoma. A few scattered gangs sprang up at the turn of the century, but they belonged to a new era.

Oklahoma was being settled rapidly.

Never before had a people formed themselves so quickly into an organization with a common cause.

On May 25, 1895, the Kickapoo Reservation, lying east of Old Oklahoma and comprising most of western Lincoln County, was opened by the last great run.

In the extreme southwest corner of Oklahoma, the counties of Harmon, Jackson, and Greer and part of Beckham had been a part of Texas, known as Greer County. The Organic Act of 1890 had defined Oklahoma Territory as extending to the south fork of Red River. On March 16, 1896, the supreme court upheld the 1890 act, and Texas lost Greer County.

The surplus lands of the Comanche, Kiowa, and Plains Apache and those of the Wichita, Caddo, and affiliated tribes were settled by a land lottery August 6, 1901. Although only 2,080,000 acres of land were available, over 160,000 persons registered for claims.

With the rapid increase of population, business interests, and property rights came such growth in the business of the courts that on May 2, 1902, two additional judges were added to the Oklahoma Territory judiciary, and the new court divided Oklahoma Territory into seven districts, with the Territorial Supreme Court composed of the justices of each district and each member acting as the trial court justice within his own district. The number of United States commissioners had gradually increased, and these officials handled much of the business that would have been transacted by justices of the peace and county courts under state governments.

Swiftly now came other openings. Lying along the eastern border of the Cherokee Outlet were the Ponca and Otoe-Missouri holdings. An act of Congress on April 21, 1904, divided the lands, abolished the reservations, and attached the areas to the counties in which they were located.

On June 6, 1906, the portion of the Kiowa-Comanche-Caddo holdings reserved from settlement as common grazing grounds for the Indians in the opening of 1901, was dissolved, and several small "pastures" aggregating about 80,000 acres were attached to the white man's land.

The Osage Indians and the Kaw Indians at the northwest corner of the Osage Nation had resisted all attempts toward allotment of their lands. They were so bitter toward the plan that the Dawes Act of 1887 was not made applicable to these reservations. The Osage and Kaw holdings covered some 1,600,000 acres. They maintained an elaborate form of government. But two factions developed within the tribes. The half-breeds wanted allotments, the full-bloods fought against it. Discovery of oil on the reservation, and large sums of money owed white traders for years, complicated matters. The political strife grew. The Indians fell prey to white shysters. On June 28, 1906, Congress provided for individual division of the lands and funds to the Indians.

Oklahoma was separated into two regions: Oklahoma Territory, the areas opened to settlement, as the west half; Indian Territory, the land of the Five Civilized Tribes, as the east half.

The torrential movement of the white man into Oklahoma Territory, jumping the population from 398,331 to more than

700,000, and the steady drift of whites into the Indian Territory, increasing its population from 180,182 to 392,060,
pointed to the eventual doom of the governments of the Five
Civilized Tribes. Since 1893, the Dawes Commission had negotiated with the Indians to resign their tribal titles and take
allotments. In 1898, they agreed to the plan and were brought
under United States laws. Existing towns were incorporated,
new townsites reserved, the Nations divided into recording
districts for filing of deeds, mortgages, and legal papers.

New railroads built into the Nations to connect the two
territories. Track mileage in Oklahoma Territory increased
from 900 miles in 1900 to 2,888 miles by 1906. Oil production
and mining had begun at the turn of the century. As early as
1897, Cassius M. Barnes, the fourth territorial governor, reported that Oklahoma had made a crop record "which aston-
ishes the world." Eastern capital was coming in. The free
homes bill of June 17, 1900, wiped out any indebtedness of
the homesteader to the government for his quarter-section
farm.

By 1901, statehood was the leading issue, and without declaring itself for either single or double blessedness, the territorial legislature adopted a strong memorial to Congress:

Oklahoma's population was "increasing with unexampled
rapidity." It had an area of 40,000 square miles, $150,000,000
in wealth "produced in a single decade from the wild prairie
and wilderness," 2,000 common schools, six "great" institutions of learning, and more churches in proportion to population and wealth than "elsewhere in the world." "Such a people
ought not to be longer held in political subjection."

It added that the Indian Territory was "supplemental" to
Oklahoma. It referred to 350,000 whites and blacks there without political rights, "peasants of the soil to 70,000 persons of
Indian extraction" (notwithstanding they had come against
the wishes of the Indian) and pointed out that these "disfran-
chised" residents could not levy taxes for roads, schools,
colleges, and asylums.

The whole period was a preparation for single statehood. And yet, the two territories, in natural resources, features, and developments, were the exact opposites to form a single state. Even the natures of the two populations were different. The chiefs of the Five Civilized Tribes met in an attempt to have the Indian Territory brought in as a separate state. They drew up a constitution and designated the area as the state of Sequoyah.

Congress refused to act on the matter. Representative Hamilton, of Michigan, introduced an enabling bill authorizing the admission of the two territories as one state. He told the House, when the debate began on January 24, 1906:

"These territories are rich in corn, cotton, wheat, coal, gas, and oil, and their cities, staked out upon the level plain but a few years ago by a virile population drawn from all parts of the union, have sprung like magic into opulence and power, equipped with every device of energy and luxury. . . . Indian names, once synonyms of savage warfare, have become the musical names of municipalities, of civilized progress."

Representative Charles C. Reid, of Arkansas, pointed out that Oklahoma Territory alone "possessed more wealth than any state when it was admitted to the union" and 200,000 more people. It had more school children "than many states today have population."

Representative Beall, of Texas, declared the government had made a pledge to the Indians that their lands should never be embraced in or annexed to any other territory or state and that without their consent it was proposed to merge them "with other people and another territory." He added, however, that Congress had been driven by necessity to agree to the union because it would be a "greater crime to longer deny a majority of the people of the two territories the right of self-government."

And Oklahoma Territory's delegate to Congress, Bird S. McGuire, argued: "If we propose to civilize the Indian, if it is the policy of the American government to better his condi-

tion, the quickest method, the surest plan to succeed would
be immediate statehood for these people."

Congress passed the enabling act June 16, 1906. A Constitutional Convention, meeting in Guthrie, provided for the new
state a complete court system, the judicial power to be vested
in a supreme court, district courts, county and municipal
courts, and justices of the peace. The constitution was ratified
by a large majority vote of the people; Charles N. Haskell was
elected as first governor; and at 10:16 o'clock the morning of
November 16, 1907, President Roosevelt signed a proclamation declaring Oklahoma to be a state of the Union.

With the extermination of the outlaw gangs, the work of
the United States marshals had dwindled to small cases and
routine. With statehood, law enforcement was turned over to
local authorities, police departments, and sheriffs' offices, except for offenses committed in violation of federal laws.

Many of the marshals remained in law enforcement work:
Bill Tilghman, who became chief of police in Oklahoma City,
sheriff of Lincoln County, and city marshal of Cromwell,
where he was killed by a drunken prohibition officer during
the oil boom of 1924; Heck Thomas, who became first chief of
police at Lawton, but soon returned to the United States
marshal's office, accepting and carrying out hazardous tasks for
the government until his death August 15, 1912; Bud Ledbetter, who held the record as the oldest long-termed officer of
the Southwest, performed his last duties as sheriff of Muskogee
County and spent his last days in the hills where he had captured the Jennings gang; Chris Madsen, who transferred to
the marshal's office of the western district of Missouri, returned
to the Indian Territory as deputy marshal of the southern district, then was chief deputy under the "wolf-catchin' " marshal,
John Abernathy, who served the western district of Oklahoma
from 1906 to 1910. Madsen succeeded Abernathy until the
office was filled by an appointment by President Taft, and was
chief deputy under Marshal Cade from 1911 to 1913. He con-

tinued his federal service in various capacities until he retired, in 1933. He died at Guthrie in 1947, at the age of 90.

Others were modest. When their jobs were finished, they went back to their quiet occupations and died, forgotten heroes in a land they served so well and for so little praise.

In 1908, 520 territorial convicts were transferred from Lansing, Kansas, to the old federal jail, at McAlester, which Oklahoma had rented for a state prison.

Among them was Arkansas Tom.

After he had served seventeen years as a model prisoner, his brother, a minister at Carthage, Missouri, set to work to obtain a pardon. When Nix left the marshal's office, in 1896, he had returned to the wholesale mercantile business, finally moving to Joplin. He was now living in St. Louis, dealing in stocks, bonds, and investments, and the brother came to him there with the report of Tom's perfect conduct in prison. Time had mellowed Nix's feelings in the matter, and the prison report caused him to use his influence in the convict's behalf and secure the assistance of other United States officers who had participated in the arrest and prosecution. Arkansas Tom was released on parole November 26, 1910.

He came straight to Oklahoma City and reported to Bill Tilghman. He wanted to "make amends and show the people that a bandit can turn over a new leaf."

Tilghman found work for him with a wholesale grocery firm in eastern Oklahoma. Later, Nix gave him a clerical job in his St. Louis firm and found him "apparently very accurate and trustworthy."

A year later, he returned to Oklahoma City to work for Bill Tilghman. This was in 1914, and Tilghman, Nix, and Chris Madsen had formed the Eagle Film Company and arranged for making a motion picture entitled, "The Passing of the Oklahoma Outlaws." Arkansas Tom played his part.

Two years later he returned to Missouri to visit his people. He became involved in a bank burglary at Neosho; was arrested and convicted and sentenced on March 12, 1917, to the state penitentiary at Jefferson City for a term of eight years.

He was discharged from the Missouri penitentiary November 11, 1921. In Oklahoma, his parole was revoked, but he never returned to the state where he had ridden, robbed, and killed with the notorious Doolin gang. He held up a bank at Asbury, Missouri, and on August 16, 1924, was slain by Joplin police while resisting arrest.

He was the last outlaw.

Bibliography

Admire, J. V. "April 22, 1889—The Crack of A Gun—A Great State Is Born." *Kingfisher Free Press,* April 17, 1939. (Published serially in the *Free Press* in 1905.)

Alley, John. *City Beginnings in Oklahoma Territory,* University of Oklahoma Press, Norman, 1939.

Alliance Courier, March 22, 1894.

Anonymous. *The Dalton Gang of the Far West,* n. p., n. d. (apparently written in 1892 shortly after the Coffeyville raid).

Barnard, Evan G. *A Rider of the Cherokee Strip.* Houghton Mifflin Company, Boston and New York, 1936.

Best, Frank J., "A Railroader Looks Back on 1889." The *Guthrie Leader,* Golden Anniversary Edition, April 16, 1939.

Bierer, A. G. C. "Early Day Courts and Lawyers." *The Chronicles of Oklahoma,* VIII (1930), pp. 2-12.

Blackwell Times-Record, November 12, 1896.

Canadian County Republican, June 1, 1894.

Candee, Helen C. "Social Conditions in Our Newest Territory." *Forum,* June, 1898.

Canton, Frank. *Frontier Trails* (an autobiography). Edited by E. E. Dale, Houghton Mifflin Company, Boston and New York, 1930.

Carroll, Lew F. "An Eighty-Niner Who Pioneered the Cherokee Strip." *The Chronicles of Oklahoma,* XXIV (1943), pp. 162-170.

Chambers, Homer S. "Early Day Railroad Building Operations in Western Oklahoma," *The Chronicles of Oklahoma,* XXI (1943), pp. 162-170.

Chapman, Berlin B. "Dissolution of the Wichita Reservation," *The Chronicles of Oklahoma,* XXII (1944), pp. 192-209, 300-314.

Chapple, Joe Mitchell. "The Story of Oklahoma," *National Magazine,* April, 1908.

Cherokee Advocate, April 25, 1894.

Cherokee Messenger, March 31, 1905.

Coffeyville Journal, October 14-26, 1892.

Coming Events, June 28, 1894; August 2-9, 1894.

Crawford, W. D. "Oklahoma and Indian Territory," *New England Magazine,* June, 1890.

Cunniff, M. G. "The New State of Oklahoma," *World's Work,* June, 1906.

Daily Ardmoreite, June 13, 1894.

Daily Oklahoman, January-December, 1894; April-December, 1895; May-March, 1896; August-October, 1897; August 29, 1898; March-August, 1904; April 22, 1909; January 8, 1911; July 14, 1911; August 18, 1912; February 21, 1915; August 21, 1921; November 12, 1922; December 9, 1938.

Daily Oklahoma State Capital, January-December, 1893; January-December, 1894; January-December, 1895; January-December, 1896; January-December, 1897; April 8, 1898; August 1, 1903.

Dale, Edward Everett, "End of Heroic Age Came When Oklahoma Ranches Gave Way to Homesteads." *Daily Oklahoman,* April 23, 1939.

———. "Land Lottery of 1901 Set New Style In Openings," *Daily Oklahoman,* April 23, 1939.

Dale, Edward Everett, and Morris L. Wardell, *History of Oklahoma,* Prentice-Hall, Inc., New York, 1948.

Dalton, Emmett. *When the Daltons Rode* (written in collaboration with Jack Jungmeyer), Doubleday, Doran & Co., New York, 1931.

Davis, Clyde Brion. *The Arkansas,* Farrar & Rinehart, New York, 1940.

Dollar, G. "The Oklahoma Boomer," *Strand Magazine,* September, 1897.

Doyle, Thomas H. "Single versus Double Statehood," *The Chronicles of Oklahoma,* V (1927), pp. 18-41, 117-148, 266-286.

Draper, Wm. R. "The Forty-Six State," *Munsey's Magazine,* May, 1903.

————. *The Land Boomer: A Personal Experience Story of the Rush of Speculators, Homeseekers and Settlers to the Great Southwest* (pamphlet), Haldeman-Julius Publications, Girard, Kansas, 1946.

————. *The Last Government Land Lottery: A Reporter Tells What He Saw on the Oklahoma and Indian Territory Frontier in the 90s* (pamphlet), Haldeman-Julius Publications, Girard, Kansas, 1946.

Eagle-Gazette, January-June, 1894.

"Ed Short, Fearless Gunman," *Daily Oklahoman,* February 29, 1920.

Edmond Sun-Democrat, November 12, 1897.

Elliott, David Stewart (Editor, *Coffeyville Journal*), *Last Raid of the Daltons: A Reliable Recital of the Battle With the Bandits at Coffeyville, Kansas, October 5, 1892.* Copyrighted and published by the *Coffeyville Daily Journal,* 128 W. 9th, Coffeyville, Kansas, Oct. 22, 1892.

El Reno Democrat, April-July, 1894.

El Reno Globe, April-November, 1895.

El Reno News, September 4, 1896; February 17, 1899.

Enid Daily News, June 8, 1894.

Enid Daily Wave, January-August, 1894; April-September, 1895.

Ex parte John Curtis Barber No. A-11064, July 21, 1948, 87 Oklahoma Criminal Reports 201.

Fanning, Pete. *Great Crimes of the West* (The Dalton Gang, pp. 184-192). Published by Pete Fanning, 951 Eddy Street, San Francisco, California.

Forbes, Gerald. *Guthrie: Oklahoma's First Capital* (No. 3, Historic Oklahoma Series), University of Oklahoma Press, Norman, 1938.

Foreman, Grant. *A History of Oklahoma,* University of Oklahoma Press, Norman, 1942.

Fort Smith Elevator, May 8-15, 1891; September 18, 1891; June 10, 1892; September 13, 1895.

Frame, Barnaby. "Pint-Sized Peril." *Inside Detective,* June, 1946.

French, J. L. (Edited by). *A Gallery of Old Rogues.* Alfred H. King, Inc., New York, 1931.

Gish, Anthony. *American Bandits: A Biographical History of the Nation's Outlaws From the Days of the James Boys, the Youngers, the Jennings, the Dalton Gang and Billy the Kid, Down to Modern Bandits of Our Own Day, Including Dillinger, "Pretty Boy" Floyd, and Others* (pamphlet), Haldeman-Julius Publications, Girard, Kansas, 1938.

Gittinger, Roy. *The Formation of the State of Oklahoma, 1803-1906,* University of Oklahoma Press, Norman, 1939.

Glasscock, C. B. *Bandits of the Southern Pacific,* Frederick A. Stokes Company, New York, 1929.

Graves, Richard S. *Oklahoma Outlaws: A Graphic History of the Early Days in Oklahoma; the Bandits who Terrorized the First Settlers and the Marshals who Fought them to Extinction; Covering a Period of Twenty-Five Years,* State Printing and Publishing Company, Oklahoma City, 1915.

Guthrie Daily Leader, July-December, 1893; March-December, 1894; April-August, 1895; March-December, 1896; August-December, 1897; April 9, 1898; April 16, 1939; April 16, 1952.

Guthrie Daily News, July-November, 1889; June-September, 1893.

Hafen, LeRoy R., and Carl Coke Rister, *Western America,* Prentice-Hall, Inc., New York, 1941.

Harger, Charles Moreau. "The Next Commonwealth: Oklahoma." *The Outlook,* February 2, 1901.

Harlow, Victor E. *Oklahoma,* Harlow Publishing Company, Oklahoma City, 1935.

Harmon, S. W. *Hell on the Border: He Hanged Eighty-Eight Men.* Phoenix Publishing Company, Fort Smith, Arkansas, 1898.

Harrel, Melvin. "The Dalton Gang" (3 Parts—May, June, July, 1953), *Northfork Sparks and Flashes.*

————. "The Outlaw Was A Lady," *Northfork Sparks and Flashes,* July, 1951.

Harrington, Fred Harvey. *The Hanging Judge.* The Caxton Printers, Ltd., Caldwell, Idaho, 1951.

Hawkeye, Harry. *The Dalton Brothers and Their Gang: Fearsome Bandits of Oklahoma and the Southwest,* Kerner & Getts, 530 Locust Street, Philadelphia, Pa., Copyright, 1908, by I. & M. Ottenheimer.

Hendricks, George D. *The Bad-man of the West,* The Naylor Company, San Antonio, Texas, 1941.

Hennessey Clipper, April-August, 1895; March 12, 1896.

"Holding Up a Train," *The Complete Works of O'Henry,* Garden City Publishing Company, Inc., Garden City, New York, 1937.

Horan, James D. *Desperate Women,* G. P. Putnam's Sons, New York, 1952.

Hough, Emerson. *The Story of the Outlaw: A Study of the Western Desperado,* Outing Publishing Company, New York, 1907.

Humphrey, Seth K. *Following the Prairie Frontier,* The University of Minnesota Press, 1931.

Hunter, J. Marvin, and N. H. Rose. *The Album of Gunfighters,* Hunter and Rose, Publishers, San Antonio, 1951.

In re Jennings. Circuit Court, Eastern District of Missouri, in Chambers, November 12, 1902, 118 Federal Reporter 479.

In re Terrill. No. 63, Circuit Court of Appeals, Eighth Circuit, 144 Federal Reporter 616.

Indian Chieftain, August 27, 1891; January 23, 1896; January 20, 1898.

Indian-Pioneer History (Foreman Collection, Vols. 1-113).
  Vol.   1 (Daltons, p. 475);
   "   2 (Daltons and Jennings, p. 247, p. 476);
   "   4 (Killing of Bill Dalton, pp. 114-115; Dalton gang, p. 466);
   "   5 (Bill Doolin robs bank at Pawnee, p. 187);
   "   8 (Doolin gang, headquarters at Ingalls, p. 325);
   "   10 (Daltons, p. 59, p. 342; Bill Raidler, Ol Yountis, Newcomb, Doolin, p. 415);
   "   13 (Dalton gang, p. 374; cave used as hideout, p. 465);

"   15 (Daltons and Doolin, p. 262, p. 289);

"   16 (Al Jennings, p. 267);

"   18 (Dalton boys and Bill Doolin, pp. 29-39);

"   20 (Doolin gang, p. 144);

"   22 (Dalton boys, p. 289);

"   23 (Dalton boys, p. 110, p. 212);

"   27 (Bill Dalton, p. 118);

"   37 (Bill Doolin, p. 421);

"   49 (Doolin, Daltons, p. 520);

"   53 (Al Jennings, p. 7; Bill Doolin, pp. 120-122; pp. 175-176; Daltons, p. 307);

"   60 (Red Buck, p. 5);

"   61 (B. Dunn, p. 179; Christian gang, p. 266);

"   63 (Dalton gang, Yeager and Black, p. 18);

"   66 (Bill Doolin, p. 147);

"   71 (Jennings gang, p. 512);

"   73 (Red Buck, p. 205; death of Bill Dalton, p. 217);

"   74 (Dalton gang, p. 266, p. 315; Jennings and Christian gangs, p. 435);

"   75 (Dalton boys, p. 39);

"   77 (Red Buck, p. 44; Bill Doolin, p. 274; Bill Dalton, p. 276; Doolin gang, p. 385; Bob and Bill Christian, p. 387; Dalton gang, p. 462);

"   79 (Jennings gang, p. 72; surrender of Jennings gang, p. 73);

"   80 (Jennings brothers, p. 430);

"   81 (Daltons, Jennings gangs, p. 424);

"   83 (Dalton gang, p. 187; killing of Dalton gang, p. 475);

"   85 (Bee Dunn, p. 353; Al Jennings, p. 426);

"   91 (Casey gang, pp. 246-258, p. 352);

"   92 (Dalton gang, p. 29, p. 63);

"   98 (Jennings, p. 39);

"   99 (Dalton gang, p. 316);

"   101 (Black and Dick Yeager, p. 463);

"   102 (Dalton gang, pp. 34-36, p. 79, pp. 84-85; hideouts, p. 353);

"   105 (Al Jennings, p. 259, p. 332);

"   106 (Bill Doolin, p. 115; Dalton boys, p. 317);

"   107 (O'Malley-Jennings gang, p. 11; Al Jennings, p. 374);

"   110 (Ol Yountis, p. 143);

"   112 (Al Jennings, p. 252; Dalton gang, p. 36);

"   113 (Dalton boys, p. 46, pp. 406-409; pp. 417-418).

Ironsides, R. P. "Desperate Battle With Outlaws," *Frontier Times,* September, 1951.

James, Marquis. *The Cherokee Strip: A Tale of an Oklahoma Boyhood,* The Viking Press, New York, 1946.

————. *They had Their Hour* (Chapter XVI, The Life and Death of Dick Yeager), Bobbs-Merrill Company, Indianapolis, Indiana, 1934.

Jennings v. United States. Court of Appeals of Indian Territory, October 26, 1899, 53 Southwestern Reporter 456.

Jennings, Al. *Through the Shadows with O'Henry,* The H. K. Fly Company, Publishers, New York, 1921.

Jennings, Al, and Will Irwin. *Beating Back,* D. Appleton & Company, New York, 1914.

Jones v. Territory. Supreme Court of Oklahoma, February 13, 1896, 43 Pacific Reporter 1072.

Kingfisher Free Press, April-August, 1895; December 27, 1906; April 17, 1939.

Lake, Stuart N. *Wyatt Earp, Frontier Marshal,* Houghton Mifflin Company, Boston and New York, 1931.

Lamb, Arthur H. *Tragedies of the Osage Hills,* The Osage Printery, Pawhuska, n. d.

Lemon, G. E. "Reminiscences of Pioneer Days in the Cherokee Strip." *Chronicles of Oklahoma,* XXII (Winter, 1944-45), pp. 435-457.

M'Clintock, R. M. "Politics in Territorial Days," *Daily Oklahoman,* April 23, 1939.

M'Kiddy, J. H. "Cherokee Strip," *Daily Oklahoman,* April 23, 1939.

McDaniel, Ruel. "Saga of the Frontier's Strangest Outlaw," *Crime Detective,* March, 1947.

McGinty, Billy. *The Old West,* The Ripley Review Publishers, Ripley, Oklahoma, n. d.

McReynolds, Robert. *Thirty Years on the Frontier,* El Paso Publishing Company, Colorado Springs, Colorado, 1906.

MacDonald, A. B. *Hands Up!: Stories of Six-Gun Fighters of the Old Wild West* (as told by Fred Sutton), Bobbs-Merrill Company, Indianapolis, 1927.

MacMartin, D. F. "Confessions of a Sooner—A Story of the Seamy Side of the Run of '89," *Daily Oklahoman,* April 23, 1939 (from *Thirty Years of Hell*).

Marshal, James. *Santa Fe, the Railroad that Built an Empire,* Random House, Inc., New York, 1945.

Masterson, V. V. *The Katy Railroad and the Last Frontier,* University of Oklahoma Press, Norman, 1952.

Masterson, W. B. (Bat). "Famous Gunfighters of the Western Frontier," *Human Life,* July, 1907.

Milam, Joe B. "The Opening of the Cherokee Outlet," *The Chronicles of Oklahoma,* IX (1931), pp. 268-286; X (1932), pp. 115-137.

Mootz, Herman Edwin. *The Blazing Frontier,* Tardy Publishing Company, Dallas, Texas, 1936.

————. "Rose of Cimarron," *The Pony Express,* December, 1945.

Mueller, Harold R. "Four Score Years A Fighter," (the life story of Chris Madsen), *Daily Oklahoman,* November-December, 1935; January-March, 1936.

Murray, W. H. "The Constitutional Convention," *The Chronicles of Oklahoma,* IX (1931), pp. 126-138.

"Mystery of Cimarron Rose Among Best Kept Secrets of Oklahoma," *Southwest Magazine,* January, 1951.

Newsom, J. A. *Life and Practice of the Wild and Modern Indian: The Early Days of Oklahoma,* Harlow Publishing Company, Oklahoma City, 1923.

Nix, Evett Dumas. *Oklahombres* (as told to Gordon Hines), Eden Publishing House, St. Louis and Chicago, 1929.

North Enid Tribune, April 12, 1894.

Oklahoma City Daily Times, April-November, 1889.

"Oklahoma City Was Born in One Day," *Daily Oklahoman,* January 3, 1943.

Oklahoma Daily Star, April-May, 1895.

Oklahoma Hawk, March 1, 1893.

Oklahoma Red Book (2 vols., Oklahoma City, 1912), I, pp. 423-425, President's Proclamation; pp. 426-436, Organic Act; pp. 512-513, Map of Openings; pp. 623-674, Sequoyah Constitution.

Oklahoma Statutes 1951 (2 vols.), I, pp. 18-44.

"Oklahoma Territory's First Marshal Selected 'He-Men' for His Deputies—and He Needed 'Em in Those Days." *Daily Oklahoman,* March 1, 1953.

Oklahoma Times Journal, January 2, 1894.

"Outlaw Girls Sassed the Judge," *Guthrie Leader,* April 16, 1939.

Pawnee Scout, January 26, 1894.

Pawnee Times, January 19-26, 1894.

Pawnee Times-Democrat, September 13, 1894.

Peery, Dan W., "Captain David L. Payne," *The Chronicles of Oklahoma,* XIII (1935), pp. 438-456.

————. "The First Two Years." *The Chronicles of Oklahoma,* VII (1929), pp. 285-286.

Perkins Journal, September-December, 1893.

Railroad Gazette, September 16, 1892.

Railway Review, June 1, 1888; July 12, 1889; October 4, 1889; January 17, 1892.

Raine, William MacLeod. *Famous Sheriffs and Western Outlaws,* Doubleday, Doran and Company, Garden City, New York, 1929.

————. "The Greatest of the Sheriffs," *Empire Magazine,* May 3, 1953.

Rainey, George. *The Cherokee Strip.* Co-operative Publishing Company, Guthrie, Oklahoma, 1933.

————. *No Man's Land: The Historic Story of a Landed Orphan* (Privately printed), Enid, Oklahoma, 1937.

Rascoe, Burton. *Belle Star, the Bandit Queen.* Random House, New York, 1941.

Ray, Clarence E. *The Dalton Brothers: A Tale of Adventures in the Indian Territory, Together with the Desperate and Startling Criminal Career of the Gang,* Regan Publishing Corporation, 26 East Van Buren Street, Chicago, n. d.

Records of the Kansas State Penitentiary, Lansing, Kansas.

Records of the Missouri State Penitentiary, Jefferson City, Missouri.

Records of the Oklahoma State Penitentiary, McAlester, Oklahoma.

Records of the Ohio State Penitentiary, Columbus, Ohio.

Records of the United States Penitentiary, Ft. Leavenworth, Kansas.

Reeves v. Territory. Supreme Court of Oklahoma, June 30, 1900, 61 Pacific Reporter 828.

Rhodes, May Davison. *The Hired Man on Horseback: My Story of Eugene Manlove Rhodes,* Houghton Mifflin Company, Boston, 1938.

Ridings, Sam P. *The Chisholm Trail,* Co-operative Publishing Company, Guthrie, Oklahoma, 1936.

Rister, Carl Coke. "Free Land Hunters of the Southern Plains," *The Chronicles of Oklahoma,* XXII (1944) pp. 392-401.

————. *Land Hunger: David L. Payne and the Oklahoma Boomers,* University of Oklahoma Press, Norman, 1942.

————. *No Man's Land.* University of Oklahoma Press, Norman, 1948.

Rock, Marion Tuttle. *Illustrated History of Oklahoma,* C. B. Hamilton & Son, Topeka, Kansas, 1890.

"Rock Island Lines Had Troubles, Too, In Early Oklahoma." *Daily Oklahoman,* March 1, 1953.

Sabin, Edwin L. *Wild Men of the Wild West,* Thomas Y. Crowell Company, New York, 1929.

Sarchet, Corb. "The Territorial Governors" (7 parts), *Daily Oklahoman,* March 1, 1953.

Scott, Dr. Angelo C. "From April, 1889, to April, 1989," *Daily Oklahoman,* April 21, 1935. (Written in 1921 and published in the *Cornhill Magazine,* London, in April of that year.)

————. *The Story of Oklahoma City,* Times-Journal Publishing Company, Oklahoma City, 1939.

Seely, O. C. (Publisher). *Oklahoma Illustrated.* The Leader Printing Company, Guthrie, Oklahoma, 1894.

Shirk, George H. "The Start of the Law." *Daily Oklahoman,* April 29, 1951.

Shirley, Glenn. *Toughest of Them All.* The University of New Mexico Press, Albuquerque, 1953.

South and West, September 3, 1896.

Stansbery, Lon R. "Cops and Robbers, Famous Battle of Ingalls in 1893 Broke Power of Bill Doolin's Gang," *Tulsa World,* March 21, 1937.

Stewart, Dora Ann. *Government and Development of Oklahoma Territory,* Harlow Publishing Company, Oklahoma City, 1933.

Stillwater Gazette, August 7, 1891; April-December, 1892; March-December, 1893; February-August, 1896; September 5, 1933.

Stillwater Populist, January 19, 1894; July 25, 1895.

Sutton, Fred E. "Fill Your Hand" (As told to A. B. MacDonald), *The Saturday Evening Post,* April 10, 1926.

――――. "Rose of Cimarron: The Passing of the Doolin Gang of Outlaws," *Daily Oklahoman,* May 8, 1921.

――――. "They Died With Their Boots On, Saying . . ." *Dallas Morning News,* May 10, 1931.

Territory of Oklahoma v. Tom Jones, No. 323, District Court of Payne County, Oklahoma Territory.

"The Story of Oklahoma," *The Nation,* April 4, 1889.

Thoburn, Joseph B., and Muriel H. Wright, "Agitation for Territorial Government." *Oklahoma: A History of the State and Its People,* Appendix LVI-2.

――――. *Oklahoma: A History of the State and Its People* (4 vols.) Lewis Historical Publishing Company, New York, 1929.

Tilghman, Zoe A. *Marshal of the Last Frontier,* The Arthur H. Clark Company, Glendale 4, California, 1949.

――――. *Outlaw Days,* Harlow Publishing Company, Oklahoma City, 1926.

――――. "The True Jennings Story." *Daily Oklahoman,* March 25, 1951.

Tulsa World, July 24, 1932; September 10, 1933.

Tuton, J. O. "Old Greer County—An Empire in Its Own Right." Daily Oklahoman, April 23, 1939.

U. S. Statutes at Large, XXVI, XXVII, XVIII.

Ward, William. *The Dalton Gang, the Bandits of the Far West,* Published by Westbrook, n. p., n. d.

Waters, L. L. *Steel Trails to Santa Fe.* University of Kansas Press, Lawrence, 1951.

Watonga Republican, July 19, 1893; November 15, 1893.

Weekly Oklahoma State Capital, September-December, 1893; January 6-27, 1894; December 2, 1894; March-July, 1895; January 25, 1896; March 21, 1896.

Index